MW00534934

Advance praise for *Gray Love*

"Everything you wanted to know about late-life dating and mating . . . and then some, from wide-ranging personal accounts."
—Susan Gubar, author of *Late-Life Love: A Memoir*

"Cupid's got a lousy sense of humor. We just keep longing for romance and companionship—even in our nineties. Love's a drive—like thirst and hunger. And this book shows the yearning (and resignation) among older folks with touching delicacy and exquisite sophistication. It's a treasure."
—Helen Fisher, chief science advisor to Match.com, author of *Anatomy of Love: A Natural History of Mating, Marriage, and Why We Stray*

"These are fresh, new voices that give dignity, pathos, humor and warmth to the search for love, or finding love, in the third or fourth quartile of life. This is a book that people of a certain age should read—but also people who will, I hope, reach a certain age—because they should know that love and passion can exist way beyond reproductive years."
—Pepper Schwartz, author of *50 Great Myths of Human Sexuality* and on-air relationship expert for the television show *Married at First Sight*

"An inspiring collection of personal stories from individuals seeking emotional and physical relationships in their later years. Their honest, insightful, and poignant narratives are a worthwhile addition to age studies."
—Ellyn Lem, author of *Gray Matters: Finding Meaning in the Stories of Later Life*

Gray Love

Gray Love

Stories About Dating and New Relationships After 60

EDITED BY

NAN BAUER-MAGLIN

DANIEL E. HOOD

RUTGERS UNIVERSITY PRESS

NEW BRUNSWICK, CAMDEN, AND NEWARK, NEW JERSEY;

AND LONDON AND OXFORD, UK

Library of Congress Cataloging-in-Publication Data

Names: Maglin, Nan Bauer, editor. | Hood, Daniel E., editor.
Title: Gray love : stories about dating and new relationships after 60 /
    edited by Nan Bauer-Maglin and Daniel E. Hood.
Description: New Brunswick, New Jersey : Rutgers University Press, [2023] |
    Includes bibliographical references and index.
Identifiers: LCCN 2022010948 | ISBN 9781978827271 (paperback) |
    ISBN 9781978827264 (cloth) | ISBN 9781978827288 (epub) |
    ISBN 9781978827295 (mobi) | ISBN 9781978827301 (pdf)
Subjects: LCSH: Love in old age. | Older people—Sexual behavior.
Classification: LCC HQ1061 .G7135 2023 | DDC 306.73084/6—dc23/eng/20220405
LC record available at https://lccn.loc.gov/2022010948

A British Cataloging-in-Publication record for this book is available from the British
Library.

⊖ The paper used in this publication meets the requirements of the American
National Standard for Information Sciences—Permanence of Paper for Printed Library
Materials, ANSI Z39.48-1992.

www.rutgersuniversitypress.org

Manufactured in the United States of America

Contents

PART II
The Complications and Pleasures of Elder Relationships

Gray Love

Introduction

Put simply, now that you're past 50, dating is a different experience than it was when you were in your 20s or even your 30s. You've changed, the culture has changed, and who you're looking for is likely to be quite different as well . . . Online dating isn't for everyone, but it's where the people are. Millions of them, in fact. And the fastest-growing group among them is people over 50. —Pepper Schwartz, Dating After 50 For Dummies

I used to think that elder love, if it even existed, was confined to rocking chairs or golf carts, that it had to be a dull business because of the physical limitations of age.
—Nora Johnson, "Age Is No Obstacle to Love, or Adventure"

Later-life relationships are born of loss.
—Susan Gubar, Notes on Late-Life Love: A Memoir

It's just over—I've closed up shop. I'm extremely happy on my own.
—Jane Fonda

Gray Love: Stories About Dating and New Relationships After 60 narrates forty-two stories of older people's lived experience looking for love on and offline, sometimes finding companionship, sometimes not, and sometimes giving up on the need and the pursuit. Many of the stories describe experiences pre-COVID-19; some have been revised to reflect the time of the pandemic. *Gray Love* is divided into two parts: (I) To Be or Not To Be in a Relationship: Tales of Humor, Disappointment, Rewards, and Personal Insight and (II) The Complications and Pleasures of Elder Relationships.

1

Forty-five people contributed to this volume: thirteen men and thirty-two women. Four pieces are authored by couples. Contributors' ages range from fifty-nine to ninety-four—one going on sixty, eleven are in their sixties, twenty in their seventies, another eleven in their eighties, and two in their nineties.[1] The people writing here represent a significant segment in the United States. People over sixty account for 22 percent of the total population—73 million in all—and that number is expected to rise to 26 percent by 2030. *The New York Times* writes, "the U.S. Census Bureau predicts that between 2010 and 2050 the number of people aged sixty-five to eighty-nine will double, and the number over ninety will quadruple."[2] According to a 2020 Pew Research Center report on single Americans, about a quarter of U.S. adults live alone and spend most of their day alone, but the number is much higher for older women—roughly half of women over sixty-five are without partners. For men, that number is only 21 percent. At age sixty-five, men are more likely to be married than are women (75 percent vs. 58 percent).[3] This disparity only increases with age.

Regarding dating, the same Pew report indicates that half of all people ages fifty to sixty-four and three-quarters of those sixty-five and older are *not* looking for dates currently. A majority of women over forty say they aren't looking to date right now compared with 42 percent of men forty and older.[4] Nonetheless, the longing for connection as old age encroaches is palpable both here in *Gray Love* and in podcasts, memoirs, and literature about people in their later years.[5] Roger Angell, writing at age ninety-plus in *The New Yorker*, captures that hunger:

> "Getting old is the second-biggest surprise of my life, but the first, by a mile, is our unceasing need for deep attachment and intimate love. We oldies yearn daily and hourly for conversation and a renewed domesticity, for company at the movies or while visiting a museum, for someone close by in the car when coming home at night. This is why we throng to Match.com and OkCupid in such numbers—but not just for this, surely. Rowing in Eden (in Emily Dickinson's words: "Rowing in Eden—/ Ah—

the sea") isn't reserved for the lithe and young, the dating or the hooked-up or the just lavishly married, or even for couples in the middle-aged mixed-doubles semifinals, thank God. No personal confession or revelation impends here, but these feelings in old folks are widely treated like a raunchy secret. The invisibility factor—you've had your turn—is back at it again. But I believe that everyone in the world wants to be with someone else tonight, together in the dark, with the sweet warmth of a hip or a foot or a bare expanse of shoulder within reach."[6]

This desire for intimacy, Angell says, leads these "oldies"[7] to online dating services "in such numbers." Cynthia McVay's piece, "Looking At 60," begins *Gray Love* by voicing the fear of aging alone: "Let me tell you what it's like to be lonely, about the fear of growing old alone, or just dying alone, falling off a ladder alone."

According to Forbes as quoted in DatingNews.com, as of June 2018 the United States alone had 2,500 dating sites, and about 1,000 new ones are launched every year. It's estimated that worldwide there are nearly 8,000 dating sites.[8] According to the 2020 Pew report on online dating, 48 percent of eighteen to twenty-nine-year-olds say they have used a dating site or app at least once; whereas only 19 percent of adults ages fifty to sixty-four say they have used a dating site or app, and for over sixty-five, it is 13 percent.[9] Scott Valdez, of VirtualDatingAssistants.com, recognized that "for most seniors, online dating is a new experience. It didn't exist when they were last single. [However], senior singles in America make up one of the fastest growing demographics in online dating."[10]

Those who write here about searching online most often have tried Match, but other sites are also referred to: Adult FriendFinder, BlackSingles, Chocolate Singles, Christian Mingle, eharmony, EliteSingles, The 50 Plus Connection, Fitness Singles, Jdate, MeetMindful, OkCupid, OurTime, PerfectMatch, Plenty of Fish, SeniorPeopleMeet, SilverSingles, The Right Stuff, Tinder, and Zoosk.[11] Susan Bickley found a partner in 1974 through Single Book Lovers (SBL); thirty-seven years later she tried Match. SBL, like Match, had a questionnaire—for Bickley, the most important answer was one's five favorite books. SBL was done entirely by traditional mail and telephone calls to the two founders; Match, as we know, works with instantaneous swipes and messages. Stacey Millett, who signed up with what she called a "relationship whisperer," and Isabel Hill, who used a new-age matchmaker, were both mentored by these consultants in their use of online dating sites.[12] Eighty-eight-year-old Natasha Josefowitz was signed up for a dating app by her personal trainer; however, she prefers meeting people the old-fashioned way: "The shadchans (Yiddish for marriage broker) of yesterday had correct information and could be relied upon." Others connected through blind dates, were set up by friends or family, or reached out to someone they knew in the past. Amy Rogers met an attractive writer at a conference; two years later she found that person again—now a different gender—on Facebook; they had one date. Tired of "job-interview-style internet dates," Candida Korman reconnected with a boyfriend thirty years after first meeting him at a mixer. They had a "terrible mismatch all over again" before they went their separate ways.

Meeting someone informally through family, church, or neighborhood networks has been in decline since World War II. Meeting online is displacing all other ways to meet.[13] Melani Robinson, in a book about her more than one hundred online dates at fifty, says there are very few places to meet people: "Going to clubs or bars, or rock-climbing, we don't do that like younger people do on a regular basis."[14] It is hard to meet people offline in your fifties; even harder in your sixties and later!

I. TO BE OR NOT TO BE IN A RELATIONSHIP
Tales of Humor, Disappointment, Rewards, and Personal Insight

The stories in Part I dive into the subject of elder dating: the question and the process, the desire and the dilemma. They pose the question: "Do I want to find a relationship?" The answers are varied: yes, no, and maybe. This section's stories tell of dating encounters on the internet and in person. Some see the dating process as a learning experience. For others it is painful, disappointing, and exhausting; for others it is humorous; for some it is an adventure or a gift; for yet others a lesson about one's self. As Alice Freed wrote, it added new textures to her life. For many it is all those things combined or serialized.

Some of our contributors decided to stop searching online. Others, though discouraged, decided to try yet again. Still others simply appreciate their singleness and are not interested in finding a partner. To put it more prosaically, Freed, after many years of searching, declared that: "I am happier than I realized at the end of each day with no one else's socks to trip over in my bedroom." How the pandemic has affected these desires and decisions also finds voice in *Gray Love*.[15]

The pieces in Part I focus on the process of dating from start to finish, while those in Part II are about actually finding someone at the end of the process. Many of the writers are critical of the process, including Susan Ostrov Weisser in "Not Jane Eyre's Story" and Phyllis Carito in "Discovery through Online Dating Sites: A Woman's Perspective." Weisser identifies online dating as a business deal, a marketplace—an exchange she does not want to enter, as does Stacey Millett in Part II: "I treated this partner quest like Amazon shopping, where you customize searches and peruse 'product' details that meet your specifications." A recent article in *The Atlantic* compares online dating to shopping for, say, a sweater: "Once you decide on the sweater you want, you can get it. But with dating, the sweater has to agree, too."[16]

To enter the dating "marketplace," one must first write a profile, as described by Nan Bauer-Maglin and Neil Stein. Vincent Valenti in Part II lists twenty-eight traits he wants in a partner and more than twenty aspects about himself he wants someone reading his profile to know. Interestingly, "online dating users ages 50 and older are more likely than users ages 18 to 49 to say that it is very important that the profiles they looked at included the person's race or ethnicity (26% vs. 16%) or their political affiliation (21% vs. 12%)."[17] On Facebook, Jonathan Ned Katz "advertised" himself, looking for a man who would like to meet an artistic eighty-two-year-old historian. Stein worked on his profile so that it clearly reflected his sensibilities: "The result was a narrative that was intended to bring a self-deprecating, witty and ironic tone to what I viewed as an incredibly artificial and dull process." Having posted his profile, Stein is at first "intoxicated" by his endless choices, all of whom are one click away, but then admits that it's also a problem: "With a seemingly endless supply of potential partners available why would I (or anyone) settle for someone who didn't hit all the marks." William Wiesner calls it a candy store for older men.

Laura Broadwell confesses that the thought of dating in later life "terrifies me to no end." As a woman in her sixties, she would not know what to wear—not a superficial issue, especially for older women. Phyllis Carito offers general advice for a dating game that is nothing like she had known in her first go-round: "Dating was in the purview of the man and traditional dating meant the woman knew her role was to be a lady who waited demurely for the man, who acquiesced to the man, and who was always treated to every dinner, movie, etc."

In her midsixties, Stephanie Brown had thirty-nine first dates, all of whom turned out ultimately to be "Mr. Wrong," or "Mr. Even Wronger," but she asserts that "none of these relationships, full or demi, and none of these dates, single or six, involved regret. I got something from everyone." Elizabeth Locke sums up her online experience at age seventy-eight: "I have recently signed off; but I have fifteen years of experience—some dismal and some hilarious . . . I never found anyone permanent. Looking back at the parade I see a lot of humor in my experiences; if nothing else, I see myself more clearly as a result. Perhaps others may find the recital pathetic, laughable, or even instructive." Candida Korman needed to repeat an earlier mistake in order to think about finding an appropriate man. And Amy Rogers wants to make sure that she reads the menu more carefully if she dates again, that "there'd better be more than the promise of snack food waiting for me when I get there." In her midseventies after an in-person rejection from an OkCupid match, Margie Kaplan still asserts her

"Ok-ness." Instead of jumping off a bridge, moaning to a friend, or watching a Hallmark movie, she has a drink and a delicious dinner by herself.

Actors Jane Fonda and Sharon Stone have both decided to stop looking for a partner; Fonda, age eighty-two, as quoted above, declared "It's just over—I've closed up shop. I'm extremely happy on my own."[18] Stone, age sixty-two, is also done with dating, preferring to spend time alone, or with her friends and her three sons.[19] Many of the women writing here have said "no" to partnering as well, often after a search that was disappointing and dispiriting. While Eugene Roth's advice in Part II is to beware of "maniacs" online, his more profound advice is to watch out for your own fantasies: "given one's hopes, the killer you are likely to encounter is disappointment. So know what you desire and listen for the signs that your desires are not within your counterpart's capacities. And if the signals of incapacity sound, flee. *Sturm und drang* may be exciting, but peace and quiet are blessings and far better for the older person's constitution than the wild fluctuations of adrenaline provoked by dating online."[20]

After maybe 150 different dates, Alice Freed is finished with internet dating, although she still checks her messages, curious to know of new dating sites on the horizon. Hedva Lewittes, after the recent death of her husband, having tried one momentary alliance to test the waters, decided to go it alone—for now, at least.

A number of the men writing here have also stopped looking. After his wife, Astrid, died, Rett Zabriske wondered about looking for a new partner; his American circle urged him to do so; his Danish circle was silent. He decided he would rather enjoy his friends and is "content to remain married to Astrid with all the memories." Widower Irvin Peckham came to embrace his solitude after a disastrous geographical relocation and a disappointing relationship. William Wiesner, after a divorce and years of dating, has come to recognize his single state as a choice, as a new social phenomenon among older people; nonetheless, he is somewhat wistful about the loss of a long-term intimate relationship.

There are several reasons older people opt out of the dating game, but the predominant one is feeling too old to date. A quarter of non-daters over fifty and a third of non-daters over sixty-five are more likely to say that they feel too old, compared with 4 percent of those younger than fifty.[21] Certainly it is not unrealistic for women to feel older age as an inhibiting factor in dating—for example, some of Nan Bauer-Maglin's friends encouraged her to color her gray hair. Older men tend to seek younger women; whereas, for women, dating younger men is not usually socially acceptable.[22] A 2018 Medicare study quoted in *Science Magazine* asserts that "the desirability of a woman peaks at age 18 and declines with each year thereafter. Meanwhile, the desirability of a man rises with age until hitting a peak at age 50, before beginning to decline. In other words, a younger woman is more likely to be attracted to an older man than a younger man is to be attracted to an older woman."[23] Looking online, octogenarian Natasha Josefowitz realized that "no one seemed interested in a woman in her late eighties." Phyllis Bogen, at ninety-two, is at a loss about how to go about finding a companion. Now, given COVID-19, she chooses not to try to figure it out.

In "Aging Out of Dating," Erica Manfred, seventy-plus, says it is about age and appearance: "And late-life internet dating is particularly cruel, because judging potential partners by their looks never ends. What does end is looks. Women are as guilty of this as men. But who still looks good in their seventies or older? Not many of us." Susan Weisser quotes an online dating ad from an "Obese Older Man seeking Beautiful Young Girl." She says while "this boiled down to youth and looks . . . he did at the end graciously concede that he would settle for a beautiful *older* woman as a second choice." She quotes another man who is repulsed by the puffy arms of women over fifty.[24] Closely related to this is the issue of sexual desire. Manfred describes how, at sixty, she went on the internet to find sex: "I was long past menopause and supposedly long past my sexual prime. My body didn't know this, however." By seventy she lost interest in men and sex. In her search for a romantic partner, Judith Ugelow Blak had to admit that she lost her libido. That admission, at age sixty-eight, while it could be troubling, had positive implications for Blak—if she decides to look again, she will no longer lead with sex (having once thought it was a path to love).

Older people don't date for other reasons besides age bias but in smaller numbers as compared to younger people: 38 percent of older non-daters say having more important priorities is the dominant reason they are not looking for a relationship or dates (compared to 61 percent of younger non-daters). Fourteen percent say they are too busy (compared to 29 percent of younger non-daters), and 12 percent feel no one would be interested in dating them (compared to 24 percent of younger non-daters).

Another reason older adults stop looking is their negative experience with online dating. The Pew report found that "users ages 18 to 49 are *more likely* than those ages 50 and older to say their online dating experience has been at least somewhat positive (59 percent vs. 50 percent)."[25] Linda Wright Moore calls the search on online dating sites "soul-crushing" for older African American women. For herself and her friends, men who come even close to dateable are in "short supply." And as an Asian American woman, Jean Leung confronts prejudice in the dating world. "Dating when you have passed the half-century mark is tough enough, but when one is trying to climb out of the cave of widowhood during a pandemic, being a minority in a prejudiced country adds a complicated layer."

Assessing the virtues and downsides of online dating in general, the Pew report notes that "while a majority of online daters have never forged a committed relationship with someone they first encountered through dating platforms, 39 percent of online dating users (representing 12 percent of all U.S. adults) say they have been in a committed relationship or married someone they met on a dating site or app." Only 5 percent of those over sixty-five say they are in a committed relationship or married someone they met on a dating site or app.[26] And for women who have used a dating site or app, they "are more likely than men to say they have found it very or somewhat difficult to find people that they were physically attracted to or seemed like someone they would want to meet in person."[27] Age, as Leung says, makes it even tougher.

In "Looking at 60," Cynthia McVay digs deeply into the pain and negative effects of living alone especially as one ages: "Living alone, being alone, has physical and mental health consequences, too. We know [that] people who live alone live shorter lives. Social isolation is the equivalent of smoking fifteen cigarettes a day. Lonely bodies are in stress and produce cortisol, which takes a toll on the body's systems." Nonetheless, she also questions the notion of compromise and giving up one's autonomy and independence. It is a conundrum. To conclude, many of the writers in this book have stopped looking while others keep trying.

II. THE COMPLICATIONS AND PLEASURES OF ELDER RELATIONSHIPS

The first seven pieces in Part II describe finding "the one." Using an online app, Jan Jacobson started dating men and then switched to women. Stephanie Speer and David Levy met each other at a "death café." Sandi Goldie and Jim Bronson had been college friends; after two marriages each to partners they had lost to death, they reunited. Yes, one can begin again, and yes, there can be more than one true love in life. In his sixties, Vincent Valenti did not think he could begin again; instead, he resigned himself to becoming an urban monk. OkCupid's algorithm led him out of the desert. Stacey Parkins Millett describes a fifty-year search over her adult years to find "the one." Eugene Roth found a partner after the third online try. And as mentioned earlier, Isabel Hill found hers with the help of a matchmaker.

The twelve essays remaining in Part II explore issues that most relationships encounter at any age, as well as some that are unique to elder relationships. These include having had previous partners and a complicated and deep personal history; family and friends' reactions to an older person dating; alternative models to marriage (such as sharing space or living apart); having more than one partner at the same time; one's aging body, appearance, and sexuality; and the pressure of time and the specter of illness and death. The stories here are about inventing a relationship at sixty, seventy, eighty, and ninety.

Coming together late in life often means learning to live with ghosts. For Nan Bauer-Maglin, the ghosts share the bed; for Doris Friedensohn and Paul Lauter, both in their eighties, the ghosts decorate the wall. Writing in the *New York Times* about sharing an apartment after age sixty, Jan Benzel is asked how she could "live in an apartment with the ghosts of the big life that happened before me?"[28] Age brings baggage, but it can also be enriching.

Families often react negatively to these late pairings. Susan O'Malley's daughter told her that the grandchildren wanted nothing to do with the mid-eighty-year-old man she was dating—even though he had been a friend of the family. They did not want a substitute grandfather. Later, they relented.[29] There are also money concerns: If one pairs up late in life, will that take away from the children's inheritance? Most adults want to please their children, but not at the expense of companionship in their elder years. After all, they are more than just parents and grandparents!

Ways to be together that do not always involve marriage or even full-time living together are addressed by three pieces here. With their dogs and cherry plants, Barbara Abercrombie and her partner choose to live apart together (LAT), as do Susan Bickley and her partner.[30] Tierl Thompson and Idris Walters explain their choice of living separately: they do not want to lose "ourselves in each other twenty-four seven. We have often said we don't want to lose the people we fell in love with—our independent selves." These are words that come from an older person's experience and understanding, but it must be noted that it requires a certain level of financial comfort to maintain two abodes. Consider also Wiesner, who, although now in a relationship of more than two years, still calls himself single. These different arrangements indicate that there is a continuum of relationship types rather than a binary single or married status, especially among people over sixty.

Two pieces, "Parallel Matches" by Anonymous and "Reflections on 'Old Love'" by Sarah Dunn, describe having more than one serious relationship at the same time. Interestingly, both authors hid their names (Dunn is a pseudonym)—clearly this is still behavior people don't feel comfortable admitting in print. Both pieces are about men who are seeing two women—perhaps an indication of the uneven numbers of women to men after sixty. In her book *Aging Thoughtfully: Conversations About Retirement, Romance, Wrinkles, & Regret*, Martha Nussbaum discusses several movies about older women. She suggests the movies are based on a lie: "the staggering lie that love arrives only in neat couples, and that a person can love only one person at a time. One would think that especially when one is over 60, this might be understood as we often see (reluctantly) that one person cannot meet all our needs."[31] Dunn has accepted her arrangement (being second to another woman) as perhaps the best she can do at age eighty-four, but she does not always sit easily with it.

Illness, disabilities, old bodies, aches and pains—one's own and those of a possible partner—all are concerns here. The issue of exposing one's aging body is one that reverberates in *Gray Love*. After her mastectomy followed by the death of her husband, when Mimi Schwartz contemplated dating at seventy-one, intimacy seemed like a leap for her "even if I still had two breasts." Of course, having a breast removed can happen at any age; however, "breast cancer incidence and death rates increase with age until the seventh decade."[32] In Bernadine Evaristo's novel *Girl, Woman, Other*, Penelope is reluctant to show her seventy-year-old body to the man she has dated for eighteen months: "It had been a long time since she'd been seen in a state of undress by anyone other than the matronly bra-fitter at Marks & Spencer. . . . Her thighs, chunky and pock-marked, were no longer the stream-lined contours of old, her breasts weren't the pumped-up balloons of her youth, and she'd spent sleepless nights wondering if she should dye her lady garden for him." In another novel, *Lillian in Love* by Sue Katz, Lillian, age eighty-four, loses herself in her first physical encounter with Sarah, age seventy-nine, despite her so-called deficits: "She

presses her breasts against mine even more firmly as we continue dancing. I realize that my limp has faded. I'm not thinking of any of my deficits. Not my neuropathy, not my sagging butt, my floppy upper arms, or
my sloping 84-year-old back. I'm just surrendering to Sarah's lead and getting lost in the dance."[33] Desire overcomes embarrassment.

The pieces in *Gray Love* written by men do not address the authors' feelings toward their aging body, but the issue is not restricted to women
alone, as is evident, certainly, in Philip Roth's writing. In *The Dying Animal*, the protagonist imagines what a younger woman might say about his
sixty-two-year-old body to a girlfriend; this is obviously how he sees it as
well: "But what about his skin? Didn't he smell funny? What about his long
white hair? What about his wattle? What about his little pot belly? Didn't
you feel sick?"[34]

Ellyn Lem in *Gray Matters* says that "there is much debate in literature
and gerontology research whether old age signals a freedom from the
demands of the body or whether the body continues to desire with no expi-
ration date, albeit with modifications of its execution."[35]

Susan O'Malley, in her seventies, speaks glowingly of sex with her partner who is in his eighties. When intimacy between older persons is referred
to, this passage from Elizabeth Strout's *Olive Kitteridge* is often quoted:
"They were here, and her body—old, big, sagging—felt straight-out desire
for his. . . . What young people didn't know, she thought . . . oh, what
young people did not know. They did not know that lumpy, aged, and
wrinkled bodies were as needy as their own young, firm ones . . ."[36] While
accommodation must be made for infirmities, elder sexuality is certainly
enjoyed, contrary to what is often assumed.

Elderly women face a dilemma when they date men their age or older:
most do not want to become a caretaker of a new partner. Bonnie Fails,
age seventy-six, describes the frailty of the eighty-five-year-old man she
has moved in with, leaving Texas for Ohio. Phyllis Raphael, writing in *tiny
love stories,* worries about his dying when she does not hear from her older
"guy." She is in her eighties, and he in his nineties. "When we're not

together, we're on the phone, worried when one of us gets sick, more worried than we were when we were young—and immortal."[37] Angela Page's title asks the question: "'Til Illness Do Us Part?" At sixty she formed a partnership with a man who was seventy-eight. Quite soon he became seriously ill. As painful and stressful as the situation was (especially in light of the opposition of his son), Page felt ethically obliged to stay until the end. After an early friendship, Thompson and Walters reconnected fifty years later. In their seventies, they are keenly aware of "advancing years and the inevitable, eventual decline of our health." These days, Thompson thinks about mortality, fearful sometimes that something will happen to Idris or to herself. "How long do we have together?" is something she asks often.

Those people, sixty, seventy, eighty, and over, who decide to reach out for intimacy and take the risk of elder relationships are happily surprised, as Barbara Abercrombie is: "I'm astonished to find myself at age eighty with a boyfriend I'm in love with and attracted to, who makes me laugh a lot, who has turned into my best friend, and is one of the most adventurous traveling companions I've ever had."

Embrace the moment fully is the message. Dustin Beall Smith describes: "We did not shrink in the face of all the obvious and often comic absurdities of late love: the ghosts of former loves; the incremental loss of hearing and even memory; the incessant entropy of human flesh and bone—any one of the realities that might have served as a persuasive excuse not to act, a convincing argument that it was too late for love." One can also embrace the choice to live alone, as Hedva Lewittes decides: "What makes sense to me at this point is not to strive for or seek fulfillment through someone else, but to pay attention to and move forward on my own path." Or as Linda Moore has done—choose a solo path but leave the door open for a future relationship: "For me, solitude and flying solo make sense— though the romantic in me still believes a charming companion may be just around the bend."

Gray Love: Stories About Dating and New Relationships After 60 tells multiple stories about the most common of themes—that of searching for and perhaps finding love. Forty-two stories talk about dating, starting or ending a relationship, embracing life alone or enjoying a partnered one. The stories they tell are all from a perspective seldom encountered when talking about love—that of not being young.

NOTES

Jane Fonda's quote was taken from an interview with Dan Heching for *The Daily Mail* on September 8, 2020.

1. More details about *Gray Love* contributors: Place of residence: New York State, 20 (New York City, 13); New Jersey, 7; North Carolina, 3; Ohio, 2; Florida, 2; California, 2; Pennsylvania, 2; England, 2; Oregon, 1; Virginia, 1; Wisconsin, 1; Canada, 1; and Denmark, 1. Most identify as white; two as African American, one as Chinese American, and one as Latina. In terms of sexual orientation, most identify as heterosexual, two as gay men, one as lesbian, and one as bisexual. Some have designated their religion as Jewish or Christian, often clarifying with words like "born Protestant" or "culturally Jewish," while others wrote: none, atheist, Buddhist, Dharma practicing, mixed religion. Others did not answer the question at all.

2. Dionne Searcey, Alan Rappeport, Trip Gabriel, and Robert Gebeloff, "The Graying of the American Economy Is on Display in Iowa," *New York Times*, February 3, 2020, https://www.nytimes.com/2020/02/02/us/politics/iowa-economy-2020.html; Ellyn Lem, *Gray Matters: Finding Meaning in the Stories of Later Life* (New Brunswick, NJ: Rutgers University Press, 2020), 4; Federal Interagency Forum on Aging-Related Statistics, *Older Americans 2020: Key Indicators of Well-Being*, Washington, DC, U.S. Government Printing Office, 2020, https://www.agingstats.gov/docs/LatestReport/OA20_508_10142020.pdf.

3. Pew Research Center, "Nearly Half of U.S. Adults Say Dating Has Gotten Harder for Most People in the Last 10 Years," August 2020, https://www.pewsocialtrends.org/2020/08/20/a-profile-of-single-americans. See also, Paula Span "The Gray Gender Gap: Women on Their Own," *New York Times*, October 11, 2016, https://www.nytimes.com/2016/10/11/health/marital-status-elderly-health.html.

4. For a breakdown of race, education, and sexual orientation of single Americans, see https://www.pewsocialtrends.org/2020/08/20/a-profile-of-single-americans/.

5. For the many titles of nonfiction studies, memoirs, novels, poems, tv, videos, films, and podcasts of aging love, see Gubar, *Notes on Late-Life Love,* and Lem, *Gray Matters,* as well as Susan J. Douglas, *In Our Prime: How Older Women Are Reinventing the Road Ahead* (New York: W. W. Norton & Company, 2020). Before the COVID-19 pandemic, ABC announced that they were planning a version of *The Bachelor* for seniors sixty-five and over called *OK Boomers,* https://www.ksl.com/article/46721997/ok-boomers-a-bachelor-for-seniors-is-headed-to-abc. The podcast *Dating While Gray* on WAMU launched in January 2020—just one of the social media sites with stories and interviews about dating, finding partners, and seeking love.

6. Roger Angell, "This Old Man: Life in the Nineties," *The New Yorker*, February 17, 2014, https://www.newyorker.com/magazine/2014/02/17/old-man-3.

7. We use the terms *old, elder, older adults,* and *senior* to designate anyone age sixty and over.

8. Hayley Matthews, "27 Online Dating Statistics & What They Mean for the Future of Dating," Dating News, June 7, 2018, https://www.datingnews.com /industry-trends/online-dating-statistics-what-they-mean-for-future/.

9. Pew Research Center, "The Virtues and Downsides of Online Dating," February 6, 2020, https://www.pewresearch.org/internet/2020/02/06/the-virtues-and-downsides -of-online-dating.

10. "How Seniors and Millennials Date: A New Comparative Study on Dating Habits," MedicareAdvantage.com, https://www.medicareadvantage.com/senior-dating-study.

11. There are many sites that rate senior dating sites: https://www.datingadvice.com /senior/best-silver-dating-sites; https://www.consumeraffairs.com/dating_services /#types-of-dating-sites; https://www.after55.com/blog/senior-dating-sites-comparison/; https://www.aarpethel.com/relationships/the-best-dating-sites-for-those-over-50?; and https://sixtyandme.com/best-senior-dating-sites/.

12. For example, the online-dating service ViDA (Virtual Dating Assistants) is one example of assistance with online dating. "Men and women (though mostly men) from all over the world pay this company to outsource the labor and tedium of online dating . . . Profile Writers,' who create seductive and click-worthy profiles based on facts our clients have supplied about themselves, and 'Closers,' who log in to clients' dating accounts at least twice a day to respond to messages from matches." Chloe Rose Stuart-Ulin, "You Could Be Flirting on Dating Apps with Paid Impersonators," QZ.com, April 26, 2018, https://qz.com/1247382/online-dating-is-so-awful-that-people -are-paying-virtual-dating-assistants-to-impersonate-them/.

13. Michael J. Rosenfeld, Reuben J. Thomas, and Sonia Hausen, "Disintermediat- ing Your Friends: How Online Dating in the United States Displaces Other Ways of Meeting," *Proceedings of the National Academy of Sciences* 116, no. 36 (September 3, 2019): 17,753–58. For a history of dating, see Moira Weigel, *Labor of Love: The Inven- tion of Dating* (New York: Farrar, Straus and Giroux, 2016).

14. New York City News Service, *Sex, Apps & Bingo: Seeking Love After 50,* online video, https://sexappsandbingo.nycitynewsservice.com. See also Laura Petrecca, "Navigating the World of Online Dating After 50," AARP, January 28, 2019, aarp.org /home-family/dating/info-2019/online-dating-after-50.html.

15. Sara Konrath, "What the Pandemic Has Done for Dating," *The Atlantic,* Decem- ber 31, 2020, https://www.theatlantic.com/ideas/archive/2020/12/what-pandemic-has-done -dating/617502/; Arwa Mahdawi, "Lockdown Lesbianism and Not Sleeping with the Enemy—The Biggest Covid Dating Trends, *The Guardian,* November 10, 2020, https:// www.theguardian.com/commentisfree/2020/nov/10/lockdown-lesbianism-and-not -sleeping-with-the-enemy-the-biggest-covid-dating-trends; Helen Fisher, "How Coro- navirus Is Changing the Dating Game for the Better," *New York Times,* May 7, 2020, https://www.nytimes.com/2020/05/07/well/mind/dating-coronavirus-love-relationships .html; Anna Brown, "Most 'Single and Looking' Americans Say Dating Has Been Harder during the Pandemic," Pew Research Center, April 6, 2022, https://www.pewresearch.org /fact-tank/2022/04/06/most-americans-who-are-single-and-looking-say-dating-has -been-harder-during-the-pandemic/.

16. Ashley Fetters and Kaitlyn Tiffany, "'Dating Market' Is Getting Worse," *The Atlan- tic,* February 25, 2020, https://www.theatlantic.com/family/archive/2020/02/modern -dating-odds-economy-apps-tinder-math/606982/. See also, "There are those which

basically allow you to browse through profiles as you would boxes of cereal on a shelf in the store. Others choose for you; they bring five boxes of cereal to your door, ask you to select one, and then return to the warehouse with the four others. Or else they leave you with all five." Nick Paumgarten, "Looking for Someone: Sex, Love, and Loneliness on the Internet," *The New Yorker*, July 4, 2011.

17. Pew Research Center, "The Virtues and Downsides of Online Dating."

18. Heching, "Jane Fonda, 82, Reveals She Has 'Closed Up Shop.'"

19. Harry Clarke-Ezzidio, "Sharon Stone Says She's 'Had It' with Dating," CNN, October 15, 2020, https://www.cnn.com/2020/10/15/entertainment/sharon-stone -done-dating-scli-intl/index.html.

20. Many sites give advice. See CNN's Dating over 50 site, https://www.huffpost .com/voices/topic/dating-over-50. There one finds such articles like "The Top 3 Dating Mistakes that Ruin a Single Woman's Chance of Finding Love after 50!" by Lisa Copeland, https://www.huffpost.com/entry/the-top-3-dating-mistakes-that -ruin-a-single-womans_b_595146b8e4b0c85b96c65b88.

21. Pew Research Center, "The Virtues and Downsides of Online Dating."

22. No woman in this collection writes about connecting with a younger man, as does eighty-two-year-old Sophy Burnham about her attraction to a thirty-year-old man in "At What Age is Love Enthralling?" Modern Love, *New York Times*, February 8, 2019, https://www.nytimes.com/2019/02/08/style/modern-love-at-what-age -is-love-enthralling-82.html.

23. Elizabeth Bruch and M. E. J. Newman, "Aspirational Pursuit of Mates in Online Dating Markets," *Science Advances* 4, no. 8 (August 8, 2018), https://advances .sciencemag.org/content/4/8/eaap9815. See also "How Seniors and Millennials Date," MedicareAdvantage.com.

24. Nancy Jo Sales, a reporter on women's experience of the internet, asserts an extreme position, in a conversation on Slate: "In tech theory, they talk about how behaviors affect attitudes.... Just by doing this one behavior of swiping on females' faces and bodies and deciding in that split second whether or not there's someone you want to have sex with or date, you're being conditioned to believe that it's OK to do that, that's acceptable behavior, to treat women that way, as objects.... I think dating apps are rape culture." Nancy Jo Sales, "How Dating Apps Feed into Racism, Sexism, and 'Rape' Culture,'" Slate, June 4, 2021, https://slate.com/culture/2021/06/nancy-jo -sales-interview-i-think-dating-apps-are-rape-culture.html.

25. Pew Research Center, "The Virtues and Downsides of Online Dating."

26. According to the Pew Research Center, "This too follows a pattern similar to that seen in overall use, with adults under the age of 50, those who are LGB or who have higher levels of educational attainment are more likely to report finding a spouse or committed partner through these platforms." Pew Research Center, "Nearly Half of U.S. Adults Say Dating Has Gotten Harder for Most People in the Last 10 Years."

27. Pew Research Center, "The Virtues and Downsides of Online Dating."

28. Jan Benzel, "How Love Divides Up 800 Square Feet," *New York Times*, December 29, 2019.

29. Dina Gachman, "My 70-Year-Old Father Joined Tinder," *New York Times*, June 19, 2021, https://www.nytimes.com/2021/06/19/style/my-70-year-old-father-joined-tinder .html.

30. "Increasingly, some couples choose to cohabitate rather than marry again, and statistics for this demographic are on the rise.... There was a 75 percent increase

between 2006 and 2017 in people over fifty living with someone outside of marriage. The total is 4 million, with 900,000 being over 65." Pew Research Center report, quoted in Ellyn Lem, *Gray Matters,* 138. See also Francine Russo, "Older Singles Have Found a New Way to Partner Up: Living Apart," *New York Times,* July 16, 2021, https://www .nytimes.com/2021/07/16/well/family/older-singles-living-apart-LAT.html.

31. Martha C. Nussbaum and Saul Levmore, *Aging Thoughtfully: Conversations about Retirement, Romance, Wrinkles, & Regret* (New York: Oxford University Press, 2017), 168. See also Book Karnjanakit, "I Used to Think There Was One Way to Have a Relationship. Then I Discovered Polyamory," *The Lily,* October 10, 2021, https://www .thelily.com/i-used-to-think-there-was-one-way-to-have-a-relationship-then-i -discovered-polyamory/?. A 2020 Pew Research Center survey found that "some 46% of 18- to 29-year-olds and 40% of 30- to 49-year-olds say open relationships are acceptable. By contrast, 22% of 50- to 64-year-olds and 17% of those 65 and older say the same." Pew Research Center, "Nearly Half of U.S. Adults Say Dating Has Gotten Harder for Most People in the Last 10 Years."

32. American Cancer Society. Breast Cancer Facts & Figures 2019–2020. Atlanta: American Cancer Society, Inc., 2019, https://www.cancer.org/content/dam/cancer-org /research/cancer-facts-and-statistics/breast-cancer-facts-and-figures/2019-2020.pdf.

33. Bernardine Evaristo, *Girl, Woman, Other* (New York: Black Cat, 2019), 442–443; Sue Katz, *Lillian in Love* (Arlington, MA: Consenting Adult Press, 2017), 46.

34. Philip Roth, *The Dying Animal* (New York: Vintage Books, 2002), 8. See also Lynne Segal's analysis of aging male sex in literature. The title and subtitle indicate her take. Lynne Segal, "Philip Roth Is Wrong about Elderly Sex: Macho Novelists Wail about the Loss of Potency. But Intimacy Can Be Deeper Than They Imagine," *Salon,* November 17, 2013, https://www.salon.com/2013/11/17/philip_roth_is_wrong _about_elderly_sex/.

35. Lem cites research from the United States that indicate that 40 percent of people aged sixty-five to eighty are sexually active. Lem, *Gray Matters,* 123. Faith Hill says "that people report having the best sex of their lives in their 60s—they've had decades to figure out what they like." Faith Hill, "What It's Like to Date After Middle Age," *The Atlantic,* January 8, 2020, https://www.theatlantic.com/family/archive /2020/01/dating-after-middle-age-older/604588/. See also Maggie Jones, "The Joys (and Challenges) of Sex After 70," *New York Times Magazine,* January 12, 2022, https:// www.nytimes.com/2022/01/12/magazine/sex-old-age.html. Joan Price is an advocate for ageless sexuality: https://joanprice.com/. For short stories about "old sex," see Arlene Hayman, *Scary Old Sex: Stories* (New York: Bloomsbury, 2017).

36. Elizabeth Strout, *Olive Kitteridge* (New York: Random House, 2008), 269–270.

37. Phyllis Raphael, "My Nearly 90-Year-Old Boyfriend," *tiny love stories: True Tales of Love in 100 Words or Less* (New York: Artisan, 2020), 196.

Prelude

Prelude

Looking at Sixty

Cynthia McVay

In the moist, dark, cool night, I ran from a distant parking lot to a table for eight at a sold-out cabaret show. No one else had arrived to claim seats. I'd come by myself but was happy to meet new people. I can make conversation with almost anyone, and generally do.

Settled in, I perused my phone.

"Is this seat taken?" a man asked.

I looked up. His hand was on the back of a chair. I don't remember what he looked like or what he was wearing. All I remember was the feeling of hope.

"No," I said, smiling.

"Great, thanks," he said, as he swung the chair to the neighboring table, joining his group of friends.

Soon, with one nod after another, the table was stripped. I found myself alone at the long table, no chairs to offer even possibility.

The lights dimmed. Laughter and music filled the room; a familiar melancholy swept over me.

I try to separate how much of my pain is some hue of shame from the desire to actually be with someone. I enjoy doing things on my own, my way. I'd relish the independence if I weren't reminded constantly that it is socially unacceptable. Over a quarter of us live alone, and yet I am considered anomalous, an outlier.

"Just you?" the restaurant hostess says.

"Yes." *Just* me.

Without a built-in mate, a single person must proactively plan, make an effort, to ensure she has someone to go with—or eat at the bar. A good friend can fill that partner role, but it's not the same as just rolling over in bed or looking across the breakfast table and saying, *How about a movie tonight?* I could stay home or organize outings with friends, both of which I do frequently. I have single friends who rarely venture out on their own. Many are booked solid for weeks, months of weekends, to avoid being caught without a plan. I value flexibility over security, and so I take risks. It was my decision to go solo to the cabaret, but still.

This is what it's like to be lonely and what propels me to keep trying—yes, clichéd and elusive as it is—to find love. Then, after yet another failed attempt, wanting to give up, feeling spent and confused and empty, after giving away another piece of myself.

I drive home from New York City to the Hudson Valley late at night after an evening out, after another disappointing date, or several, none individually nor collectively worth the four-hour roundtrip. Having consumed a glass of wine hours earlier, I am not tipsy but tired, hurtling up Interstate 87 at close to midnight. I wish someone were in the car with me to keep me company, keep me *awake*, maybe even driving *us*. What if I hit a deer? Get a flat tire? Who do I call? Who is my go-to person?

That's what I seek: Someone who cares whether I make it home alive. Someone with whom to unpack my day. When I arrive home, I will bury my face in my puppy Dexter's soft rib cage and sob, but while I'm driving, I just want to heave this aloneness into this dark night. It seems so basic, so obvious, to love and be loved, but why is it so hard?

At forty-nine, I was half-involved (half in, half out) with an alcoholic man, fully aware I would turn fifty single. Sure enough, a few months before my fiftieth birthday, after eight yo-yo years, I broke up with him for the fourth and final time. I turned fifty surrounded by friends and family, but alone in the world, unhitched.

That man was the closest I've come to finding a life partner. He wasn't perfect, *we* weren't perfect, but our early morning rhythms and priorities aligned. We jumped from bed onto the land together. We wrestled poison ivy from apple trees and bittersweet from dogwoods. He brought an old tractor and ran it in my field. A student of falconry, he taught me how to identify raptors. We built things—arbors, a four-tree bed, barnwood walls. He had tools and skills; I had enthusiasm and ideas. We explored the Hudson River in kayaks and trails with our Labradors. We traveled well together to Curaçao, China, and Normandy. He had an intuitive eye for art, and we shared a rustic, organic taste. He was tall, had good hair and broad shoulders. We laughed deeply and frequently. When he nicked his finger with the chainsaw—is nicking even possible with a chainsaw?—and I drove him to the emergency room, he told me to go home so I could catch the sunset.

I didn't miss the sunset, but I missed him at my fiftieth. He'd been married thirty years before we met; he was a grown-up. He did so much right that I kept hoping he'd get that last bit—sobriety—but the circular arguments, the swirl of lies, the red face, the empty vodka bottle rolling in the back seat of his car, the alcohol leaking from his pores, erased all the good. I was hurt that he would not choose me over a secret, stiff drink and angry at him for wasting my last "good" years—most of my forties. It'd be downhill from there, physically, for me. My face and body would go through changes that I'd heard described but wasn't prepared for. I would never meet anyone again. I would grow old alone.

A day hasn't gone by when I don't think of him. I see him every time a hawk lands in the field. As much as I don't want to, I compare subsequent men to him. He unwittingly became the benchmark. I want *him* minus the drinking.

Here I am, ten years later, looking at sixty. I survived my fifties, having gone out with—what?—twenty more men, wondering whether I would ever find my guy. I have dated widely: CIA operative, chocolatier, sculptor, animator, salesman, architect, air force vet, investment banker, physicist, economist, tech entrepreneur, baker, producer, carpenter, composer, writer, cowboy, puppeteer, photographer, professor, blueberry farmer; white, Black, Latino, East Indian, West Indian, Native American, Jewish; midwestern, New Yorker, southwestern, southern, African, French; tall, short, skinny, broad, redhead, bald, curly, frizzy, flat, always capped.

I have met men out and about doing things I love; through friends' introductions, and I was totally comfortable with online dating long before most, having consulted for Match when many thought it creepy. I am not recently widowed or divorced, nor am I technically a spinster—I was married briefly and am a mother—but I've been effectively single *forever*. Over decades, I've been on thousands of dates and been in hundreds of relationships of varying degrees and non-degrees of intimacy.

I have been in love, want to be in love, but mostly, more recently, I have been in *like*.

Is it asking too much to want not just an equal, but a partner, someone who wants to build something together? I acknowledge there will be compromises, but what am I willing to give up? Do I become the caregiver for a man my parents' age with debilitating health issues or play cougar to a younger man who likely still has or wants children? Do I support a man's unsustainable lifestyle after being a single working mom for two decades? Do I stomach mansplaining? Lies? Disfunction? Narcissism and addictions? Compulsive, bipolar schizophrenics and depressives? Men on spectrums or with syndromes? Do I forgo physical attraction? And on that score, as an aside, I'm not sure I know what chemistry is anymore. So many men don't even know the basics of seduction. Women friends confess that they are *attracted to no one*. Others tell me that they *train* their men, but if they don't know how to kiss, where do I start?

Would I settle for a good, regular conversation?

Let me tell you what it's like to be lonely, about the fear of growing old alone, or just dying alone, falling off a ladder alone. Getting a cough alone. Imagine the monotony and consumption of being allowed to live with all your thoughts in the news-surround pandemic, tear-gassed Black Lives Matter protests, raging wildfires, the turbulent election week, the Trump-crazed years stoking fear and paranoia and anxiety and sadness and grief, with no one to offer comfort. No one to hug, to touch. And then living with the guilt of knowing that I have it better than most, especially those essential workers who witness the death of strangers and loved ones daily, or who are bagging groceries wondering *when*.

And then having my oldest childhood friend take her own life.

This is the formula for loneliness. It starts with being single and living alone—in the country. Add to that working alone as a writer; that is, not working remotely, not checking in with the team or client, but completely solo. That was my pre-pandemic life, so not much changed when COVID had us in lockdown, as I entered my sixtieth year. Being alone most of the time was and is my norm. While I cherish my independence and space—both mental and physical—I am a social creature. The solitude can be overwhelming. On occasion, as an antidote, pre-pandemic, I took my work to a café, just to be around other people, but mostly I would get my fix of humanity in the evenings, going out with friends, attending performances or lectures at Bard or Vassar, readings at local bookshops, movies at Upstate Films, dinner at favorite haunts.

When the pandemic struck, I no longer had those evening distractions populated with friends and other humans. The isolation's grip halted the search for romance. While it heightened the desire, it removed the external expectations of being in a relationship.

The pandemic has prompted a new conversation about loneliness and isolation.

And it forced the friendship hand. I noticed who called and who didn't. Married and partnered friends, people connected to others through work, or who were living with family, bemoaned their isolation on Facebook, but I rarely heard from them.

Once I texted a friend saying I was very sick and sad. She wrote back, "Call me when you feel better."

It was a chilling, gray, rainy spring. When I was hitting rock bottom during the pandemic, I reached out to people who might be even more alone than me. I headed out for a walk or to the garden. I yanked a weed. Maybe I ate it.

Nature has always been my salve. It's hard to imagine an easier place to self-isolate than my field: abundant fresh air, no sidewalks to negotiate, no terrifying, radioactive elevator buttons to push. I am fortunate to live as I do: in a converted two-hundred-year-old "green" barn that I brought to the property, a meadow spilling out the back door. I built my life around being outdoors: gardening, hiking, and inhaling views. I forage, cook, and eat. In spring, I scour the landscape for morels, wild asparagus, watercress, and fiddlehead ferns. How long can I live in a field by myself?

I love my independence, and yet being a single woman at my age—at any age—is no cup of tea.

There are safety issues. Although I am tall and able-bodied, I cross the street when a man approaches. I pull out my car keys before I leave the movie theater to avoid fumbling for them in the parking lot. In St. Croix, where I recently bought and renovated a house, I am warned to not walk the beaches by myself, which I do daily, and look forward to. People wonder whether it's scary living at the end of a long driveway alone. Some ask me if I own a gun. Four men have given me axes.

Or take logistics, life's mechanics. There is no one to hold the seats while the other person gets popcorn. No one to watch the luggage while the other parks. Hotel rooms and organized bike trips carry premiums for single travelers. Who's my snorkel buddy? And traveling solo is more difficult, less fun, and less memorable (like movies and books) without shared observations and discoveries, an articulated narrative.

Not to mention that cooking for one either means you stop cooking or eat for two.

And then there's chauvinism. Although I've renovated six historic homes as both general contractor and designer, most tradesmen conde-

scend, intimidate, or get defensive if I ask a question—which I do, frequently, wanting to understand and learn.

Living alone, being alone, has physical and mental health consequences,
too. We know people who live alone live shorter lives. Social isolation is
the equivalent of smoking fifteen cigarettes a day. Lonely bodies are in
stress and produce cortisol, which takes a toll on the body's systems.

I find that being single is exacerbated by active exclusion from "normal" social circles. Where is basic empathy and inclusivity? Singleness—
like race or ethnicity—defines us, more than all other qualities. Until
recently, rarely would a married couple include me in a night out, and generally only in larger potlucks or cocktail parties. I was *disinvited* from a
dinner party when my boyfriend could no longer make it. Last year, coming out of a theater alone, I bumped into married friends who were going
for dinner, who didn't think to ask, *Would you like to join us?*

Is something wrong with us single women? It's not because we aren't
interesting or can't hold our own. Having had a substantial career as a
management consultant—retail, fashion, media, innovation—and exten-
sive experience in construction and design, as an artist, writer, forager, gar-
dener, environmentalist, athlete, having traveled widely and thought
deeply, I can engage on any number of topics with men and women of any
age and persuasion. I am not an awkward single woman at the table who
only talks "female things," whatever that means. Handbags? The last time
I was sexually assaulted?

I believe many assume we are to blame for our divorces, just as women
are held accountable for all that goes wrong everywhere (like in corporate America or even when husbands or other men act badly), while men
are given the benefit of the doubt. Are we menacing in our singlehood?
Are we reminders of what might be in an unhappy couple's future? There's
the self-serving fallback: *we are threatening.* To be clear, I don't flirt with
the hitched men at the table. I am on my gender's side. I'm not interested
in married or partnered men. I consider it a lose-lose-lose.

So, we single women hang out together.

Some of the fear of being single is a branding issue. People perceive us as damaged goods. Let me assert, in self-defense: Roughly a dozen men have expressed interest in spending a lifetime with me. But I drove them away and ended those relationships because I woke up one day and realized I'd rather be drinking my café latte alone. I believe I have still not met the man I am meant to be with so I will not waste time with someone who isn't, who detracts from rather than contributes something to my life, to the conversation. Nor would I return to anyone in my past; not a single one, in my estimation, is *the one who got away.*

"I'm surprised no one's snapped you up!" says a handsome man I'd just met. I know he means well, but he's implying that it's the man's decision.

Then there's the valid concern, the self-doubt inherent in being alone, that maybe something *is* wrong with me—*us.* I'm sure all those men I dated could tell you—and they would be right—I am cold and lacking in affection. Why would I be anything else with a man whom I find unattractive?

It's not as if I come from a "broken" family. Rather, it's possible I witnessed in my octogenarian parents' marriage one that worked so well that my aspirations are high. My father gazes with delight at my mother while she tells a story, hanging on every word. My parents are both fascinating, bright, attractive, stylish, and competent. They grew together and operate as a single organism, a true partnership, ever expanding and engaged in the world. Even after they've been together all day, I can hear them comparing notes as they lie in bed. I want what they have.

And, of course, meeting young and growing old together is different than finding a mate later in life, which requires merging two separate lives (families, routines, homes, locations) and inherent complexity and logistical compromises. But that just means the partner must be worth it. Why would I share (or give up) my life, my mornings, my precious time, my body, *me,* with someone who has little to offer in return, who only drags me down?

Some friends enjoy hearing about my romantic escapades and give me an audience and counsel. But I am fully aware, after being single for decades and having gone through many potential mates, that there is, understandably, less interest, and I suspect, more skepticism as time goes by. *What is wrong with me?* Even I am less interested. Even I am skeptical. I generally don't bother to tell anyone about the latest squeeze until I feel like he will last at least a few months. My family has welcomed a parade of men who thought they were special because they were invited to Thanksgiving. Little did they know that they'd followed many who'd come before, and the family was merely another test of stamina and character they rarely passed. None made it onto my Facebook page.

I acknowledge that it is mostly my own doing, my choice. But I also know I am not alone in my aloneness. There are a lot of us. We are part of a broader growing trend, and yet invisible. According to the Pew Research Center, between 2014 and 2017, 23 percent of adults sixty and older live alone and spend most of their day alone. And it gets worse as we get older; more of us, and more women, will live alone. In New York City, the percentage of people living alone hovers around 50 percent. Some older singles, recently divorced or widowed, relish their newfound independence, but I think few would give up the opportunity to find the right mate if it weren't so much work, so discouraging—if they believed someone was out there for them.

My affectionate, silky English Setter, Dexter, stands in for the partner I can't seem to find and friends I rarely see. Dexter makes me laugh, forces hour-long daily walks, gobbles up dubious items excavated from the freezer. #Dexter occupies my Instagram feed, lap, and bed. But Dexter doesn't have much to say. So, I keep trying.

Most single women I know have given up. They purport that most of the single men our age have issues—real, insurmountable ones. One friend swears by widowers. "All the good men are taken," she says. She has her eye on a few happily married men. I am circumspect about widowers. I can't think of married male friends, or husbands of women friends, as *contenders*. Waiting in the bleachers for a woman to leave this life—or her marriage—strikes me as unsavory. Besides, despite a widower's enduring track record, compared to, say, a serial bachelor, I don't feel I could fill the shoes of an adored woman who was taken away prematurely, nor do I relish being jealous of a ghost. I avoid the topic altogether by avoiding widowers, but that is becoming difficult as they appear with greater frequency in the graying dating pool.

I live on an eighty-three-acre defunct apple orchard in the Hudson Valley my daughter named Field Farm. Over the years, I have shared this mesmerizing meadow with hundreds of people through dinner parties, poolside and firepit gatherings, and men I was involved with, some of whom were helpful, most of whom told me what I should do. But it is hard to keep this place up all on my own. I am physically capable of doing much of it, but the motivation is becoming difficult to muster. I hire a guy named Frank on an hourly basis for small projects or to make firewood of a toppled apple tree, while I jump on my John Deere tractor in the adjacent field.

In this pandemic moment, while everyone is fleeing to the suburbs, to the Hudson Valley, for a place like mine, I search for New York City real estate online. I am on the split-rail fence about whether I want to end up back in the city, where everything is walkable, accessible, and less maintenance. There will be more contenders, romance, distractions, people, in the city, although I lived there for twenty years and never found a partner there either. I would hate to leave this land, which has been so kind to me, the exuberant gardens I have created and nurtured, the vistas that offer me solace, particularly during the pandemic. But I fear I cannot manage all this upkeep by myself for much longer. Friends are moving into the local town and giving up their backyards.

I realize that I'm not just deciding about a romantic partner but also about how and where to grow older. I should find a caretaker—that's what I should do. But finding a caretaker is almost as hard as finding a lover.

To Be or Not To Be in a Relationship

TALES OF HUMOR, DISAPPOINTMENT, REWARDS, AND PERSONAL INSIGHT

Not Jane Eyre's Story

Susan Ostrov Weisser

In all the romantic books I read as a teenager, the heroine doesn't look for love but finds it anyway. Elizabeth Bennet, Jo March, Jane Eyre, and so on, would never dream of seeking out a man for love or making the first move, much less serial dating. Before I was twelve, I knew how the story went: someone of great personal value (and sometimes monetary value as well) notices how special you are, usually through your good looks but possibly because of your personal charm, wit, and fine mind. I secretly believed I had at least the last three, if only the right man were there to recognize and reward this. Female virtue helped as well—that would have to be faked— but Catherine Earnshaw of *Wuthering Heights* did without it.

It was hard at first for me to shake the feeling that actively seeking men through online dating was unwomanly, and it seemed a mark of being undeserving. But then modern popular wisdom is in complete conflict with the traditional story. You are supposed to be the can-do go-getter who "looks for men for fifteen hours a week," to quote the advice of an article on dating. Hard work will pay off, and if you don't have what you want, it's probably your fault.

The fact is that once you've exhausted your workplace colleagues, social network of friends, and relatives who are willing to recommend you, places to go are in short supply. You're supposed to try the hardware store, museums, and massage classes. Or you're told to live your life and let it happen, be Zen. If it succeeds, it's either fate or a sign of your maturity (a proxy for virtue), and if it doesn't, it's because you didn't work hard enough at pretending you weren't trying.

One odd characteristic of online dating is that it's one-on-one. The prospective couple doesn't mix with anyone else either of you know, whereas pre-digitally, you were more likely to go out with someone who fit in with your existing family or social circle right off the bat. Now you don't get much of a chance to try that out with all these little intimate "us only" dates, so there's a tremendous burden on each party to be "just perfect" for the other one. How do you know what might fit when there's so little to go on?

One guy I approached on Match wrote back to say that we had already met once and it had been a "marginal no-go" for him. Since I didn't remember him, I'd say it was a "definite no-go" for me. But the language cracks me up. It's like a business deal is being negotiated.

Speaking of dating as a marketplace, I ran across the funniest ad not meant to be funny: "Obese Older Man Seeks Beautiful Young Girl." This could have been marvelous irony, except that the profile seemed dead serious—it was a male rant about why women complain that men judge them on *their* looks yet reject obese him, combined with a detailed explanation of what he wanted in a woman. This boiled down to youth and looks, though he did at the end graciously concede that he would settle for a *beautiful* older woman as a second choice.

One aspect of online dating I find horrifying is the need to talk on the phone to these strangers. It's not that I'm shy; it's that I'm allergic to the boredom of chatting with someone I don't know, unless this someone is funny or fascinating. The initial conversation is such a sacred cow that you're considered troubled if you want to bypass it. Usually, it involves something like the following: Where do you work? How do you get to work? How long does that take? I'd rather fax the information in.

I'm at my worst when someone I barely know calls "just to chat." It seems churlish to say "Hey, we haven't even met yet, and I have to give up my precious evening time to make silly small talk?" Of course, this is not a Good Attitude. I can chat with the best of them, but while I do, I often have one eye on the TV or the article I'm reading: my brain needs more stimulation than hearing what a fabulous, high-achieving child they have, often with a younger wife. One of the nicest compliments a man ever gave me was that I was the only woman he wanted to talk to on the phone without also reading the day's news (apparently, that included his girl-friend). It may not have been true, but I knew what he meant.

"I just wanted to hear the sound of your voice," Pete said—for Pete's sake! We'd known each other all of a week or so. If the sound of *your* voice is not what I crave, this kind of attention does nothing for me.

Joe said that women older than fifty are not very attractive in general. "Let's face it" (he's sixty-three). "I especially feel repulsed by their arms. They tend to have what I call 'puffy arms.' You can always tell a woman's age by her arms." Oh. So good to know.

By now you've cleverly gathered that I regularly offend men who like me. I went out with a gentleman who took me to the Yale Club for our first date, and then was ready to go back to my place or at least hang together around my neighborhood for several more hours. He was sweet and pleas-ant looking, but since we had absolutely nothing to say to each other dur-ing dinner, I cheerfully announced I was going home at 7 P.M. The next day he called to scold me—he'd driven into Manhattan all the way from Queens because he assumed he'd be home late, and I'd ended a Saturday evening date (that started around 4 P.M.) at 7 P.M. "Who does that?" he wanted to know. When I admitted I didn't really think we were going to work as a couple, he accused me indignantly of "not being flexible," some-thing I'm used to hearing.

My sad conclusion: I'm not really flexible, and I don't want to be.

One odd thing I've noticed lately in dating is the way men either talk about themselves without asking me any question beyond "What do you teach?" As soon as I say, "English," they immediately launch into their grades in the subject or their fear that I'll correct their grammar. Many speak over me when I try to add to the conversation, never noticing that I'm trying to get a word in. It could be worse: the Conversational Dominator who talks over you and the Conversational Narcissist who talks only about himself can be effectively combined for the ultimate alienating experience. I'm not sure if this is a male thing, actually, since I haven't dated females (I definitely would if a cute one asked me)—maybe it's a dating thing. Or maybe it's that men believe that asking women personal questions on early dates is rude or intrusive. I wish I knew. I asked my daughter if she thinks this tendency to talk exclusively about oneself and/or step on another person's conversational turn is a gender thing. She says she knows women like this (and I do too—and also men who don't). Perhaps, she says, it's particularly true of men of my own generation, because at that time women in their youth were trained to listen and appreciate, and therefore these men expect it.

One night I went out with Robert, who neither dominated the conversation nor talked only about himself, but whose responses to my own conversation were so distant that he could have been on another planet. Twice I asked him what he was thinking, because after I spoke, he screwed up his face and literally turned it a bit away. The next day he wrote that he "does not want to get involved" with me. Was it my age, five years older than he was? I'll never know, which doesn't keep me up at night.

More recently, I agreed to a Zoom meeting with a guy named Chet, who'd pressed for it. The Zoom conversation was less than sparky, mostly dull exchanges of facts, when Chet suddenly asked for my astrological sign. "Um, I think it's Gemini," I said, "but I don't have much interest in astrology, actually."

"Well, I'm a Leo," he went on, as if he hadn't heard the last part, "and I'm not sure how a Gemini and a Leo would get on in a love relationship."

"I'm the last one who could tell you," I said.

Hold on a second, cried Chet, "I'm googling it now." And google it he did, for more than a second, while I waited on Zoom, not patiently. Apparently, the news wasn't good, though I don't remember what our astrological problem was. In any case, he'd insightfully picked up my silent reaction to all this and accused me of being judgmental, which he resented, and the Zoom "date" ended about five minutes later. The astrologers were right.

Sometimes it seems that when I tell a friend that so-and-so was not for me and they ask why, no explanation I give is sufficient. "Nothing in common" or "We don't share values" elicits "But it could be more interesting to have nothing in common!" or "You'll discover new values!'; "not attractive" is answered with, "He'll grow on you!"; "dull" with "He could be shy," and so on. I think if I said, "He has three heads," I'd be told "Are you saying you judge people by their looks?" The theory is that the world is littered with uncut diamonds who need to be dug up. Not that there aren't those: I had an interesting relationship with one very flawed diamond, myself.

What this criticism amounts to, though, is that you, a single person, don't have the right to complain about being lonely—or aren't supposed to even *be* lonely—if you aren't simply choosing from what's on offer. An analogy would be insisting on going naked if you don't like what you can afford at a huge department store—in theory you *should* be able to find something suitable and likable, so if you don't, it's your own fault. There are a lot of suits out there! And if I were twenty, or thirty, or even fifty, I might agree.

But the logical consequence of going out with everybody because they *could* turn out to be Mr. Right is that you don't have time to do anything else. It's the equivalent of holding down three jobs. I'm just too old to take the time to investigate all the nice people out there: I want at least a *little* flicker of pleasure when I'm with a guy.

The underlying message about being single at an older age is always that you're alone because you're a neurotic failure at love and haven't worked hard enough, including on yourself. You just need an attitude adjustment! The dating market and other people have nothing to do with it. On the contrary, I would say it very much does. One pertinent fact is that older women outnumber older men on dating sites. Partly this is due to men's higher chance of dying earlier than women do, but probably also because older men in general are more likely to be married than women of the same age. Though women initiate the great majority of divorces in America, men remarry sooner and at a higher rate than women after divorce, which means more women are harvesting the leftovers from other women's relationships, to put it bluntly.

Here's what happened one day when I tried to be open to possibilities.

Jerry was not unattractive and looked better on paper than most, so I agreed to lunch soon after we started emailing. Two minutes into the meal he asked what my principles were about monogamy. This is a subject I find interesting and complex, and I was curious as to what he had to say. Some guys have been recently hurt and want reassurance that you won't be banging their best friend the week after they've declared their love. Some want to tell you up front that they're married, a bravado I admire more than the man who hides it until asked. So I took the question seriously and replied that I wasn't in favor of it or against it, that I thought the structure of a relationship should grow organically. For myself, at this point in my life, I could embrace monogamy or renounce it, depending on who the person was and what they could give me.

He barely seemed to listen to my response to his question. "Well, I have a theory about it," he said importantly. I was all ears.

"Look, let me begin this way," he started, "When you were young and had a best friend, you thought that was the only friend you could have, right?" Not really, but I nodded to speed things up. "Then when you grew up you realized that it was better to have several friends, all different, right?" Oh, right. I could see where this was going.

"So, who are you f-cking?" I said.

He blanched, looked away. "It so happens that I'm against one-night stands and casual sex," he said quickly, "You have to have tender feelings for each one, and there can't be more than a few, or you don't have time for them all. I call it"—he paused—"*friend sex.*"

"Okay," I said, "So who *are* you sleeping with?" I regretted having said "f-ck" just before—too harsh.

"There's a lovely lady in California," he confided, "We are good friends and lovers, and there is someone in the New York area too. But I would like there to be someone else. What do you think?"

I wasn't sure thinking had much to do with this. But my gut was unaccountably roiling, and I tried to sort out why. "It's not that I think your arrangement is wrong, but there's something about this that bothers me," I said, "It sounds so *thought out*, like a business proposal."

"Okay, this is what I suggest: we'll meet next time at your place. I like to go to women's apartments," he continued, "I like to look at their books and pictures, get a sense of who they are. We'll chat, we'll kiss and make out and rub each other, but we won't fuck." (So much for my delicate fear of offending two minutes before.) "Then we'll see what happens."

We'll *rub* each other? That grabbed me most. The staging was built into the program: first we look at my art to get a sense of me, then we kiss to see if we like each other, then we proceed to the rub. Scrub-a-dub-dub, man and woman in the tub. I don't think so. He was looking at me expectantly, while explaining that most women thought sex should *follow* intimacy, whereas he thought it was the *pathway to intimacy*. He said this as though no one had thought of that before.

"I'm sorry," I said evenly, "But I'm afraid there's not a chance in hell that we're going to be rubbing in my apartment anytime soon."

"No?" he said. He seemed startled. And displeased.

"I just can't get with the idea that we're going to arrange the kissing and caressing as though we're making up the agenda for a corporate meeting."
Silence.

"Look," I said, "I don't think sex has to grow out of love, but it's nice when there's at least some spontaneity of desire." Any attraction I'd had evaporated in the Trumpian let's-make-a-deal atmosphere. He didn't take well to my not taking well to this, and a chill was in the air as we got the check. We split it, then split. There wasn't going to be friendship, or sex, or alas, *friend sex*.

Will I date again? I don't know. It takes a stomach of iron and a will of steel.

Discovery through Online Dating Sites

A WOMAN'S PERSPECTIVE

Phyllis Carito

It starts with a photograph, the picture chosen to hopefully show the man at his best. There are men who pose for the camera, with charismatic eyes and full-toothed smiles. Some men choose the family look with a picture of them at their daughter or son's wedding, or an endearing photograph of them holding a baby grandchild. Some men choose the tough guy look, straddling their motorcycle or hanging off the edge of a cliff, a panorama world spread out below them.

A wall of faces to explore or discount based on past attractions—mustache out or beard in, bald in or long hair out. This is limiting and it may take a few rounds of sorting profiles to be open to men with a different look. Once into the profile, the details say sixty years old, but some photographs are definitely from an earlier time. Standard dating site protocol rejects a profile without a photograph. The idea is that seeing each other entices one in and offers a more secure feeling about that other person. That may not be true, because a smile for a photograph doesn't truly indicate what burdens they still hold on to or what desires they expect fulfilled.

The key questions are answered about religion, drinking, and children, along with the description of what they would want on a first date, which is often given some serious thought. Sometimes the men are clear that they want only a friend or casual dating while others quickly request a relationship and some of those even say they are looking for a marriage. Still, this is a different process from their original dating when they were young. It is a virtual world that is attempting to duplicate the dating ritual that previously occurred more often at college, a dance, a bar, or a friend's wedding.

There is another twist to online matchmaking that women sixty or older have to recognize; it isn't the way it was when they grew up either. Dating was in the purview of the man, and traditional dating meant the woman knew her role was to be a lady who waited demurely for the man, who acquiesced to the man, and who was always treated to every dinner, movie, etc. If she was married before the changing time of women's liberation in the 1960s, then this may be the first time a woman feels empowered in a potential relationship. Women's roles and expectations have shifted, and some men have (reluctantly) shifted, too.

From tag names to photographs, to descriptive narratives, all pursuers become labeled in the viewer's mind: the Talker, the Deceiver, the Desperate, the Uncertain, the Angry, and the Unattractive.

I have found at one end of the spectrum is the Talker, who continues to communicate but never has any leanings toward meeting. Is he just lonely for conversation? Is there really another relationship he is hiding? You can even come to wonder if he is a shill. He keeps women coming back by throwing them a "flirt" or a "wink" or a "gift"—different sites use different terms for this—but it seems a way of saying, *I'm potentially interested but I'm not ready to even write a hello.* Or he answers each inquiry from the woman with a vague, "I like dancing, too." Yet, he never asks you to go dancing. The continued contact, albeit disappointing, keeps the other person tempted with possibility.

The Deceiver is one who sometimes can be exposed within a few writing exchanges or who, at a meeting face-to-face, is revealed to be a different age than stated, still married, or clearly wants only a physical relationship.

All of which may or may not be a deal breaker for the woman. You have to decide what is important to you.

For some women, a warning sign or even the signal for an immediate rejection is that a man is separated but not divorced. What these men say about this situation may give the impression that they might decide to go back to that "worst woman ever." Will they? As more profiles are read it becomes clearer how to decipher which men are looking to test their virility again and which are looking for new companionship.

The Desperate can make you feel desired because of his interest to connect quickly. He moves from writing on the site to conversation to wanting to meet: "Don't put me off." Everything he says is about immediate gratification. Be ready for a proposal of some sort. Trust your response, your gut feeling, to tell you how interested you are or if you are just enjoying the attention.

The Uncertain can truly be anyone on a dating site, as in many ways this seems an unnatural way to build care about another person. We are strangers, after all. Thinking about this reminds me to accept that the man may be as uncomfortable as I may be.

The Angry is a sad man because he thinks he wants to move forward but is still holding the burden of some woman who burnt him or some concept that women are always going to betray him. Is this something you want to take on?

Finally, the Unattractive moniker is not about looks but only about a lack of attraction between the man and woman. A connection is wanted, but there are no pheromones firing between the two or no strong desire to engage and exchange a sharing about everything. I have found, to my surprise, that some of these men, at this point in the game of relationships, may become an acquaintance or even a friend.

Part of the process of sorting through the potential suitors is an awareness of what men are saying, not about themselves, but about their caveats—indicating the potential of women they won't tolerate— women who they perceive will berate, lie, whine, etc. Most of all, they don't want someone who is still carrying the pain of any past relationships. It's not about judging, it's about interpretations, and probably unrealistic expectations, weighted with the image both the man and the woman already have in their heads. These are often based on past experiences rather than the need they each have in their heart to connect with someone.

Sometimes the wall of profiles feels overwhelming. Sometimes the uncertainty of descriptions moves the pursuer on to another profile. The hope is to glimpse something about whether this first communication is a path to connection. In the end the discovery may be more about themselves than those they meet. Participants must ask themselves if they believe they will meet the right person? Do they even believe this is the way to proceed? What effort are they putting into the process of searching through photographs and attempting to say just the right words to catch the attention of a special someone?

The process can be daunting or fun; it can reveal the deep sadness of a widower or the hidden desires of a man that can be a surprise to him depending upon past experiences molded by a traditional marriage. Now at a crossroads, when they are customarily past dating, with grown families, and retired, they find themselves still seeking to share a meal, a laugh, an embrace, and to have a social companion.

Ultimately the process will go from meeting online to a first date and maybe a second date, just to be sure. There is always going back to the virtual wall of a potential relationship. Since they are past sixty, time and loneliness are important factors, so the wall will easily call to them again. I've found this myself, going back to an initial rejected connection to see if a thread from our former conversation could be picked up with that person again. Each time you go back, there is a dual pull of frustration and motivation to meet the right match.

This sometimes leads to going off the dating site for a few months and then returning, and sometimes continuing with updating and altering profiles to fine-tune your correspondence. I have also changed dating sites to see if one over another offered more compatibility for seniors. Generally, I found the process to be similar on each site, and the mix of men don't vary much from one site to another. Finding a long-term companion might be more of a challenge, but certainly virtually meeting new and different men in your life is part of the adventure of online dating.

Close Encounters
of the Fifth Kind

Nan Bauer-Maglin

A little over a year after Chris, my husband of thirty-six years, died of pancreatic cancer, I ventured onto OkCupid and Match. I was lonely, lonely for a man's companionship and caring. I was keeping very busy, going out with friends for dinner, a movie, a museum, a walk. I was also involved with two women's groups—one to discuss aging; the other, a reading and political action group—plus, I had several volunteer commitments and a big family (four children and thirteen grandchildren). I was not without company. I was without intimacy.

Before Chris, I had been married for fifteen years to another man. So, adding it up, I have had a live-in partner for fifty-one years. When Chris died, the silence became deafening, the loneliness was palpable, and the exhaustion of having to attend to all the financial transactions and household chores alone was overwhelming. I had to settle everything related to Chris's death (Social Security payments, retirement funds of his that were being held up, a refund for a trip to France we never made, among other things). In addition, I learned our car was not in my name, that the trust we had put property into had to be revised, and I wanted to rethink the names on my health-care proxy and living will—all the small and big things that go with a complicated life lived for more than seventy years.

In that first lonely year, pieces of Chris were everywhere I turned: his research, his books, his clothes, especially his collarless black shirts and his gray felt hat. I spent that year finding people who would pick up his research, men who would appreciate his dapper attire. I gave away boxes of papers and clothes. But that meant that piece by piece, the material evidence of my husband was disappearing. As I entered the second year of widowhood, I had less busy work attending to the logistical aftermath of death and also less of Chris in any tangible, material way. The loneliness, the emptiness, of the second year felt even heavier. The finality of my loss hit me hard.

So, I ventured online.

One of my friends helped me write my profile:

> Lively, energetic, petite, stylish, solvent widow, 71, seeking man in my age range for movies, plays, museums, ramen, wine, and rambles in city & country. Writer, editor, and retired English professor & administrator, grandmother several times over. Aesthetic predilection for rusty metal and weathered wood. Love Manhattan; love far-flung travel. Politically dismayed as of November 2016.

I learned later that I should have said I was younger than seventy (even though I had reduced my age by four years to seventy-one), maybe sixty-nine or sixty-eight so as not to limit who "looks" at me. Not unexpectedly, most older men want younger women. Enid, a friend with online experience, wanted me to henna my hair; gray is not good, she advised. I refused, as I wanted to remain me, even as I questioned this decision. But I was cheered by an experiment by Anne Kreamer, who posted her picture on Match first with brown hair and then months later with her natural gray. Three times as many men were interested in the gray-haired woman.[1]

My experienced friend gave me additional instructions: I should initiate conversations. She even gave me a template:

> Hi [Depressed Loser, or whatever his screen name might be],
> I really enjoyed reading your profile, particularly the part where you said you like to torture young children! Take a look at mine and let me know if you'd like to connect.

While she was obviously joking with the salutation and the content of the message, she wanted me to understand that including a specific reference to something the person had actually written would show that you read his profile and were not just sending a generic note. Enid claims, and the sites suggest, that initiating conversation increases your chances of finding a suitable match, since you're finding people as well as waiting to be found. I appreciated the advice, as I received numerous notes that just said, "Hello beautiful, want to get together?" or "We have so much in common, let's talk." I rejected these immediately, annoyed that these men likely had not read my profile.

Enid also advised that I should date at least seven men before allowing myself to get discouraged but cautioned me not to waste my time on people who the sites say are less than a 90 percent match with my profile (the percentage calculated by how the other person and I answer a series of questions). This is because the algorithms are reasonably good at estimating the suitability of the match. Before advising me, Enid had met someone on the site OkCupid. While I did pay attention to her instructions, I was somewhat skeptical; after all, she was in her early sixties—not in the no-man's-land of the seventies—it had to be easier for her.

When I questioned why the number seven, she acknowledged its arbitrariness, but she didn't want me to give up if I had a few bad experiences. It can take a long time to find someone appealing, she said, and even seven could be too few. She hoped, though, that once I had done seven, I would feel comfortable doing more.

Discouragement came after only four different encounters. Numbers One, Two, and Three wrote to me; I wrote to Number Four.

1. George[2] had a lot in common with me: Caucasian American, second marriage, stepchildren, professor. He wrote sensitive, thoughtful emails: about his wife with Alzheimer's who he took care of for three years, about his youthful attachment to the main character in Sherwood Anderson's *Winesburg, Ohio*, with whom I, too, identified

in high school. We went on two dates. He kissed me at the end of
each date—to my surprise. I liked talking to him but was a bit taken
aback by his age—eighty-five (listed online as seventy-nine). I was
uncomfortable with this number, having just been through a death
and not wanting to grow attached to someone who could be close to
death or to the infirmities associated with aging. He disappeared
after the second date. Relieved that I did not have to make a decision,
I was nonetheless hurt as I waited for some communication. (I now
understand that kind of wordless vanishing is called *ghosting*.)

2. Buni, a South Asian American, was sixty-one, never married, no
   children, with a forty-year career in technology. We met in an upscale
   part of the city. He wore NYC regulation black. We had raw oysters
   and cold white wine. It was quite pleasant, but our lifestyles proved so
   very different. It made no sense to continue.

3. Samson, a former literature teacher, now photographer with leftist
   sentiments, divorced, with children and grandchildren, whose age
   and ethnicity were similar to mine. I especially liked the rugged
   aesthetic visible in his photography, but he was extremely verbose and
   intense. I felt he was throwing words at me that walled me into
   silence. When I told him I did not like Shakespeare, he was shocked.
   He was sure I must have had a traumatic experience while reading
   Shakespeare as a teenager; he had a hard time believing me when
   I said it was purely a matter of taste. Probably also a matter of my
   women's literature background, when we opposed the domination of
   dead white men in the literary canon. He later wrote a long email
   trying to ferret out the deep reason for my dislike. He exhausted me.

4. Mathias, African American, sixty-five, was an artist, divorced, with a
   daughter. After Number Three, I had been planning to take a break,
   but I liked what he wrote in his profile: he was open to women older
   than he; his reading preferences were refreshing—personal, political,
   and up to date. He answered my inquiry saying he hoped I understood that he felt he should try to develop a love relationship with a

woman of color. I did; in fact, I had trepidations myself about the work needed to connect across culture and experience. We did not pursue it.

After Number Four, I decided to pull back for a while. However, because my Match subscription was good for a few more months, I kept getting regular messages about men "just right for me," determined by those aforementioned algorithms. It was hard not to scan these email blasts. And so, one night I opened one. While it indicated that Mr. X and I were only 88 percent matched, I was taken with the fact that he was a widower (I am partial to widowers) and had a very long marriage that he declared were "mostly" great years. I liked his honesty about what the ups and downs of any long-term relationship were, so I immediately penned him a message saying I identified with him in terms of loss and also with his characterization of marriage. But as soon as I sent it off, I realized that I had not read his entire profile page. I quickly scrolled down to the final paragraph where Mr. X declares his dedication to Christ as son of God and the forgiver of our sins. As a lifelong atheist, I panicked at my carelessness and quickly sent an "oops" message about our different views on religion. So that ended that.

Now after two months of dating online, here is what I know:

I miss my husband now more than ever. It is so difficult to find someone who could be a partner, even if I do not expect the connection to be similar to the one I had. Men have it easier: they have a wider range of ages to choose from, including much younger women. Also, the ratio of widows to widowers is about four to one. I suspect that ratio is even greater for older widows. I still want male companionship, though not necessarily for marriage or cohabitation. I wish I were attracted to women; there are so many great women out there. I remain lonely but reluctant to continue the search; it has exhausted me.

If I ever do go back to online dating sites, I will promise any man who writes or dates me that I will not write about him for publication. I do not want to further jinx my chances. I am writing this now because that is what I do; I write about my life and experiences in order to take some control. After this essay, I pledge that I will not publish anything more about my dating life.

NOTES

1. Thanks to Avis, Elliot, Florence, June, Yael, and Dan for editorial comments. https://www.womansday.com/style/beauty/a52199/sexy-gray-hair/.
2. The names of the men have been changed.

Confessions of an Online Dater

Neil Stein

Yes, it's true, I was an online dater. For much longer than either I or, certainly, the women I met would have liked. That part of my love life has been thankfully moved to my desktop trash bin. But every now and again I have the urge, and it all comes back to me in waves like a tsunami.

I first went online after a breakup with a woman that I had met in a conventional way—through mutual friends. After a mourning period, I decided that I was ready to meet someone new. I had read about Match, so I subscribed. Creating and posting a profile felt like a task that I was well suited for. I would be able to capitalize on my senses of humor and irony. Add to that, I was reasonably confident that in any email exchange my grammar and spelling would be more correct than not. What a winning combination that would be. I would be a hit!

And to some degree, I was. I contacted and was contacted by an array of women. And therein lies an inherent problem with online dating. With a seemingly endless supply of potential partners available why would I (or anyone) settle for someone who didn't hit all the marks? I know that's not a very attractive remark, but this is, after all, a confession.

At first, the process was intoxicating. It gave me a rush of excitement. And when you're the new kid on the block, there's a lot of interest. It seems that true love is just around the corner. But it soon became apparent to me that I was in for a longer haul than I had expected. And a process that had been exciting and full of promise at the outset soon became drudgery—merely a means to an end.

It didn't take long for me to learn the ropes. Of course, I had too many long dinners with women I knew I wasn't interested in. But I eventually had the sense to stick to just drinks whenever possible. I like to drink, so almost always, while I may have been disappointed with my date, I enjoyed myself. Occasionally, I would go on a second date with someone in hopes that the spark that wasn't there in the first place would miraculously appear. That never happened. Although I had at other times in my life experienced falling for someone over an extended period of time, while online dating I wasn't prepared to invest the time to see if love would grow—not when the chance for instant infatuation was just one click away.

As for my own profile, which included some basic biographical information along with a description of what kind of person I was, I took the approach that I wanted it to reflect my personality—that upon meeting there wouldn't be any huge discrepancy between the real me and the cyber me. The result was a narrative that was intended to bring a self-deprecating, witty, and ironic tone to what I viewed as an incredibly artificial and dull process. I was also trying to break out of the standard, cliché-driven, dry tone that I found in many of the women's profiles I had read. (I couldn't bring myself to read what the "competition" was offering so I'll never know if my profile was strikingly different than other men's.) Looking back, my approach may have been a mistake. I think I may have been viewed as too glib, too supercilious, too flip, or too something for which there is no word. In trying to stand out, it's possible all I did was distinguish myself as an asshole.

But I did get a lot of responses from women saying that they laughed and got a kick out of reading my profile. It was not infrequent that these were from women who were either much older than my parameters and/or lived thousands of miles away. Still, it gave me a boost, at least in the beginning.

And then there is the photo. If someone is really interested in meeting this way, a photo or several must be posted along with one's profile. It's a sad fact that in the online dating world the visual holds sway over every-thing else. How you look trumps many other characteristics. It's hard to be charmed by a narrative, so the reader is usually moved by what he or she sees.

I chose two pictures that I thought were representative of how I looked. Not too bad. I don't think anyone screamed when they saw them. And occasionally I would get a compliment (thank you, thank you!). I naively thought that women were less interested in looks than men; that as long as all the body parts were in relatively the right place, that was enough. Not so. It turns out that many women have very specific physical require-ments. A minimum height is often required. And it is not uncommon for someone to suggest that bald men need not apply. I found that kind of bla-tant baldish obnoxious. (I still have enough hair not to be included in that category, but I have a certain solidarity with my brothers.) I can under-stand that preference, but it seems to me that there should be a more graceful way to weed out men with no hair.

And beyond looks, there was often a lengthy and precise menu of qual-ities and characteristics some women required. (I felt my back stiffen each time I read the words "He should be"—I'm a little oppositional. Well, maybe more than a little.) There were times, after reading a list of all the qualities Mr. Right ought to have, that I felt that if I could meet a guy like that, I might switch teams.

Someone must have written a book on how to present yourself in an online dating profile because so many were so similar. The overriding theme for most is that the writer's life is great . . . but it might just be even greater sharing it with someone. Optimism and self-actualization abound. The glass is *at least* half-full. These are exactly the kind of people who, when I see them coming, I cross the street. For me, life is much more nuanced and filled with angst. There are days that I don't even *see* that glass. Makes me interesting—human, I think. Some other common denominators are the use of phrases like "all the city has to offer," "fine cuisine," and my favorite, "he should be as comfortable in a tux as he is in jeans." Apparently, these women are bent on limiting themselves to meeting members of the philharmonic. Who talks that way?! I was so uninspired by this kind of writing that I began using the very presence of those phrases as a reason to move on. Was that wise? I'll never know.

And of course, there was the occasional "he should be generous." Now, I'll admit that we could be talking about the "generosity of spirit" generous. And I'm right there for that. But sometimes there was a hint that what was being sought was a different kind of generous, like the "spend your money on me 'cause I'm so hot" generous. This quest for generosity was not infrequently combined with the desire to meet a "gentleman" who knows how to treat a "lady." Although I have fairly decent manners and am reasonably courteous, I'm certain that I'm not the kind of "gentleman" that is being referred to. And I think a "lady" and I would not have been a very good match. (Other qualities greatly in demand were to be emotionally and physically available. I couldn't help thinking that in some cases what was really being suggested was to be *fiscally* available.)

A large percentage of people using online dating sites lie about their age. That's a given. The age range of women I indicated that I was looking to meet was from fifty-five to sixty years old. I was contacted by a variety of women up to sixty-five years old. Surprisingly, against all statistical odds, there seem to be more fifty-nine-year-old women in New York City than any other single age (except, perhaps, for forty-nine-year-olds). Not that I was above misrepresenting my age, as well. I was sixty-one years old when I went online but shaved a few years off, presenting myself in my profile as fifty-nine. But I have a hard time lying, at least face to face. So, if I saw someone more than once, I made a point of getting the age thing out of the way. And I can cling to the virtuous notion that at least my photos were current. Almost anyone who dates online has stories of dates showing up who look little like the pictures that are included in their profile. I used to wonder what's going on in someone's head when they do that. Do they think that no one will notice the extra thirty pounds? Or ten years? I've come to believe that these people have a very healthy self-regard. They presume that their personal charm will make the extra weight and/or extra years moot. That certainly might be possible if the dating, or more accurately, the meeting, wasn't in a crucible where there is such a focus on "where is this leading?" It's difficult, at least it was for me, to block out the question: "Can I see myself being with this person *forever*?" Not exactly the most relaxed environment in which to get to know someone.

So, maybe you're wondering how a misanthrope such as I could ever have met someone who would have me. Well, I got lucky . . . very lucky. One of my Match dates was with a woman who, when we met for a drink, informed me that she had just started seeing someone she was very interested in. (That directness and honesty translated into her also having been truthful about her age—fifty-seven at the time we met.) Rather than cancel, she decided to tell me this in person. I had said in my profile that I was looking for someone who was "better looking, smarter, and nicer than I am." She appeared to be all of those. I was disappointed but didn't dwell on it. A few weeks later she called me. Things hadn't worked out with the other guy, and she asked me out for dinner. And that was just the beginning of many, many more dinners together.

C and I were a couple for nearly five years. After some time after our parting, I began to want to meet someone again. And funny thing is, the dating thing is like riding a bike. You just have to *want* to hop on the seat again.

Advertisement for Myself

Jonathan Ned Katz

During this time
of inspiring political resistance
against years-long,
systemic police brutality
against Black people,
during a national viral pandemic,
during an economic meltdown
bigger than the Great Depression of 1929,
may seem an odd time
to publicly seek
a new intimate partner.
But, because I'm serious
about meeting
and getting to know
appropriate,
single,
gay guys
that would like to meet this
eighty-two-year-old historian and artist,
I've decided to let you know.
that I'm looking for hellos

from such guys
within regular visiting distance
of Greenwich Village.
A friend advised me recently
that it shows strength
to let people know
that I'm interested
in meeting and greeting
appropriate,
single,
gay gentlemen.
My friend's comment
encouraged me
to let you know
that I'm interested
in messages here
from such guys.
So pass this along
to your wonderful,
single,
gay male friend.

NOTE

This piece first appeared on Facebook in May 2020.

What Would I Wear?

Laura Broadwell

Part 1

For many years now, I have been a stay-at-home worker, a Zoomer ahead
of the times. Even before COVID-19 made hermits and multitaskers of us
all, turning our kitchen tables into office space, I "commuted" from my
bed to my desk each morning, ready to start my day. So, it's no surprise that
my typical work attire has been casual, sometimes bordering on the eclec-
tic. This morning, for instance, I threw on a warm, furry bathrobe, cotton
leggings, and festive Christmas slipper socks, even though that holiday
has long since passed. I gave my dark, graying hair a quick brush and
avoided makeup altogether. Later when I run out to do errands, I'll slip
into a pair of trusty jeans, a sweater, well-worn boots, and one of three sets
of favored silver earrings. Over the years, I've fallen into an all-too-
predictable comfort zone, both in mind-set and appearance—a pattern
that's had both its upsides and potential downfalls.

For the most part, I've embraced my casual way of life and its associated style of dress for nearly two decades now. Rather than worry about
what to wear to the "office" each day, I've focused on adopting and raising
a daughter, caring for elderly parents, deepening my spiritual life, tend-
ing to friendships. For better or for worse (depending on how you view
things), I've mostly—and unabashedly—been single, so dressing up and
pulling together a cute outfit has not been a top priority.

To be fair, I am not—and never have been—an enthusiastic or casual dater. In my sixty-four years on the planet, I've had my share of long-term relationships, ambiguous partnerships, and cherished friendships with men. I've even had my celebrity crushes. But I've never been completely comfortable with the concept of dating, and the thought of doing so in later life terrifies me to no end. By comparison, I know people my age who actually *enjoy* the dating process—combing through dating apps, dressing up, and meeting perfect strangers. If one date doesn't work out, they simply move on to the next. Impressed by their resilience, I call them professional daters.

On occasion, however, I'll find myself fighting off a bout of regret should I see a couple with that certain glow, that divinely fated relationship. I wonder how it might feel to have that rare soulful bond, a special connection of my own. In these moments, I think that maybe, just maybe, I could venture out of my comfort zone and take a chance at dating. But, at the age of sixty-four and counting, I seriously wonder, *What would I wear?*

When I was younger, in my twenties and thirties, long before I became a mother, I was more cavalier in my approach to dressing up. Feeling more confident in my body, I might have thrown on a short, fitted skirt, a sleeveless top, and a pair of suede pumps for a night out with friends. I might have painted my lips a bright scarlet red or attempted a smoky eye just for fun. In those days, I walked with a certain levity, even a bit of swagger. Back then, the weight of my emotions had yet to wear me down. I had fewer worry lines, fewer disappointments, and ten fewer pounds to camouflage. Of course, I had my problems and insecurities then; it's just that life—and my wardrobe issues—seemed simpler.

These days I dress not to stand out but to cover up, to feel more invisible. I dress to hide the various assaults on my body sustained over the years—the surgeries in my fifties and sixties that caught me off guard; the death of my parents (and younger family members) that struck me repeatedly with blows of grief. I dress for comfort and dependability as a way to center—and protect—myself from the world. I dress as a woman in her sixties, not sure how to change her style.

Not long ago, I spoke to three friends about the topic of dressing and dating. My friend Shawn, though partnered for years, had this to say: "I think comfort is necessary when you go on a date at our age. It's respectful to be clean and neat and have a bit of polish, but not to the extent to where you feel vulnerable or on display. Haven't we spent enough of our lives being judged by our physical appearance?" Another friend, Lisa, married for decades and now single, added this: "I've been told that we don't need much makeup at our age. It's best to let our eyes tell the story."

Each of these points resonated with me, distinctly. For starters, I'll admit that part of my reluctance to date comes down to judgment. In my experience, women are held often to a higher standard than men and judged more critically—and perhaps disproportionately—by our physical appearance. We have to try harder to look good, despite all of our accomplishments. As we age, we are given less of a pass than men are. We are unfairly overlooked by youth, a favored commodity. And while I've worked hard for years to develop a sense of self-worth and confidence—based less on looks and fashion and more on my character and values—I'm still at the mercy of these cultural constructs, ingrained deeply within me.

So, when it comes to the topic of dressing and dating, I find myself asking these questions: What would a potential partner think of me when eyeing me up initially—and would I be willing (or tolerant enough) to open myself up to such scrutiny? If I were to attempt to improve my dressing game, with a pair of fitted pants, a scarf, sunglasses, and some makeup—dressing for comfort *and* polish, as Shawn suggests—would I appear to be somewhat of an imposter? Would a set of new clothes, an upgraded image, conceal the very essence of who I am: a woman in her sixties, who is prone to feeling vibrant and youthful one day, defeated and tired the next? Would a pair of new shoes be enough to disguise my mistrust of men, based fairly or unfairly on my past? Would my eyes be able to tell my story—and if so, which story would it tell?

My friend Mary has known me since I was twenty-three and a university student in California. For many years, Mary has heard my tales of life, travel, work, and family, and has been part of the narrative on more than a few occasions. Since we've both been independently single for vast stretches of our friendship, we've laughed (and cried) over our love lives, our exes, our dreams, our indecisions. So, when I asked Mary recently what I should wear if I were to go on a date at my age, she answered—directly—with her trademark humor, "Some black lingerie?" Her response made me laugh and cringe simultaneously, as I gazed on the snow falling softly outside my window, threw on an extra sweater, and thought, black lingerie would have to wait for another day (or maybe forever).

PART 2

Several months have passed and a bleak winter sky has given way to the gentle unfolding of spring. In a wave of energy this morning, I washed my front windows, swept up dry leaves, and folded a stack of purple sweaters, black jeans, and gray socks, worn to oblivion in the cold. As I felt the warm sun filter in, I drew a sigh of relief—and as I looked out my window, I sensed that my vision was slowly improving, getting clearer. A few months ago, I had one of those unexpected medical events that creep up on you when you're living life in your sixties. Unbeknownst to me, a layer of scar tissue had formed on the retina of my right eye, so for weeks on end, I was banished to doctors' offices, to operating rooms, and to my home to recover from surgery. I struggled with blurry vision, a sensitivity to light, and a reluctance to leave my home. The simple thought of socializing, much less *dating*, exhausted me. I wondered what a path forward might look like.

But with the arrival of spring, and an emergence from the darkness of vision problems, I've found a world bathed in color, in light. The signs of hope and renewal—and synchronicities—are everywhere. Earlier this morning, I looked out my window to find two mourning doves perched on the fire escape, their soft, drawn-out calls piercing the still city air. It's been said that when a pair of doves come to visit (as they do each spring), they are a symbol of devotion, friendship, and love—a beacon of healing, forgiveness, peace. An indication to move on.

On this morning in early spring, I stood wrapped in my bathrobe, watching those puffed-up, slender-tailed birds court, preen, and chase one another across leafy yards, devoid of self-consciousness, free. In their grayness, their nakedness, their sheer commitment to the moment, they shared a dance, a journey, however temporary. In my shared grayness, and with my teacup in hand, I turned from the window smiling, ready to start my day.

Something from Everyone

Stephanie M. Brown

I've been at this for nine years. Much to my surprise, I'm still single.

Since 2012, I have gone on thirty-nine first dates. Of them, thirteen have led to three dates or more.

Along the way, I have learned a few things about dating, like don't fall in love with someone via email, and its pandemic corollary, don't get infatuated with a voice. Also, almost everyone looks older and homelier in 3D than in pictures, but so do you, depending on the light. Simply discount your expectations the way a stock analyst does an earnings forecast.

From my dating tallies, five became demi-relationships, depending on how you count them. I do if they involved sex of some sort. Two of my dates turned into epic relationships. These involved a lot of sex, along with financial entanglement in one case, and planning for the future that turned out to be one-sided in both cases.

One of the epics and one of the demis also involved heartbreak. But none of these relationships, full or demi, and none of this dating involved regret. I got something from everyone.

Here is my registry of gifts—mostly intangible but occasionally pricey— from men I have met.

BIG STUFF: SEXUAL HEALING

While he eventually revealed himself as spectacularly, devastatingly, operatically Mr. Wrong, my first lover gave me immense, profound, extraordinary gifts that have kept on giving. His initial gift was confirmation of my sex appeal, after decades off the market, and his biggest gift was actual sex.

Eleven years before his death, my husband's kidneys robbed his penis of performance. I believed that love was more important than sex in a long-term relationship, as was his ability to serve as a one-man entertainment center, doing "sit-down standup" at the end of my long, hard workdays. I figured that sex was an inevitable sacrifice required by the medical interventions that would extend his life by twenty or more years. Besides, I thought lust was long gone at my age. I was wrong on both counts.

Mr. Eventually Wrong started out as a professional acquaintance and, about a year into my widowhood, evolved into a golf partner. At sixty, I developed a simmering crush that transported me into giddiness when he suggested we meet for a golfless drink and swept me past the fear of physical intimacy when he invited me to his weekend place in the mountains. My friends laughed when I told them I first put my overnight bag in the guest room.

Once the ointments got figured out, we began screwing like teenagers. Actually, we did it more than I ever did as an adolescent, but with hormone-fired avidity you'd think only youthful energy could manage: several times a week, several times each time.

End of fear of sex. End of thinking I was done with it, didn't need it, could only enjoy it with the man who introduced me to it and knew all my idiosyncratic preferences. Nope. There's a wealth of generic techniques out there available to anyone who cares to customize it to the person at hand, and you can ride it all the way into the sunset if you choose.

BIG STUFF: RUNNING WILD

Eventually I did meet Mr. Right, and why this one didn't work out is a short sad story. But he did give me the gift of exercise. In an effort to impress him, I started running, and the habit lasted even though the romance hit the wall.

As a horsewoman, golfer, and skier, I'd gone in for the grand gesture in sports. Running was mundane and dull. I knew this from the high school track team, the first and only sport for girls in my era. Mine was the longest event our fragile feminine bodies could handle, all of 440 yards. At practice the coaches used to pit the boys against me to make them run faster out of shame.

At age sixty-five, I met distance. With three weeks' preparation in a pair of tired trainers, I ran in a four-mile fundraiser Mr. Right had organized. I fell, I twisted my ankle, and bloodied a knee, but I kept going—little knowing this would end up a metaphor for the relationship.

Now running is a habit I can't live without. I get itchy if I go too long without slapping on high-tech sneakers and gliding down the sidewalk to the park. I run on my own, I run in groups that eat pancakes afterwards, I run in races where I go fast enough to bring home medals I share with my grandchildren . . . because you don't have to go all that fast when your competition is the women's sixty-five-to-sixty-nine age division. I look forward to turning seventy and really cleaning up.

BIG STUFF: DANCING QUEEN

I entered the ballroom first on the arm of Mr. Wrong, then with Mr. Even Wronger. At first, I was just trying to keep up with these guys. Then I started feeling a tinge of competition. Finally, I began dancing for the sheer pleasure of moving to music, but also for some degree of healing when each of the Wrongs broke up with me.

The dance plan began as prep for a coworker's wedding, evolved into white tie (not merely black) balls at ritzy hotels, and culminated in twelve

days of honing the cha-cha and aspiring to the tango on a strenuous Carib-
bean cruise. Along the way I also discovered a more gynocentric amal-
gam of ballet, jazz, aerobics, and yoga, topped with a touch of karate.
Goddess optional.

Dance now brings me joy at a level somewhere between running and
sex. Were it not for the Mr. Wrongs, I would have left it behind in third-
grade ballet class.

SMALL BUT SIGNIFICANT STUFF

I also have accumulated quite an inventory of pleasant experiences and
acquisitions, some of which live on:

- The second-best cat I have ever known. He may take the top spot
  by the time he's done.
- The most moving opera performance of my life, in front-row seats for
  Candide at Tanglewood.
- Two designer cocktail frocks, into which I fit for a whole year after the
  Dead Husband/Bad Boyfriend Diet.
- An iPhone app, Runmeter, that tipped me down the slippery slope into
  athletic data geekdom (now escalated to a Garmin GPS watch).
- A sunny piece of lawn I transformed into a copious garden that produced
  enough cherry tomatoes to choke a horse, if horses ate tomatoes.
- Two of my lowest-ever golf scores, as well as a lot of free country-club
  rounds.
- A slew of first-ever or in-a-long-time experiences: sauna, cruise,
  burlesque, canoe paddling, outdoor Shakespeare, artisanal cocktails,
  alligators, Gulf beaches, and professional ballet, among others. Some
  of them might have happened with a female friend, but probably not
  on her tab. How does this square with a feminist perspective? Well,
  I'm a socialist feminist.
- The inevitable punchline STD (pharmaceutically vanquished,
  I assure future lovers).

MIDDLING YET MEANINGFUL STUFF

I conclude with a recent medical scare. A CT scan for one purpose confirmed the suspect organ's health but unearthed potential trouble in another. Of the three people I told—not wanting to freak out others in my life until I had a good reason to—two were men I had met online within the previous year.

One was a physician from whom I'd gotten the soft dump, but he willingly lent his objective eye to review jargon-filled radiologist reports. The other was a recent contact, still in the phone conversation stage, who had confessed a medical issue of his own that unexpectedly became relevant to mine. He was a reassuring coach as I wended my way through scans and specialists.

This is not to say I've experienced nine years of Hallmark Channel movie material. I've also gotten some of the toughest lessons of my life from a few of these men.

I have learned, for example, how to figure out if the man in your life has other women in his. I finally understand that, when a man says he's not ready for a relationship, he ipso facto isn't. I now assume that the charming conversationalist I find increasingly intriguing is an alcoholic until proven otherwise. I have gained the ability to locate someone in a confidential rehab program.

I'm glad these lessons were postponed until I'd acquired the resilience to deal with them. Had I been in this classroom in my twenties, I might have flunked out.

My point, ultimately, is that all thirty-nine of these first dates were meetings with human beings, not just auditions for lovers. The fact that none of them yielded the second love of my life does not mean either these men or I have failed in some way.

Incidentally, I now know whether men and women can remain friends after the love, or at least the sex, is gone. But that's another story.

A (Mostly) Amusing
Exercise in Futility

Elizabeth Locke

Online dating at seventy-eight. Still? Actually, I have recently signed off for good, but I have fifteen years of experience under my belt—some dismal and some hilarious. I must be more optimistic than I realize. In all my efforts, I never found anyone permanent. Looking back at the parade, I see a lot of humor in my experiences; if nothing else, I see myself more clearly as a result. Perhaps others may find the recital pathetic, laughable, or even instructive.

Let me start my story by saying that I am a pretty average woman. Never an all-American beauty, I am considered attractive and do clean up fairly well. I dress neatly, if conventionally, with a touch too much color coordination. Although in high school I was tall enough to be in the back of the corps de ballet, I don't tower over most men. And I admit that the former dancer figure now has more padding than it did in the first two-thirds of my life. I have attractive silver hair, lovely light eyes, and a wicked and somewhat warped sense of humor. I have had an excellent education plus varied enough life experiences that I can at least hold my own in most conversations. I consider myself a good listener and am kind to children and small animals.

However, none of these sterling qualities contribute toward success with men. I am twice divorced, so perhaps any secret hopes of "third time's the charm" are rather misplaced. My first marriage at twenty-four was blessedly brief, but messy. My second, many years later, produced two truly delightful children, so I have no regrets. But at age sixty-three, after a divorce from my husband of twenty-three years, I set out in search of a date or three and signed up for Match. I thought I might find a friend to share a pleasant dinner with or a companion to accompany me to the opera or the ballet. That I might find love was just a distant, foolishly hopeful glimmer in my subconscious. It is only after years of online dating nonsense that I can admit that the effort was actually a rather frantic search to prove myself worthy of male attention. It took me much too long to acknowledge the incredibly hurtful impact of being suddenly deserted by my second ex-husband. I am sure I'm still dealing with the repercussions.

I may have been so stunned by the circumstances of my divorce that for the first six or eight months online I jabbered about it to anyone who would listen. Unsurprisingly, any potential dates ran as fast as they could in the opposite direction. Faces are a blur from that period, although I did meet several nice men. I certainly can't blame them for distancing themselves from the demented woman I was back then.

Although I was brave enough to write to men on Match, I was usually met with a deafening silence. I was willing to give almost anyone a chance by exchanging messages or actually meeting face-to-face; that explains why I have so many single date experiences to report. However, that is not how most people operate in the online world. The anonymity provides a shield to hide behind. It is very easy to click "skip" if a picture does not instantly catch your eye, and it's even easier to dodge having to say no to someone or let someone down gently.

I was probably not young or pretty enough for those who posted shirtless photos and listed their hair as brown even though (if they had hair at all) it was obviously gray. As I grew older it seemed that men's age requirements for suitable dates grew younger and adjectives such as "thin," "toned," and "attractive" appeared more often in descriptions of their ideal woman. Match habitually offered profiles with only one photo of the man and multiple photos of sports cars, overseas destinations, and flower gardens. I began to believe that every man over sixty owned a motorcycle or wished he did. The variations in self-descriptions fascinated me. Profiles ranged from one sentence statements conveying no information to angry rants; from flippant but amusing essays to well-crafted, sincere compositions. If I commented that I enjoyed reading a profile or that their wit made me smile, I occasionally got a thank-you but no follow-up.

I tried eHarmony but was put off by the numerous questions I had to answer, and the hoops members had to jump through in order to be able to communicate in anything but dictated formulas. No joy there. I dabbled briefly with other dating sites, even Christian Mingle, but did not attract much attention. Still game, I wrote to multiple men; few had the manners to even reply. Even though I had a relatively secure ego, eventually repeated rejection began to smart. Still, I persisted!

The opposite experience involved conspicuous spam messages strewn with suspiciously effusive declarations of adoration, almost always poorly written with multiple misspellings, sent from men who were ready to relocate immediately. I received one note from someone who called me "my angle"! My daughter's response to that was "acute or obtuse?" I'm afraid the answer is obvious.

The nadir of my Match search was a rude encounter with an attractive, sexy, and unsettling man named James, who I only met once for a glass of wine and a walk in Battery Park. Later conversations involved only egotistical tales about his sexual encounters. When he started to sexualize a child, I cut him off in horror. I regret that I did not have the sense to do so after our first encounter. There was something truly evil about that man.

Finally, I landed on a more "mature" site named Adult Friend Finder that took a refreshing approach by acknowledging that sex is a major factor in this online game. It did away with the veiled hints and sly nudges so common on other, tamer sites. People were friendly and open, and, although listening into the random chat room could get rather raunchy, there was no pressure to participate in any way. It was obvious that many of these people had been chatting for some time and had gotten to know each other as friends.

I took a chance and wrote to a strikingly attractive man in a red shirt who lived on a wilderness preserve on the opposite side of the United States—much too far away to arrange an impromptu meeting—and asked if he would like to correspond. Surprisingly, even though I never posted a picture and revealed very little about myself in my brief profile, Ray replied in the affirmative, and we began a yearlong conversation. We quickly graduated to private email and then to telephone chats. I found him fascinating—a former big-city cop turned desert shaman. As our conversations became longer and more intense, I found myself falling for him and even fantasizing about moving to what was for me very foreign territory. In the spring he arranged a business trip to Washington, DC, and then took the train to New York. At Penn Station I practically leapt into his arms. We had a delightful five days together getting to know each other. One night, much to my bemusement, Ray treated me to what he described as a shamanic journey to identify my spirit animal. He seemed to go into a trance as we lay on the floor on his special blanket and listed to taped drums. I can honestly say that I have never met anyone quite like him. Sad, I kissed him goodbye with visions of soon flying to visit him. Once home he sent me a book by a spiritual author whose work we had discussed, plus an unusual necklace that I wear to this day.

Then the situation inexplicably changed. Perhaps I should have paid more attention to my daughter's lukewarm reaction to this man. Telephone calls and emails became fewer; he discouraged me from visiting. When I called in September to wish him a happy birthday, he almost seemed not to know who I was; I had to accept that our brief romance was over. We still exchanged the occasional message, and I did see him once four years later when a friend and I traveled out west. But it was not the same. Over those years I learned that, although he said he was separated, his version of that involved still sharing a home with his wife; apparently, they could not afford to divorce. No wonder he did not want me to visit. He eventually married for the fourth time and has now vanished from Facebook, so I can't even stalk him. I won't forget him, but I remember him with mixed emotions. It would have been less painful if he had been straight with me from the start.

In the mix of all my dates, somewhere in there was one brief evening with a former Navy SEAL. I managed to take the subway to a destination far out in Queens. I arrived at his condo with a candle, a bottle of wine, and a toy for his cat. What was I thinking? Although early on he left the room and returned wearing only a bathrobe, nothing sexual happened. We drank a couple of glasses of wine, had some awkward conversation; then he announced abruptly that he had to leave to help a friend. I rushed back to the subway and home. In retrospect, that was, obviously, very risky behavior. Normally I did have lengthy conversations with someone before I agreed to meet them, almost always in a public place, but still, I took too many chances. I have been quite lucky that none of my dates ever proved dangerous. I emerged with my ego somewhat dented but otherwise unscathed.

Three other men I met on that adult site were all married. One was a banker whom I first met for dinner downtown. He proved to be a sweetheart who, I think, just wanted temporary respite from a rather cold, controlling wife. I had a quite different personality than her, and despite not having a lot in common with him, conversation was easy. Even after I moved away from Brooklyn, until just recently we continued to have an occasional festive evening several times a year. We did care about each other, but there was never any question of our situation changing.

The find from that risqué site was darling Joe. He had a genuine Irishman's gift of blarney and totally charmed me with truly silly emails. He signed on to the site ostensibly in search of sex, but it turned out that he was really in need of an emotional and spiritual connection he was missing. We met for dinner several times, and I vividly recall one quite passionate parting kiss at a midtown subway entrance. Our relationship was not otherwise physical. After only a few months of acquaintance he moved across the country. I have not seen him for many years, but he remains a genuine presence in my life. Our emails have touched on subjects from God to the antics of cats. I delight in tales of his frequent travel and get vicarious experiences of grandchildren. He sends me beautiful picture collections, poems, jokes, and prayers. I write him poetry and ask him profound questions that he always answers seriously. I respect his spiritual search, value his opinion, trust him implicitly, and love him dearly. He has helped me through some very dark days. If I had met him many years ago, I believe that he would have been the love of my life, but that was not the scenario we found ourselves in. I am very grateful that he is in my life, and he would not have been without that silly adult site.

I find it fascinating that in all my years on all the other dating platforms combined I really never connected with anyone for any length of time; but on the one site that many people might find shocking, I found six different, genuine, interesting, attractive, and entertaining men I liked very much, several of whom remained in my life for years.

The last man who contacted me before I signed off that site was Will—an extremely intelligent man: in appearance a benign, avuncular sort, in reality a complex, mysterious, somewhat narcissistic man. I was hooked after our first evening, and he has popped in and out of my life at random ever since. He now lives far away, and I have not seen him for more than eight years. I don't hear from him for long stretches of time; just as I am about to call it quits, he emerges and says he loves me. Although I frequently feel poorly treated, I can't seem to let Will go. He is the most interesting and the most infuriating man I have met in many years.

That flurry of activity occurred in the first years after my divorce. In April 2010, at age sixty-eight, I moved to upstate New York, and any dating activity changed drastically. I went from Plenty of Fish to OurTime to you name it, I tried it. Plenty of Fish was low-key and had the added benefit of being free. I got messages from moderators about in-person gatherings, but most of those events were located too far away. OurTime seemed to be a watered-down version of Match that catered to the over-sixty crowd as did SilverSingles. Christian Mingle hosted too many men who seemed too narrow-minded for my liberal Anglican attitude. I had high hopes for MeetMindful, but perhaps I did not express myself in lofty enough spiritual terms for the seekers on that site.

So, once again, mostly thunderous silence was the result of all that thrashing around. But there were some very funny and some rather strange encounters. I am only reporting a small sample of my adventures.

The strangest involved two men from Match. The first profile pictured an attractive, bearded man who said his name was Luis. Born in Massachusetts, his family moved to Sweden when he was young. He grew up there and married; after his wife died, he returned to Massachusetts for a job and stayed. On the phone I found his accent difficult to understand. In lengthy letters that grew increasingly warm in tone, Luis seemed to be implying that he was falling in love with me. This set off small alarm bells in my head, so I tried to google him. I found nothing at all. Neither Luis's phone number nor his email address produced any information. Only one person with that name turned up in the entire United States. I was suspicious, but I agreed to meet him for lunch at a very public restaurant. Luis canceled, citing work as an excuse, and I last heard from him a few days later. Then he ghosted me and dropped off the face of the earth. Despite my sense that there was something not quite right about Luis, I found him rather fascinating. I almost regret never meeting him and discovering his true story. He may not have been Luis, or from Sweden, but there was a real voice and an actual person with the ability to invent a whale of a tale on the other end of that phone.

The second incident occurred about six months later. A man named David contacted me with a similar story. He, too, had been born in the United States, moved to Sweden, and returned as an adult. Despite little encouragement from me, his messages grew intense; he expressed much interest in meeting me and stressed his willingness to relocate from his temporary residence. When googled, David also proved not to be a real person with a history that could be tracked, so I never agreed to meet him. And after a month or two he, like Luis, vanished without a trace.

What are the odds of running into two unidentifiable, mystery men with almost identical unusual tales? If they had been the same con man the episodes might have made more sense, but they had very different voices, accents, writing styles, etc. If either man had asked for money, I would have backed away immediately. Perhaps our chats told them that I was not a likely target. I have since learned that the man-from-Sweden tale is a quite common scam, but, despite my discounting the flowery language as hyperbole and my suspicions about their identity, at the time I was probably not as wary as I should have been.

I have long since signed off from all dating forums. I may still be a ghostly presence on POF, but I attracted so little notice on that site it does not matter that my profile seems to have an extended half-life there. Meet-Mindful and Zoosk keep my photograph active to no effect. An aside here: most online dating sites keep as many profiles as possible visible, and unless a former member edits his own profile stating that he can no longer read or return messages, any attempted contact simply falls into the abyss. It took me years of suffering a seriously bruised ego to figure that out and to realize that all that silence frequently had nothing whatsoever to do with me. Additionally, removing oneself completely from a site takes time and insistence and often does not totally succeed. Lastly, beware of automatic membership renewal—especially if you need to watch your pennies.

Match, out of all the dating platforms, still tries to lure me back by sending me profiles of attractive men every few days. Unfortunately, most of them live too far away to be truly available, and I choose not to pay for an additional membership. Despite all the internet discouragement, I am certain there must be interesting men out there somewhere who can hold up their end of a conversation with wit and charm. Men must exist who would respect me for who I am and would not try to cram me into their version of an ideal woman. But I have stopped searching for that rare phenomenon online.

I do know several couples that met their significant other via online dating. So, it works for some. But I am done. I will either meet someone locally or I won't. Fifteen years of throwing money I can't spare at websites whose only real purpose is to fill their coffers was frequently a waste of my time. But it wasn't a total loss; I had some truly delightful evenings and way too many mediocre meals—and some delicious ones. I crossed paths with men I would not have otherwise met. I formed attachments that teetered on the edge of love, experienced at least one heartbreak, and made a few friends, one of whom I expect to be in my life until one of us dies. I learned to cope with an almost unimaginable dose of rejection; I am delighted to discover that I have emerged with my ego mostly intact.

I am still troubled by my continued entanglement with Will; I don't seem to be able to say goodbye. I guess that would extinguish that last tiny spark of hope. So, I sometimes allow myself to seesaw back and forth between some happy emotions and some pretty dark ones.

I will be forever grateful for my lovely email correspondent, Joe, and our heartfelt connection that continues to sustain me. Most of the time I am relatively content being alone and resigned to the fact that my situation is unlikely to change. I have gained some insight into the source of my restless seeking. Perhaps I have finally realized that I am enough by myself and am worthy of love, and I understand that pale imitations and faulty connections are not acceptable.

I do not know how my experiences compare to those of other women my age. Although I thought I described myself accurately in my profiles with a modicum of humor and did not sit back and wait to be contacted, I had very little success attracting men I was really interested in. I certainly did not find a permanent relationship. Perhaps I should have asked for help presenting myself or for professional advice on how to initiate a conversation that would elicit a reply. Perhaps I am just too picky! But all in all, I think I can say that, despite not finding anything lasting, for me, internet dating was worth a try. Playing around online gave me something to do other than mope and provided me with almost endless stories to tell.

Rick Redux

Candida B. Korman

Even thirty years ago a singles weekend was retro. When a dance studio friend suggested we go, I thought . . . why not? From the start it was awful and involved a strange reunion with a distant cousin on her own spectrum; the realization that my friend's motive for attending in the first place was her latest multilevel vitamin marketing scheme; the odd postseason summer camp setting; and the fact that the evening dances were more high-school mixer than going out dancing. I was both too old to enjoy it for real and too young to enjoy it for the irony. I did my best with the outdoor activities, but after rappelling during the rock-climbing experience, I knew I wouldn't do that again.

And then . . . I was walking up a steep hill toward the Sunday afternoon cookout, and there he was. We locked eyes and laughed. It was that story-book chemistry but in different packaging. He wasn't Prince Charming, but he was clever, charismatic, and fun. He was also short, overweight, divorced with kids, and only in the New York metro area for an extended consulting contract. Rick wasn't like anyone else I'd ever met. Totally self-made and self-educated, he was absolutely original and intriguing. He drove my friend and me home from the retreat. He called that night. And that was it.

An extended on-again, off-again, long-distance, short-distance, confusion-of-expectations-about-romance-and-love relationships that began and ended a couple of times. Rick was the kind of man who could walk into a bar in any city in the world and make friends—full of confidence and easy charm—but there was a huge chip on his shoulder and a need to prove himself. I knew there was a story there, but he wasn't sharing it.

Thirty years later, he resurfaced in my life. I was no longer looking for marriage or children, and he was more self-aware, if no more willing to change. He was still a man of excess or deprivation—no moderation possible. His story began to emerge then, and, as he kept having (or perhaps finding) reasons to be in New York City, I slowly warmed to the idea of a different, no-expectations romance. He'd taken up acting as a side gig, so we went to the world premiere of an indie horror flick in which he chewed the scenery as the angry boss. He introduced me to a wild mix of friends. He shared one thing with many of them—they'd grown up as Jehovah's Witnesses and had escaped from the fold. Finally, I had an explanation for his stunted education, his casual stereotyping, and his envy of intellectuals.

He turned sixty first, and a whole lot spilled out. His father died young, so Rick had never expected to live to be sixty. It was as if every day were a bonus, and there was no need to eat healthy food, exercise, or do anything that might be interpreted as planning for a good future. There was no future.

We were a terrible mismatch all over again.

When I turned sixty—a few months after my mother died—I needed someone to tell me I was fine just the way I was, and that was something Rick could do. A friend of mine saw us together and said, "He is crazy about you!" I needed somebody to be crazy about me. I was sixty. I was alone. I was tired of job-interview-style internet dates. I was tired of being dismissed as old or short or eccentric. I needed to know that there was a man who was crazy about me.

But it couldn't last.

I was sixty and planning to be a fabulous ninety-nine. I was sixty and traveling, dancing, exploring, and taking good care of myself. Rick Redux helped me realize that being okay on my own means I want to meet a man who is traveling, exploring, and taking good care of himself. He doesn't have to dance, but that would be nice. Dating at sixty-plus is strange. Sometimes you just need a shot of "He's crazy about you!" from the past in order to face the future.

You Say Potato

Amy Rogers

I have always been hopeless at dating. I lack any ability to pick up on subtext or signals. I can't tell the difference between an ordinary invitation for coffee and the same offer that somehow conveys sex is about to happen.

So when I embarked on my first date in a decade at age sixty-two, I was determined to change it up and get it right.

It happened almost accidentally. Heading out of town for a road trip, I posted on Facebook: "Atlanta friends! I'm in town this weekend. Who wants to meet up?" A writer friend replied, "Is your dance card full? Hoping it's not." Within minutes we were booked for a food tour of the city. It would be a daytime date with a group. I was relieved to reduce the awkwardness of an after-dark dinner date fueled by alcohol and innuendo.

But this date was going to be complicated in a way that was new for me. To say a lot had changed in the three years since my date and I first met was an understatement. We'd originally connected at a writers' conference in the Carolinas, where I took part in the faculty open mic. Unlike the poets who presented elegant, finely honed work, I read "Appetites," a rollicking, memoir piece about food, sex, and my failed romance with a devastatingly handsome man who'd dumped me for a much younger woman.

After my reading, a tall woman with dark, curly hair and crinkly, kind eyes approached me. Lanky and unfussily dressed, she told me how much she liked my essay. She stunned me with the boldness of what she said next. "While I was listening to you read, I thought to myself, 'That is just exactly the kind of woman I've always wanted to be'—and then she dropped the final syllable—'*with*.'"

With. The word just hung there. It had been years since anyone paid me a compliment, and I didn't know how to respond to this one, especially coming from a woman who'd heard me say ten minutes ago that I was still pining for the man I'd lost. So I gushed, "Oh, you are so kind to say that! Thank you. I really appreciate your thoughtfulness. Thank you so much. It's always good to know that our work connects with others, isn't it?"

Late one night about two years later, I was scrolling through my Facebook feed and stopped abruptly at a profile photo of a good-looking man with a scruffy goatee and a half smile. The dark, curly hair and crinkly, kind eyes were familiar, but I couldn't quite place them. It took a minute to register.

"I thank everyone for supporting me. I now am legally 'Jackson,'" the caption stated. The next posts were mundane and manly. "Great team effort. Congrats to the Braves." I clicked through photos to see Jackson in various locations around Atlanta, sporting a fedora at a baseball game, and in a close-up selfie in a swimming pool, where his chest hair grazed the notch at the spot where his collarbone met his creased, wet neck.

I messaged: "Hi! I saw your new photo. It's good to see you looking well and happy! I look forward to reading your new work. Cheers!"

He replied right away: "I'm very glad to hear from you. You definitely captured my attention at the conference. You were so gracious, and I remember thinking you were beautiful as well as talented. I hope we shall meet again, Jackson." He added a smile emoji.

Although I hadn't felt a single drop of attraction to the person I'd met two years earlier, I couldn't deny there was a wave of it starting to build now.

Still, it would be another year before we finally connected in person.

And now here I was, getting ready for the food tour Jackson had booked
for us on a steamy summer day. I reverted to the silliness of a school girl
fretting over what to wear and how to fix her hair. I joked to a girlfriend
that for the first time in my life, I'd have no worries about birth control.
I'd aged out of my fertile years, regardless of whom I chose as a partner.

But then I had to stop and consider that for all my years of intimacy,
enhanced with bouts of sexual experimentation back in the 1970s, I knew
nothing about coupling with a trans person. Aside from the logistics of
how it would work, which of us two sixty-somethings would make the first
move? Would we assume traditional gender roles? Who would open the
car door? Who would pay? Who would initiate the first kiss?

I needn't have worried. Jackson had arranged everything. He strode
toward me on the sweltering street where the tour met up. Wearing a plaid
shirt and jeans, he enveloped me in a strong hug and said, "You look
fantastic."

"So do you," I replied. It was true.

For an icebreaker, everyone in the group revealed our favorite guilty-
pleasure food.

"Rocky road ice cream."

"Red velvet cake."

When it was my turn I said, "There is no finer food product on Earth
than honey-barbecue potato chips." Jackson chuckled.

We spent the next three hours strolling our way through a half-dozen
bars and bistros. We squeezed into a tiny eatery to devour platters of just-
fried doughnuts and deli sandwiches that we chased with beer. We dined
on courses of artisanal cheeses paired with smoked meats and carefully
chosen wines at tables so tightly packed that our knees and elbows bumped
against each other. He walked on the outside of each sidewalk and opened
every door for me, then lightly touched my shoulder as I walked through.
I sparkled from the attention. The group assumed Jackson and I were a
couple, and I liked it.

In between stops we conversed easily. "I love to travel," he said. "I really want to go to New York."

"You've never been to New York? You'd love it."

"We should go to New York together! You can show me around!" And just like that, I pictured us meandering arm in arm down Broadway.

Three stops into the tour, I realized I'd misjudged the amount of alcohol we'd have. Combined with the heat of the day, I'd become uncomfortably tipsy. By the time we reached an Italian place that rolled out a special pasta dish for our group, I could barely eat another bite. I'd expected dainty samples, but we'd had hefty portions at each stop. In my nervousness to impress my date I hadn't paid attention. Now I was bloated, sticky, and groggy.

A typical dinner date at a restaurant is predictable: cocktails, appetizers, entrees, dessert, coffee. It's orderly. It takes two hours at the absolute most. But the food tour felt like five separate dates cobbled together, each with a beginning, a middle, and an end, separated by spurts of walking and talking until the whole mashed-up thing stretched out beyond three hours and headed into four. When we blessedly reached the last stop at a boutique food store, I stood under an air conditioner vent and let it blow my limp hair off my forehead. I'd need to catch a second wind for the private activities I was pretty sure would follow soon enough. Jackson slid up behind me and pressed a gift bag into my hands. While I'd been sweating, he'd been shopping. "Don't open it yet, okay?" He grinned.

"Okay." I grinned back.

We headed back to our cars at the other end of the now-empty street. Suddenly we ran out of things to say. I'd forgotten how that can happen in the build-up to intimacy as each partner takes care not to break the fragile mood that's forming.

I chose my words carefully. I'd been taught only recently that when a date tells you, "That was fun," it's code for "You won't be hearing from me."

"That was really great. Thank you so much," I said. To make sure he knew I wasn't brushing him off I emphasized, "You should come to my town and let me host you."

"I'm glad you enjoyed it."

When we arrived at my car I leaned into his chest. He tilted his head up, gave me a one-armed hug, and stepped away. He was out of sight almost before I closed the car door. I cranked the engine, blasted the A/C, and was headed toward the highway when the text tone buzzed on my phone.

"Thank you for joining me on the food tour today. I am glad to call you my friend and I hope you will think of me as the same!"

If the phrase "friend zone" had existed when I last dated more than a decade ago, I was blissfully unaware of it. Today, I instantly understood. I had been friend-zoned. An indirect way of taking sex off the table. I felt in the pit of my stomach what it really meant: utter rejection.

After all my agonizing before and during the date, had I missed some kind of signal right in front of me, again? I replayed the day in my head. I'd been sweet, funny, smart, and appreciative with no missteps that I could see. I pulled the car over and opened the gift bag. It held several expensive chocolates, a cute refrigerator magnet, and a package of locally made, hand-cut, honey-barbecue potato chips. Jackson had paid attention to my offhand comment hours earlier, then chosen my favorite food as a keepsake of our day. It made the rejection that much more maddening.

Over the next couple of weeks, I watched Facebook for clues. Maybe he was moving to a foreign country and couldn't embark on a long-distance relationship. Maybe he was gravely ill, afraid to start a romance that would leave me sobbing and bereft when he died. Maybe he'd testified against a crime boss and had secretly fled into the witness protection program. These were the same ridiculous excuses women have conjured up forever when trying to make sense of rejection. But I was doubly confounded because this person had pursued me twice, both before and after his transition. There was no way I'd misread the signals. It had to be something else.

By fall, the photos were there. Jackson was dating a pretty brunette who looked about forty. Wearing a tuxedo, he draped his arm around her at a charity gala. They walked their dogs together in the park. They cooked meals in his kitchen and toasted each other next to a lavish Christmas tree.

But by spring she was gone. A curvy blonde appeared that summer for a few weeks. I lost track after that. I don't know who he's dating these days. I haven't checked his page in a while, although he posts a birthday greeting every November on mine.

Without an ability to imagine some sort of future happiness, we'd have no reason to put ourselves through these hapless and sometimes heartbreaking endeavors. Luckily as it turns out, that's actually where I excel. I can envision an endless menu of possibilities, and that skill has proved to stand the test of time. Just last year I took a class and learned how to make homemade potato chips. It's easy to customize how hot or sweet you want them to be, and they're better than any you can buy, anywhere.

And even if I never master how to decipher signals or translate subtext, I know one thing for certain: if and when I decide to go down the dating road again, there'd better be more than the promise of snack food waiting for me when I get there.

NOTE

This is a true story; several identifying details have been altered to protect the privacy of people in this essay.

Three Dates

Margie Kaplan

I'm no beauty, but meeting men and feeling attractive to them is always something I have experienced, and I'm grateful for that.

Why am I lucky that way? I am big-breasted and was shapely until postpartum spread hit in my late forties and fifties, but I don't think it's that. I'm also gregarious and funny, and I love people, music, animals, nature, and sports. I think I add to a group, and probably most importantly, I am genuinely interested in people—who they are and what their lives are like. I think that's what attracts men. People like to be listened to and taken seriously. I like to listen, but I'm not a quiet person. I contribute a lot to conversations as well.

So, I cruised through teen romances in high school and met my first husband in my senior year. He was a college senior, a very handsome rock and roll singer going into dentistry. I hadn't yet turned twenty when we married and was not yet twenty-two when we parted.

That released me from needing to get married and allowed me to be footloose and fancy-free for the next almost fifteen years. I attended college, completed graduate work, and began my psychotherapy practice. I traveled lots with the current boyfriend of the year (or two), lived in varying places, and was generally a happy soul. I never considered marrying again during those years.

Then I turned thirty-five. Having children was never a question for me; I knew I wanted them, and now it seemed, for the first time, important. The man I was dating then was ten years my junior, and certainly not in the same place as I was, so letting go and moving on, though we did love each other and enjoyed our time together, seemed like a sad necessity.

I guess I'm also a lucky person, as this lovely boyfriend, although initially agreeing with our sad disequilibrium, felt connected and caring enough to set up a wonderful, never-to-be-forgotten, romantic dinner during the next week, champagne and all, to ask me to marry him.

We did that a few months later, and by the time I was forty-one, we had two wonderful daughters.

Our marriage lasted about fifteen years, and though he eventually wanted out, and I was sad and fearful about my life ahead without him at that time, in retrospect, it allowed me an opportunity to really come in to my own in those years following.

I established a long, loving relationship (no more marriages for me) beginning about three years later that enhanced and enriched my life for the next fifteen years, and from which I extricated myself bit by bit, slowly, over a three-year period. So here I was, sixty-seven years old, unpartnered.

A sixty-seven-year-old, gray-haired woman carrying more than twenty extra pounds does not have to fight off potential suitors. My mother, who became widowed for a second time after a forty-five-year marriage, had also been successful in love and romance previously and assumed that this time would be no different. She was about seventy-seven at the time, and she booked a luxury cruise, bought lovely lingerie, and, I think, expected to return with her next partner. That didn't happen, and though my mom lived for another eighteen years, I think she became depressed for the first time in her life and declined, albeit slowly, until her death at age ninety-five.

———

There is one wonderful and poignant story that needs to be fit in before I continue. During this period, pre–internet dating, about 1991, at the begin-

ning of my mom's second widowhood, my friend and I placed a personal
ad for my mother in the *New York Review of Books*. We wrote her profile
and she got responses and had a date, about which she was quite excited.
She gussied up waiting for Mr. Right.

Before I say more, let me tell you that my mother was always an athlete,
an active traveler, a serious flirt with lots of sexual energy, and a woman
with a great sense of humor. I can remember her recounting her date. She,
or they, picked a restaurant a block and a half from her apartment, and they
headed off for this short jaunt, which unfortunately became quite a hike, as
he needed to stop to catch his breath about every five steps. This was certainly *not* my mother's speed. I think the sitting down in the restaurant
and talking went well, and then was the arduous walk home. When they
got there, she invited him up for either a drink or a cup of coffee.

They were sitting on the couch in her den, she with her legs crossed, when
he said, "You know, you shouldn't sit with your legs crossed like that."

My mother thought he was flirting and demonstrating a bit of lively
sexual energy by commenting that her upper legs were showing. So she
coyly said, "Oh yes, why is that?"

Mr. Date responded, "It's bad for the circulation." As she told it, the evening ended quite rapidly after that.

———

So, back to me. At sixty-seven, I certainly was not forlorn. My teaching
and my psychotherapy practice not only occupied much of my time but
were greatly rewarding. But male attention, and sexual activity, had also
been rewarding. As part of my extrication plan from my long-term boyfriend, I wrote a profile for OkCupid and included a current photo. I chose
this venue because, at the time (2013), it was the only free dating site I was
aware of, and I certainly didn't want to "pay" for a date!

Shockingly, not long after, I met a lovely man, who I dated and became
lovers with sporadically, for the next year. We segued after that into a genuine, valuable, nonsexual friendship that continues today.

Five years have passed since then. I'm now seventy-three, and dating has not been center stage at all in my very full, bifurcated life—New York City apartment and modest lake home in northern New Jersey. OkCupid has sent photos and profiles of literally hundreds of men over these years. I rarely look at them, but about a year ago I did, thinking it would be nice to meet an attractive-to-me man.

I have never been a game player, and as I have no idea of my password from six-plus years ago, nothing has changed in my OkCupid profile except my age, which I guess updates automatically. My grandson is no longer two, but I am pretty much living the same outline, with a few added trips, as I was when it was written.

DATE ONE

A little over a year ago, I began an online correspondence with someone who seemed like a nice fellow. We segued into phone chats to his number, with mine blocked, as friends warned me to do. He was an employed Manhattanite with fine diction; his photo was of a nice-looking man. He was age appropriate, never married, had no children.

Normally, that would eliminate him from my interest, but then, I was a *newbie* to online dating. So, we agreed to meet uptown, close to my home, at a favorite moderately priced Greek place. Mr. One arrived a few minutes after I did and pleasantly joined me at the table. It was immediately clear to me that he was not for me.

I do not think of myself as a style queen at all. I'd probably be described as an aging hippie, and I was surprised that someone's outfit would actually loom large in my eyes, but his did. He wore a deep red, broad, *old* corduroy, almost velvety jacket that I couldn't stop paying attention to. I hated it. Although I remember none of the conversation, it was instantly clear as he came into my line of view that I was not interested in him.

That wasn't the case in reverse, however, as his conversation included suggestions of several things *we* might do together. There was nothing *wrong* with Mr. One. He was not inappropriate, overly sexualized, stupid, or hideously unattractive, but he was not for me. I was drowning. How could I get out?

I noticed my watch; it was about 6:50 P.M. God, I wanted to get home to watch *Jeopardy!* So, I said that! Not my finest hour, but there it is. I said, standing up, that it had been lovely to meet him, but that I needed to leave because *Jeopardy!* was beginning in ten minutes. I'm sure he was as taken aback by me, by that, as I was by his jacket. I left cash, which he tried to reject, and headed out. He said he'd love to do something again. Can you imagine saying that after someone dumps you for *Jeopardy!*? I said we'd see, as my life was busy and filled with commitments, and I headed out and home.

We never spoke or crossed paths again. It put me off for many months from even considering looking at OkCupid's offerings.

DATE TWO

But almost a year later, I again perused OkCupid's offerings. To be honest, most of the photos and profiles that were suggested to me were completely inappropriate. Most of the men were more than ten years younger than me, and though it is said that opposites attract, I was amazed that *anyone* would consider those *matches*. I guess, at least in this app, the only one I've ever used, that people within twenty years of you get bunched into the same category, with no attention paid to profiles, history, education, wishes, goals, interests, activity choices, etc.

Mr. Two seemed rather appropriate in his age, education, and interests. His photo showed a normal, nice-looking fellow who was geographically local. We emailed briefly and transferred into phone communication for a couple of chats, which were fine, agreeing to meet at a local diner.

He was there first. He looked like his photo, but I thought that he seemed let down by my appearance, and he was very nervous. We sat down in our booth, checked over the menu, and ordered.

I felt sorry for his inflated anxiety, and hoped I'd ease it by starting a conversation, so I said, "How about telling me something special or out of the usual chatter about yourself?" He didn't pause, but said straightforwardly, "Both of my parents killed themselves."

I was aghast, put my hand to my heart, and said, "Oh my God, I'm so sorry! Did they do that together?" He explained that no, they had divorced after a bad marriage and later individually, at different times, each took their own life.

I really do not remember much after that, except that Mr. Two, who had been divorced and had no children, was the eldest of seven children raised in a Catholic home. I wondered aloud if he was close with his nieces and nephews, only to be told that not one of his six siblings, most married, had children.

We completed our repast, walked out in the direction of the subway together, chatting pleasantly, and parted. I kept feeling—and this is horrible, I know—that I didn't want to get whatever was encasing this smart, not unattractive, professionally successful person on me.

Life is not perfect in any way, and given many hours, I can complain with the best of 'em about the shortfalls of any given day, but I guess I am a very lucky person. I've had sad losses (my father when I was six, my second marriage, a brother who died much too young, pivotal people who loved and cared for me, as well as expected life endings with the passage of time), but I am happy to be alive. I love the sunrises and the day's breezes. I love laughing and losing myself in inane movies, singing out loud, and eating at Dairy Queen.

Mr. Two is probably a fine person, but he was not for me. He called me the morning after our date, which was lovely. We agreed that it had been a nice evening meetup and wished each other a good upcoming day. That was it.

DATE THREE

I spend most of my free nonworking time at the lake, not in Manhattan, so I decided that if I made another match, it would be based upon geographical convenience. So, I geographically limited my periodic perusals of the website to see if anyone available was in my northern Jersey vicinity. There were very few people to choose from in my area, but I did come across one fellow from a town nearby. We began exchanging messages through the OkCupid app, which is not easy, since the platform's messaging function has some idiosyncrasies. Every time I pressed Enter to skip to the next line, whatever I'd written previously got sent, resulting in Mr. Three receiving many partial messages. Aargh!

I suggested he share his phone number because of my tech limitations, but he said he doesn't like or feel comfortable using the phone, so we continued exchanging brief notes. He suggested meeting up and allowed me to choose where, since he didn't mind driving.

I decided on a lovely park near my home, and we set a time. It was the end of summer and the weather was lovely, so I thought a walk or at least sitting outside would be better than a coffee (which I don't drink) or a different drink inside somewhere.

Mr. Three was a widower with no children who seemed to have similar interests to me, and he appeared nice-looking from his one photo. It is weird not to have spoken to someone you are about to meet. Somenone's actual voice and natural conversation flow, I think, give a whole other dimension to any beginning relationship.

I put on a casual outdoor outfit, felt satisfied with my presentation, and headed to the park. I arrived first and sat casually on top of a picnic table, feet on the seat appreciating the lovely late afternoon. Mr. Three arrived about five minutes after our scheduled time and joined me on the table. He looked like his photo and seemed to be a serious, nice guy, mainly mourning the loss of his beloved wife, gone for three years, but with whom he had shared his whole life, work included.

He seemed open, very committed to being in touch with his feelings and staying true to them regardless of any circumstances. It was clear that he put a lot of consideration into where he was now and where he wanted to go. That was all fine with me, and we seemed to have a general give and take of life-to-life connections in our conversation.

What did I feel? Well, I kept checking my emotional pulse and listening to myself. I behaved and did not dominate the conversation. I listened and asked questions. He did too. I can't say my sexual energy was sparked, but I was not turned off or clearly rejecting him. We talked, seemingly easily, for about an hour. I was thinking of asking if he'd like to walk a bit.

About five minutes after this thought, Mr. Three climbed down from the picnic table, faced me, and said, "It's been nice meeting you."

I was aghast! "You as well," I said, and he turned and walked up to his car and headed off. Wow, I'd just been solidly rejected! I sat dumbfounded, taking it in.

I certainly have my own insecurities about why he may have rejected me—my extra weight or my casual attire, for example—but truly, other than those, I felt okay about the date. I had been pleasant, noncritical, and empathetic. I listened, shared commonalities, and made a few jokes, to which we both smiled.

After he left, I had a lengthy conversation with myself, sitting on that table. What should I do? Jump off a bridge into the waterfall nearby? Call a friend to vent my cacophony of thoughts, feelings, and sensations? Go home and turn on a Hallmark movie? It was about 5:00 P.M. and I was hungry, so after a while of breathing and letting the experience move through my pores, I got up, drove to my local pub, sat at the bar, and had a drink and a delicious dinner while watching a fabulous US Open tennis final.

As I said previously, I'm no beauty, but I've always had an internal confidence when it comes to men. I've been grateful to have had many lovely romances—some short, some of many years' duration and of various levels of commitment. It's been a while since I felt so rejected; it was truly unfamiliar. But I'm forging ahead, learning more with every step I take, about myself, about life, about love, about aging and being so grateful for all I have.

It's important to always remember that whatever comes our way, it's for us, even if we don't initially experience it that way, and it is equally important to always remember that a Dairy Queen is never far away!

Dreams and Matches in an Unsure Virtual World

Alice F. Freed

This isn't one of those self-help or how-to pieces. I just have a story to tell.

In the fall of 2001, about a year after my then-husband and I went our separate ways, when I was in my early fifties, I first tried online dating. At the time, this was far from conventional behavior for a woman like me. Instead, it was a daring foray into the unknown. For about a year, I carried on like a teenager with an embarrassing secret and finally abandoned the endeavor. Some years later, still living alone but then past sixty, I again turned to online dating, which by then was a bit more mainstream. Success, if that's the right word, continued to evade me. Despite this, I recognized that my collection of experiences had an unmistakably positive underbelly, which, as my mother would have said, added texture to my life.

I'm a sophisticated woman—financially secure, reasonably well traveled, well bred, with a PhD from an Ivy League university, feminist—a published full professor who claims mother, sister, and daughter among her favorite titles. I'm in good health, in full possession of all my faculties, have extraordinary friends and a loving, albeit small, spread-out family. I am fortunate and certainly privileged. You might know women like me. In my story, I will do my utmost to protect the identity of everyone but myself.

It all started after September 11, 2001. Plane travel suddenly presented new challenges and risks, and I realized that the magical, nearly perfect but very long-distance relationship that I was in was hard on my newly processed emotional self. I needed a clear and present companion, not someone trapped on the other side of the world. No one knew any straight, age-appropriate, available men. Everyone "good" was taken or gay. I enrolled in a wine-tasting class, learned a little about the bouquet, flavor, and structure of a good wine, but noticed that the structure of my emotional life was not improving with age. I quickly understood that it was going to be personal ads, online dating, or lonely nights alone.

It was certainly no coincidence that the decision to take the plunge was less than a month after our world shook and the World Trade Center became Ground Zero. Everyone I knew was terrified and grief stricken, appalled that we were at war, on edge but somehow determined to go on with their lives. What distinguished me from everyone close to me was that they all seemed to have a life to go on with. Everyone agreed that it was a lousy time to be alone.

World events do indeed seem to bookend my post-marriage romantic decisions. When I started this journey, the Twin Towers had just come down. More recently, from March 2020 to March 2021 (and beyond), we were all hiding from COVID-19 and sheltering through a worldwide pandemic. Neither was a good time to be alone. My virtual search for a partner has morphed into a world of virtual everything. Oh, the ironies of the gods.

Back in 2001, I started by scanning the now discontinued *New York Times* Personals. I called a few numbers, listened to a few male voices announce their own virtues as they described what sort of long brown mane they wanted a woman to have. I heard the word *slender* a bit more often than I liked; I also heard the ages "thirty-five to forty-five" coming out of the mouths of many a sixty-year-old delusional man. At the time, I was a vital fifty-something and not ashamed of my age or my looks. I cringed as I listened and knew I had to look elsewhere.

It was on the *New York Review of Books* personals page that I discovered something called "The Right Stuff: An Introduction Network," for graduates of select universities—where "Smart is sexy." I was smart, kind of sexy. And I liked smart, sexy men. That's when I also discovered that I had no shame. I keyed in "The Right Stuff" in an online search, and we seemed to be a match made in heaven, The Right Stuff and I. I am not advertising for TRS or any other service, though I do have my favorites. Members had to provide evidence of their affiliation with an Ivy League university (or other select "excellent" schools). The existence of some screening device reassured me at the time. Right or wrong, I thought it would permit me to get my feet wet without worrying too much about the sleaze factor, to say nothing of serial killers. Unfortunately, TRS had a fairly limited database.

A close friend insisted that as long as I was bothering, I should also join the much larger site Jdate. That's "J" for "Jewish." I am at best what one clever man (whom I never got to meet) called "lukewarm Jewish." Since this friend's daughter had met her beau through Jdate, my friend assured me that it had to be good. (Her daughter was twenty-five.) I joined both TRS and Jdate in early October 2001.

I started filling out the questionnaires and writing the required essays. You've no doubt heard about the dreaded college essay; that's a piece of cake in comparison. You should try sitting alone on a Saturday night, weeping for your soul mate who lives a planet away, looking for the words to describe your idea of a perfect Sunday. I knew very well what my perfect Sunday was, but did I have to tell the whole world? Imagine listing your age, height, weight, religious preference, interests, and other juicy personal stuff while reviewing the profiles of men older than you who are looking for women your daughter's age. Some of the profiles of the women sharing the marketplace with me were announcing their pantie size while I wanted to list how many articles I'd published.

At the time, I was slightly humiliated to admit that I was doing this internet dating thing, but the online marketplace seemed to be the way to go. By the time the 2020 pandemic hit, online dating was the only game in town. I have written more anonymous messages to more complete strangers than even I want to admit. I have learned to suffer the lack of response to my cleverly written messages. And better (or worse), in due course, I too learned to ignore messages from men who didn't appeal to me, although, raised to always write a thank-you note, it still feels rude.

My earliest online experiences taught me things I hadn't realized. I knew I liked people who wrote well, but "funny" turned out to be a big draw. I kept falling for jerks because they were funny. The worst experience with someone I never even met was with a man I wrote to three different times (on two different dating sites), thinking he was three different people. He presented himself under three different aliases but always had the same gift for gab. I finally discovered (when I recognized his voice on the phone) that his humor (and accompanying creepiness) had repeatedly caught my attention.

Another man I found really intrigued me. When I had his real name, I googled him (I am a trained researcher and know to check my sources). I learned that he was an MD. Sounded promising. When I entered his name, a long list of sites appeared. I clicked and I read, "It is with great sadness that we announce the passing of our colleague. . . ." I am ashamed to tell you that I burst out laughing. That was the first deceased personals connection I had made.

There were many people who showed up on more than one site; we were a virtual community—a *community of practice* is what we call this in the social sciences. People engaged in a mutual endeavor who have a similar goal and shared "practices." The same faces appeared from one site to another. These same people were of course noticing my same face over and over again as well; one kind man told me I was "ubiquitous." Didn't sound like a compliment to me.

I accidentally found myself corresponding with a man who was in the same academic field as me. We both felt terrifically exposed. Then I received a message from the ex-husband of a colleague. I recognized his face, and I knew his name. Apparently, he didn't know that I knew him— nor did he know that I had already passed over his profile when I had discovered it several weeks earlier. Later, I found a profile written by a friend's partner, looking for a woman with whom he could father a child. What was the ethical thing to do with this information? I decided to conceal this huge indiscretion from everyone I knew.

I have looked at the faces and read the descriptions, narratives, biographies, and profiles of thousands of men. Sailors and doctors. PhDs, MBAs, CEOs, MDs. Successful men. Men who have been hurt in past relationships. Men of seventy who love their five-year-old children from their third marriages and men who love their grown children from their first marriages. Men who are disabled. Others in early stages of dementia. Attorneys, engineers, judges, computer scientists. People starting second careers. Widowers. Writers, models, musicians, and artists. Who said there are no men out there? But, even with a well-tuned sense of humor and a positive outlook, it is, honestly, believe me, take me at my word, an utterly exhausting enterprise.

Anonymity remains a major issue with all these services. At first, I was writing emails from my university address, where my name was prominently displayed at the top of each message. Almost everyone else, I discovered, had clever aliases and email addresses. "Mr. Write," for example, or "openbook@___.com." Hearing my tales of woe over dinner one night, a friend offered to set me up with an email account on his business web site so I could correspond with these men directly using an anonymous email address. I became "openbook@___.com."

I have had quite a few good dinners with quite a few good men. My dreamy prospects each acquired an affectionate term of reference that I used when talking about them with my close friends. There was the Professor, the Marine, the Pharmacist, the Phantom, the Glassblower, the Israeli, the Yogi, the Widower, Jerry, Richard, and Bill. Messages arrived from all sorts of people. Several thirty-five-year-olds wrote to me and regretted that I found them too young. At least one twenty-five-year-old has contacted me. Everyone, including me, eventually, seems to shed a few years from their published age because no one pays any attention to stated preferences anyway. It is the wild wild West of dating. Naïve optimist that I am, I have almost always gotten my hopes up before meeting someone new; the experiences are, therefore, almost always depressing because they are so consistently disappointing. But only once did I have a scare.

I met a man who I thought could be a winner. He contacted me via Match.com. He was well educated, an engineer. He had done two tours of duty in Vietnam. (I decided to treat the fact that I was marching against the war while he was in Southeast Asia as a historic detail.) He had an MBA from Stanford, had been a student of yoga for twenty-five years. He was semiretired and had never married. (A red flag, but I decided I wasn't one for generalizations.) When he told me that he watched pornographic movies in the afternoons, I thought he was kidding. He said he was kidding. After emailing and talking, we made a date for a Saturday night. Drinks, dinner, and then a jazz club. I spent hours making sure I looked great. He didn't look much like his photo—he was shorter, fatter. I was determined to remain open and curious. We went out for drinks. There was a lot of touching on his part. I kept smiling. He told me horror stories from the war. I asked him to stop; he didn't. We moved to dinner. He was rude to the waiter while I tried not to notice. And then, with no warning, he leaned over in the upscale restaurant, arugula on my plate, and gave me an open-mouthed kiss. Next thing I knew, I was in the bathroom calling a friend, asking her how to escape. I had made the mistake of having a total stranger pick me up at *my* house in *his* car. My parents taught me not to get into cars with strangers. I should have listened to my parents.

I interviewed for a new matchmaking service that was about to launch its site. Someone had given them my email address. They claimed to have recruited two thousand "bright, educated, successful, upscale men" in NYC in the preceding eight months and were next looking for women. The interviewer and I met at Artie's Delicatessen on Broadway. I was entered into "Good Looking" database but never heard from them again. And then I joined, voluntarily, stupidly, idiotically, an extremely expensive British matchmaking service that guaranteed a specific number of quality matches, and flew to London for an interview. That was a total and complete waste of my hard-earned money.

I tried eHarmony and outsmarted their algorithm. My first go at their exhaustive questionnaire produced a profile category and description of me that was entirely wrong. I threatened to quit if they didn't allow me to redo the questionnaire. The second time I answered the questions much less honestly, and, with that, the description fit, but the men still didn't. I tried Match and Tinder, which is supposed to be completely anonymous, but if you are clever, you can figure things out. I also tried OurTime and OkCupid. I haven't tried Bumble or Zoosk. A few other sites have popped up that seem great, but they either have regional restrictions or are for people younger than I am.

From my early fifties to my early seventies, I had more than 150 dates. That's 150 different men, not counting the repeats. (I did not keep an exact count, but this is not an exaggeration.) Some men I met at lectures. Some were men introduced to me. Most I met online. Some I went out with only once. Some I tried meeting several times. Some men I got closer to. None—not one—genuinely sparked my interest for more than a few months. Some vanished without explanation. Sometimes I had to be the one to disappoint. I met arrogant men and humble men. I met smart men who admitted to having no steady income, rich men who had no education, educated men who had no manners, and mannered men who had no wit. Almost all were nice decent men—and all of them lonely. Hundreds of men in both New York and San Francisco, where rumor has it that there are no single straight men between the ages of forty-five and seventy-five.

I have become a bit of an expert, but I also see, many years into this process, that I am happier than I realized at the end of each day with no one else's socks to trip over in my bedroom. The man who was the indisputable love of my life stayed in my life until he died in 2019, but we were star-crossed lovers separated by time, space, and tragically bad luck. When the pandemic of 2020 hit, my goal was to stay sane, as cheerful as possible—and healthy. And in 2020, I reluctantly realized that I was, I am, at least for the time being, finished with internet dating. I discovered that I had perhaps also lost interest in any sort of dating at all.

Dreams and matches look different in an unsure, dangerous world. One thing I am sure of, though, is that I could change my mind again. There just might be wonders ahead, unexpected delights. So, with continued curiosity about what new textures will be added to my life, what new dating sites might be just around the corner, and what surprises might show up in my inbox, I'm still doing a daily check of my messages.

In Transition,
Not Seeking for Now

Hedva Lewittes

I am seventy-five. My husband, Arthur, died about a year ago. During our thirty-seven years of marriage, I grew firm roots. Nurtured by Arthur's warmth, I became more confident and open. Holding on through some serious and threatening storms, I learned to be trustworthy. We created a family and home, a secure base from which to pursue work, develop friendships, and embark on adventures. We gave each other space to do our own thing but could also return to a place of quiet comfort. We delighted in each other's sense of humor and had a lot of fun. Even with age, as Arthur began to show signs of memory loss, we were still a good team. Joint grandparenting was our crowning achievement. When my walking was impaired for months by osteoporosis stress fractures, Arthur had my back. Slowed down by his own limitations, he had more time and patience as he accompanied me to endless doctors' visits and kept our daily life going. This process of evolving together and its intimate interactions has shaped who I am, and I want more. I understand that I cannot replace Arthur's unique spirit. But must I also lose this essential part of my own self? Is a new partner, a new connection, possible?

My experience of Arthur's illness and death also shaped me. While his cognitive decline had been slow and uneven, in the last year of our marriage, it became increasingly debilitating. The dynamic between us shifted as I took on more and more responsibility for keeping him functioning and he was less and less capable of being an equal partner. About five months before he died, he had a major stroke that wiped out most of his language and his control of movement in his entire right side. He was in and out of various hospitals, rehab, and assisted living facilities. Watching him suffer was devastating, and, struggling to care for him, I was continually overwhelmed and exhausted. My transition to living on my own began while he was dying. Being home alone gave me respite and relief, which was necessary to effectively help him and for my own survival, but being apart was painful for us both. As I contemplate a new relationship, I do not want to impulsively enmesh myself or squander my hard-won independence.

COVID-19 overtook our national existence two months after my husband passed away. Initially I feared getting sick, quarantining and dying alone in the hospital. But after the first few weeks I noticed that, day to day, my sense of loneliness had not increased. I had already started to learn to live by myself. Indeed, I began to feel more normal and less the needy supplicant because now my friends and family were also more isolated and equally eager for frequent reassuring telephone calls.

Regardless of my conflicting emotions, the pandemic made finding a new partner more difficult, at least in the short run. I did have one brief encounter that only lasted for a few months but gave me some insight into what I did not want. Literally four days before lockdown I met a man at a synagogue event, and we began to have "walking dates" every few weeks. Getting together provided a welcome distraction from COVID, and our relationship was both somewhat more and less than a friendship. There was an easy flow to our rhythm, choosing the paths and pace of our walks. Nonetheless, it soon became clear that although we were members of the same congregation, ours was not a match made in heaven. Because of social distancing, the relationship may have lasted longer than it might have under other circumstances. There was no pressure for physical intimacy, given our age and health issues. But he was staunchly apolitical and, from my perspective, this was a major barrier. He cared more about what he ate for breakfast than voting rights. I realized that I was attracted to people who were passionate about something beyond their own immediate needs. Further, I recognized that I was not willing to compromise my beliefs just for companionship and/or because I was lonely.

My retirement, delayed first by the exigencies of caring for my husband and then by the economic crash at the beginning of the pandemic, finally happened at the end of 2020. I appreciated having control over my own time. I had a plan, plenty to do, and enjoyed teaching one course and writing. Nonetheless, with the virus's winter surge, the pandemic added new dimensions to my early experiences of being alone. Snowstorms and a succession of cold, gloomy days, combined with COVID isolation, rigorously tested my ability to manage.

Emerging out of my marriage's cocoon, I felt vulnerable. The term *single*, in essence, only tells us who or what isn't there. I was no longer married, but my relational self still needed people. Changes in my relationships, perspective, and needs were complicated by the pandemic restrictions. My aging, mostly coupled friends hunkered down for safety. Getting along or not, they typically took for granted the benefits of being able to eat dinner with each other or that there was someone close by for emergencies. They were frequently unaware of how the tendrils of loneliness crept into my psyche and everyday life. My single friends, who, like me, were living alone, resonated with my feelings. Their self-sufficiency was instructive. But they had in the past worked out ways of being on their own and had built networks that provided some support even within the confines of the lockdown. Unlike them, as a recent widow, I had not chosen my status and still missed the presence of an intimate partner with whom I felt safe and known.

Being alone in the pandemic intensified my desire to be in a primary relationship. Nonetheless, I am not seeking right now. For now, I am headed in the direction of developing a life of my own. With vaccinations in my arm and spring in the air, I hope to move on from survival mode and regain some resilience. I need some healing and renewed energy.

Travel can be restorative, and I hope to take to the road. I need a vacation from the house I shared with and where I mourn my husband. I would like to visit, walk, and share a meal with my scattered friends, get beyond the defensiveness, and reconnect.

I also began the transition out of my career as a college professor in the middle of the pandemic lockdown. Although I left my job, my identity came with me. I am eager to expand my work beyond academia, shift to a more personal voice as a writer and build on my past activities and interests. For the last two years, I have been involved in a political group centered around a Jewish social justice perspective that integrates my political activism with my Jewish roots. After a career of being in front of the classroom and in charge of meetings as a chair and director, I was content to be a foot soldier, making calls to legislators, writing postcards, and generally helping out. During the pandemic, breathing meditation, a practice I began about fifteen years ago, enabled me to get some distance from my feelings of panic and despair. Looking inward, I connected to a visceral sense of my own core and imagined my backbone was made of shiny steel. I anticipate that I will continue to explore contemplative workshops and retreats.

Reflecting a mindfulness perspective, I want to feel complete and whole in my present life, so I do not plan to make looking for a mate my raison d'être. This is not just a philosophical position. Spending my time on dating apps, checking my email, messages, and Facebook is not the retirement I had envisioned. I am confident I have a lot to give someone special. I am less confident about my aging body but recoil at the prospect of making myself over to be "acceptable" in the marketplace. Finding a new partner is not, in my opinion, accomplished by promoting a best-case scenario of myself or fantasizing and checking off items on my wish list. The nitty-gritty and chemistry of intimacy cannot really be anticipated outside of the actual interaction. However, I do have thoughts about the kind of relationship I want at this stage of my life. I see it as a mutually created process that involves gaining appreciation and acceptance for what each person can and cannot offer and developing attachment and trust step by step. Taking the next step requires emotional and interpersonal courage. With a fellow vaccine veteran, holding hands, snuggling, hugging, back rubs, and orgasms would be lovely. I do not foresee moving in with someone or linking up legally or economically. But I would like us to be part of each other's day-to-day existence; to keep track of each other's life maps; to regularly prepare and eat dinner together in and out of the house. I am not expecting a one-person, all-purpose entertainment companion, but I hope we can introduce each other to new passions and pleasures that could expand our horizons. Caring for each other emotionally is a must. Taking care of each other physically, the elephant in the room. My involvement in Arthur's illness grew out of the commitment and obligation of years of being a family. In forming a bond with someone new who is also aging, it is of course impossible to predict the amount of time we would have together or our capabilities to help each other. Finding a balance between caring for yourself and someone you love is a challenge, especially as you get older.

Looking to the future, I imagine getting to know a new partner in the context of my post-pandemic retirement journey. Indeed, building on my past, I met both my first husband (we divorced after a few years) and Arthur in political and community activities. However, I think of finding a new primary relationship as an intention rather than an immediate goal. The concept of intention, an idea I have studied and written about,[1] is based on the philosophies of Buddhism and mindfulness. Jon Kabat-Zinn, founder of the Mindfulness-Based Stress Reduction program at the University of Massachusetts Medical School, describes intention as follows: "People need to kindle vision of what they really want for themselves and keep that vision alive in the face of inner and outer hardships, obstacles, and setbacks."[2] The mindfulness attitude of nonstriving contributes to following an intention. Kabat-Zinn writes, "Almost everything we do, we do for a purpose to get something or somewhere." He continues, "The best way to achieve your goals is to back off from striving for results and instead focusing carefully on seeing and accepting things as they are, moment by moment.[3] While Kabat-Zinn discusses intention as a way to sustain a meditation practice, I find it a relevant and hopeful approach to my current situation. It helps me to deal with uncertainty and leaves room for me to be deliberate, to feel grounded, and to draw on the wisdom I have gleaned in my seventy-five years. At the same time, it encourages an openness to learning and to new ways of being with people. What makes sense to me at this point is not to strive for or seek fulfillment through someone else but to pay attention to and move forward on my own path. Being willing to be on my own, lonely though it is, gives me the integrity to find (or not) a new relationship that works for me.

NOTES

1. H. Lewittes and L. Morris, "Intentional Learning, Mindfulness and Mindset," *International Journal of Pedagogy and Curriculum* 28, no.1 (2021): 37–55, doi.org/10.18848/2327-796CGP.

2. J. Kabat-Zinn, *Full Catastrophe Living* (New York: Bantam Books, 2013), 37.

3. Kabat-Zinn, *Full Catastrophe Living*, 26–27.

"Do You Get It Yet?"

Rett Zabriskie

Human beings, from the beginnings of consciousness, have been and remain slow learners with great hopes. From God asking Adam and Eve in Eden, "What part of 'No' did you not understand?" to the politician who absolutely denied whatever it was, we continue, as individuals and as a species, to fumble. While much good occurs, all human experiences have at least a tad of not so good, even with our best loves. Knowing this, it is a witness to the triumph of hope over experience that so many who lose a partner after the age of sixty find such joy and energy in the prospect of a new romance.

My wife Astrid died in 2007. She was Danish, I'm American, and we shared love and life in both Denmark and New York for thirty-five years. As with any marriage, the ways in which we were individually and collectively slow learners provided unique insights into the ways life can get messed up. But I regret not a single moment. The initial lust, the inevitable wars—most ending in genuine growth—and the ever-increasing ability to both enjoy each other and be helpful to those around us were and remain meaningful. We loved each other. We loved being married and rejoicing in each other's work. And we loved doing it double, having it all: family, work, and social life in Denmark as well as New York.

During Astrid's bout with colon cancer, fifteen years before she died of something else, we had the serious conversations about what it would mean to be a caregiver in our old age and about being alone when one of us finally departed. For both of us, those conversations rooted our consistent joy for our life together even deeper. When she died, the shock of her going from vibrant life to dead from cerebral hemorrhaging in thirty hours was disorienting. That shock matured in the weeks after the funeral and became an awareness of how much I had actually lost. When I was in pastoral counselor training, they taught us that good marriages exist in three parts. First, marriage begins with the two people who make the couple. Then they have, each of them, their own separate personal lives, with their accomplishments, their specific challenges, and their individual parameters. But there is also the third part, the marriage, that is just as real and just as challenging as each personal life but requires the presence of the two people to exist. The shock of being suddenly alone and the constant tears that erupted without warning regardless of context, time, and place, seemed, at first, overreaction. As the weeks became months, as I learned to do the housekeeping tasks she had done, and as the friendships in our social circle rebalanced with some growing stronger and some disappearing, I perceived that I had not lost half my life—I had lost two-thirds of my life. Not only was Astrid dead and unavailable, but that third reality, our marriage, with all its own peculiar specifics and gifts, was also gone completely. I was not just without a partner. I was without a partner and without a framework for living.

Each surviving spouse arrives at this lonely place, of course. But each surviving spouse will have his or her own way of reacting. About a year after Astrid's death, I began to wonder whether I desired or felt life required me to have a partner again. I was encouraged in that direction by almost all of my female friends and most of my male friends. There was a marked advocacy for it in my American circle and a deliberate, reticent, silence on the subject in my Danish circle, reflective of the cultural tone of both. During the first four years of my widowhood (yes, the word applies to men in that situation), I twice spent twelve to fourteen months in serious relationships. The first was a classmate from more than sixty years ago; the other a Dane with an interest in Søren Kierkegaard. The classmate and

I discovered why we never dated in school. The Dane and I discovered other interests and complications that made Kierkegaard not enough reason to stay together. I remain friends with both women, and we see one another regularly, yet all remain single.

For the past ten years (other than during the COVID-19 pandemic time), each week has included an event with one of (currently) seven female friends. Lunch, weekend at some destination, theater, museum, etc. The weeks often hold an additional similar event with a male friend or a couple, but on the whole, I find I prefer the company of single women. Occasionally, one of us wonders what a closer relationship might look like, but in no case does the conversation get beyond speculation. In formulating ways to express what I think and feel, two notions have become clear. First, I loved Astrid deeply, which does not mean we did not fight. There were days—and occasional weeks—throughout our thirty-five years together that could not be described in any way as either acceptable or pleasant. However, I believe those difficult times are necessary to create a good marriage. Human beings are slow learners, and they do not learn to know another person deeply without significant conflict over issues that matter. Being a true partner takes total investment along with massive amounts of time. Second, at my age, even with good prospects, I no longer have any reasonable hope of having enough time left to create a meaningful marriage.

So, I continue with slow learning, and the new lessons continue to emerge. Friendship is about meaningful life, not the filling of personal needs, whether for a nurse or a purse or whatever. Those practical necessities are to be secured in other ways. One human caring for another can well mean deciding *not* to share bathrooms, bedrooms, or kitchens. It makes economic and educational sense for parents and their young children to share these things. For old folks, not so much. For the life left to me, I will be content to remain married to Astrid with all my memories and hopes for God's redemption. For the daily round, I will be content to live with those I encounter, slow learners all, and rejoice in gratitude for the gift of today and for meaningful life.

On the Road

Irvin Peckham

My wife of forty-one years died of a particularly virulent cancer nine years ago. She was diagnosed in January 2011. She was dead by August 11. I have learned how to go forward by drawing on my love for Sarah. I wrote a book several years ago about going through her death and the dark period after. It's a good book, but I can't read it. I wrote it, as I write most things, to externalize and understand what was going on inside me. When I write, it's like talking to Sarah, the closest friend I've ever had.

We were married in 1970, before we moved to Canada when I was drafted. We moved to California three years later; then to Omaha, Nebraska, where I took my first university position; and from there to Baton Rouge, where she died. She was beautiful: a talented artist and a librarian. This essay is about how I have learned to live without her and, perhaps more importantly, how I've learned to live by myself.

Certainly, other widowers and widows share the experience of trying to find another partner. It is a major problem for those of us who have been left behind. I desperately wanted another partner. I am sensual; I like sex. I like making love and holding a woman I love next to me. I like having breakfast with her, having her listen to my concerns and tell me hers. I love loving someone. This kind of love seems to me like the bedrock of the human condition. Learning how to go to the other side, where one lives alone, is quite a trick, which is what this essay is about.

Me

I was a working-class academic. I grew up in a rural farmhouse with no running water and an outhouse. We went to the bathroom quickly in our Wisconsin winters. Middle class, to us, meant the Clarks up the road; they had running water. I went to a one-room schoolhouse. I joke that I was salutatorian in eighth grade—there were two in our class. I was an athlete—a wrestler—in high school and college until I became a hippie in my junior year at the University of Wisconsin. I could write books about my hippie years in Madison, which is where I met Sarah.

Sarah came from a well-known family in Madison. They were upper middle class socially but middle middle class economically. Most of her male relatives, except her father, had their doctorates. Her great-uncle, Harold Groves, was Robert La Follette's running mate for president on the Progressive Party ticket in 1924. Harold and his wife, Helen, were close friends of the Frank Lloyd Wrights. I was only a working-class young man trying to understand the conventions of educated, middle-class Americans, the ones who overpopulate postsecondary institutions.

Sarah and her family taught me how to be middle class, which, in part, entailed the rejection of my working-class origins, leading to guilt over my social-class betrayal. I don't think in my twenties I really understood what I was doing as I changed what Pierre Bourdieu, the French sociologist, calls *habitus* (e.g., one's language, dress codes, eating habits, entertainment, books, preferred music), but I remanufactured myself to move into the hypereducated, upper middle class. At the nether end of my life, I'm glad I made the choices I did. I couldn't have wished for a better life than the one I had with Sarah and as a college professor. But I respect my origins and understand how middle- and upper-class privileges depend on the exploited labor of the working classes.

Despite the weed I smoked and the acid I took in the sixties, I hung on to an athletic frame of mind, one I still hold. I like my body. I exercise regularly. I used to be a runner; now I'm a mountain biker and pickleball player. I watch my weight. I would like to drink more, because gin or vodka smooth out my solitary space, but drinking also puts on weight. So, I watch my alcoholic intake carefully. I eat lots of fruit and vegetables, fish, and, rarely, red meat.

MISTAKE

I don't like to think about the time between Sarah dying and when I began to come to terms with myself. After Sarah died, I fantasized about having another partner like her. I knew that was stupid, that one should meet potential partners where they are, not where one wants them to be. In fact, my first new relationship was a serious attempt to do that. Lisa was a Tea Party fanatic—and I'm a quasi-Marxist communitarian, in the older sense of the word. I loved my relationship with Lisa, but it was never going to be the right one. For one thing, I wanted her more than she wanted me. She may also have held my age against me. I was in my midsixties; I think she was in her midfifties. In the beginning we were both in love, but I think I wore her out after a few months. I thought she was beautiful, and she probably thought I was just okay. As I reflect on our relationship now, I think she just wanted a lover for a while, whereas I wanted someone to love. She had also been married three times; me, once.

In the next couple of years, I dated several women via Match, one of whom I liked quite a bit. We had a strong relationship for several months, but I think ultimately ours was the reverse of my relationship with Lisa. I knew that Cheryl wasn't the woman with whom I wanted to spend the rest of my life; Cheryl sensed my hesitation and called our relationship off. Although I have since moved from Baton Rouge, I have remained good Facebook friends with both Lisa and Cheryl (although Biden's win over Trump has strained my relationship with Lisa). There is at least this: I have two more friends in my life.

I know others have developed successful relationships with people they have met through online dating sites. I may have gone out with twenty

women via Match, but Lisa and Cheryl were the only ones with whom a
relationship was even halfway possible. I realize my percentage does not
speak well of me. I could write quite a bit about Match, but I generally want
to avoid those memories. Most of my attempts to find a partner online
were silly. We were like billiard balls bouncing off each other, unwilling
to let the other inside.

People on Match seem to be jockeying for position, trying to find the
most attractive and interesting person they think might find them worth
their attention. Clearly most of us overestimate ourselves. I was surprised
at many of the women who thought I would be interested in them. I am
sure there were an equal number of women who were surprised that
I thought they would be interested in me. I was irritated by the way I would
waste my time going through all the available women and sending notes
out to the wrong ones (the ones who clearly couldn't imagine hanging out
with the likes of me).

In addition, I dislike being suckered. The people who operate online
dating sites don't care about making real matches. Their sites are basically
con games; their owners make millions from people's fantasies. Match gen-
erates about $500 million a year in revenue from lonely searchers. After a
couple of years, I left Match. I decided I would rather meet a possible partner in a real-life situation, spy someone across the crowded room. But
because I am a person who enjoys solitude, this Hollywood-style fantasy
was highly unlikely. Even before COVID-19, I didn't like crowded rooms.

Sometime later, it happened. I saw her at a national conference for writing teachers. I was standing in line for coffee when I saw this attractive
woman—long hair, sweeping dress, intelligent face—looking at me, or so
I thought. I assumed I was imagining things and ignored her, although I
glanced at her now and then. By the time I got my coffee, she was gone.
A year later, I was at another national conference of writing teachers. After
the presentation, I made a couple of comments (my normal behavior) and
I saw the same woman looking at me from across the room. After the

session, I went over to her and said, "I think I know you." I did. A few years before, she had been a visiting professor in the writing program I directed at LSU. We met again the next day, exchanged email addresses, and soon a relationship was on.

Mia and I began our relationship via email because she lived in New Jersey, and I was in Baton Rouge. We traded a few weekends; she came to Baton Rouge, and I went to New Jersey. She told me about seeing me at that first conference, while I was in line for coffee. We thought it was funny that here we were in bed a year later. During one of my flights home from New Jersey, she texted me about an open academic position near her. I thought for a few moments and texted back: Ok, I'll apply. That was stupid. I was a full professor at a major university applying for an associate professor position at a lower-ranked university. Aside from this academic social-class demotion, I loved teaching at LSU and had many close friends there. I would be leaving that for the chance of a long-term relationship with Mia.

I had early warning signs that a relationship with Mia wouldn't work. Our weekend sex was great, but I saw raw edges to her that I didn't like. The worst one was her sexual history. She referred to her twenties as "cock-jumping." She rammed through two marriages, got involved in some scandal in graduate school, and after her second marriage, maybe in her later thirties, she started having relationships with women. She was still living with her previous lover, Leslie, though she explained that she and Leslie no longer had a sexual relationship. Leslie had developed a disability, and Mia was taking care of her.

My relationship with Mia lasted about a year. Then we started to rub each other raw. Leslie made it clear that she didn't like me staying at their house for the weekend. Despite Mia's stories, I was more interested in sex than she was. She found all sorts of things about me that irritated her, like my toenails, pubic hair, and disdain for her habit of watching reality TV shows. I think she just didn't like men. I don't blame her.

Down and Back

Breaking up with Mia was difficult, a replay of my earlier relationship with Lisa. I hated the way I lost control of myself when I fell in love, like hitting an icy spot while driving down the road and spinning into a ditch. After my experience with Mia, I decided it was better to learn how to live alone. I quit my university position, listed my house for sale, and drove with Lola, my newly rescued dog, from New Jersey to the virtual end of the road in Panama, where I had a place to cabana-sit on fifteen secluded seaside acres for two months. I wanted to be one hundred percent by myself (with Lola) for a long time. The poet Marianne Moore wrote that the best cure for loneliness is solitude. Jesus took off into the desert. Buddha hung out for a few years underneath a tree. Thoreau went to the woods. I'm no Jesus, Buddha, or Thoreau, but I thought isolation would be a good way to get right with myself, undistracted by relations with anyone other than Lola. I realized there was a hole in my logic, predicated on the assumption that to be human, defined by Kenneth Burke as symbol-making bipeds, is to be in linguistic relationships with others. But I wasn't too interested in arguing my case. I just wanted to get in touch with myself by traveling in a car with Lola through places where I didn't know anyone, a solitary condition magnified by my not being able to speak the native language.

As I discovered later, there was another condition of my solitude: I didn't have any maps of the countries though which I was traveling, an obvious metaphor for my spiritual journey. I assumed that when I got to Mexico, I would get a map at the border, and likewise at the borders of Guatemala, El Salvador, Honduras, Nicaragua, Costa Rica, and Panama. Little did I know—people in Mexico and Central America don't seem to use maps. In addition, the GPS only worked sporadically. I ended up driving through Mexico and Central America mostly by stopping and asking in my limited Spanish the best way to get to the next town or country: "Donde es el mejor ruta a Vera Cruz?" I would phrase the question with the help of my *Spanish for Idiots* book and then generally be unable to understand the answer. "No comprendo," I would say. "Puedo hablar solo un poco de español," and they would point this way and that way, and I would follow their arm directions to the next town—or next person, to whom I would admit I was once again lost.

I knew that going down to South America with my bare-bones Spanish would be difficult—and it was. My plan was to stay near Las Escobas del Venado for two months, take Spanish lessons, finish a couple of books I was working on, and then drive back, Spanish-fluent. I would be isolated; the primary source of fellowship would be a beach bar about twenty minutes from where I was staying. I spent about a month of isolation driving down, two months of relative isolation while there, and another month of isolation on the way back. By the time I got back to New Jersey, I was more fluent in Spanish, and I knew how to be alone.

The Pleasure of Being Alone

When I am driving through another country, I focus on landscape through which I'm traveling. I am outside myself. I generally take back roads to avoid fellow travelers. I like to drive slowly and pay attention to the landscape and farmhouses. I think about the people who live inside them. While driving through eastern Colorado last summer, I was struck by the vastness of the landscape and the distance between farms, thousands of acres between them. I would drive for twenty minutes between one farmhouse and the next, for ten minutes without meeting another car. I remember passing one abandoned farmhouse that sat about a quarter mile off the road. It was standing alone with no sheds or barns. The windows were gone. I thought of it as courageous and beautiful. Lola had been moving around in the front seat, her sign that it was time to pee. I pulled off the side of the road. We got out and she ran off to find a good spot. I stood there and listened. This was early fall, and the fields were plowed, leaving nothing for birds. There was no sound. The silence was palpable. I breathed it in, if one can breathe silence. The absence of life and the empty house leaning into the west wind were paradoxically beautiful. After a while, a car appeared on the horizon. I called Lola, we got back in the car and continued east toward home.

Home now is Harrisonburg, Virginia, where my daughter lives. There, I am not as alone as when I'm traveling. I am comfortable in a funky farmhouse I bought in the middle of industrial Harrisonburg. The house is cool inside. An old hippie, a bit younger than I, redesigned and rebuilt the downstairs interior. He was a good carpenter. My house has a warm feel to it and a backyard that my two dogs love. I enjoy being in my house, waking slowly in the morning, talking to the dogs, exercising while listening to CNN or Eric Clapton, taking a warm shower and eating a slow breakfast, writing emails or writing to myself in my diary, playing my guitars and singing, pickleballing or mountain biking, walking my dogs, going over to my daughter's house for dinner and another episode of *The Durrells*, one or two of my three adorable granddaughters in my arms, coming home, reading or writing with maybe a little weed and cognac on the side, going to bed, dreaming wild dreams, and waking up again.

Who could not be happy like this, even alone? I have learned—and perhaps it has been my greatest lesson—how to be alone. My advice to people who have lost their partners in later life: get in your car with your dog and drive to Panama and back while listening to Kerouac's scroll version of *On the Road*.

Dark Clouds and Silver Linings

William Wiesner

I am eighty years old and have been single for close to half of my life. I was sure that I'd be married within five years of my divorce. I was twenty-nine when I married my wife, and for twelve years, until I was forty-one, it was mostly good. We had two daughters and lived paycheck to paycheck until my wife decided to leave. It was an amicable, mediated divorce, but there was heartbreak on two levels. My marriage was over, and I was afraid that I would be more uncle to my kids than father. Fortunately, my relationship with my daughters has remained close. Even though I was the noncustodial parent—they were with me five nights out of fourteen. Still, I quickly realized that I didn't like being single. I started dating a lot in the hopes of finding a new life partner.

Dating first as a middle-aged and then as an older man is only a little different than dating as a young man, but some of the considerations are very different. There are very few casual get-togethers with new people at my age, but there are occasional singles' groups and parties. There are also print ads as well as online matching sites. The net effect is that it is easy for a single man, even a senior, to meet as many women as he might like. In fact, the older I get, the more I feel like a commodity since there are so many more single women than there are single men. At times it feels like being in a candy store with too many choices; this may sound good, but it is uncomfortable and leads to being overly picky.

Another negative is age consideration. At a certain point I realized that if I met someone, I could no longer hope for a silver anniversary. When I was fifty, I could comfortably date someone ten years younger than me. But at eighty, would that be fair? I'm pretty healthy and everything works, but if I started a relationship with someone who is seventy, would that be fair to her? When she is eighty, I could well be a doddering ninety-year-old or maybe not even here. The other side of the coin is the health of a potential partner. I don't want to be responsible for taking care of a sick elderly woman for the rest of my life, one I've known only a few years.

Money is another concern. I have my savings, and I'd like to leave what I have to my children and grandchildren. At some level, her financial situation and her health insurance must be considered.

I have dated a lot. Dating has been good. I learned some things that strengthened me in ways that were not true when I was married. I learned that there were women who found me attractive. I learned that I wasn't such a bad lover, after all, and I learned I could take care of myself.

I lived on Long Island with my wife for five years after moving from Vermont, and after the divorce, for the first time in my life, I didn't have a close friend. When we separated, I was without a support system. Fortunately, being single led to making male friends. For example, a colleague I didn't know well called and said, "I hear you're separated, I've been through that. Would you like to have lunch sometime?" This was a lifesaver! We had lunch within a week, and we had lunch together almost every weekday for at least ten years. On weekends we did what single guys do—went looking for women. We also did some "hunting" independently of each other, and on one of his forays my buddy made another male friend. I was jealous, frightened that I may have lost my one close friend! But it was an unnecessary reaction.

Soon the three of us went out together. We all wanted to post singles' ads like the ones we'd seen in various newspapers, but we were anxious about looking foolish. Our camaraderie gave us strength. Since we were all educators, we were able to write an ad that reasonably described the three of us. We received twenty-one replies. We sat down with them and dealt them out, seven replies to each. After reviewing all of them, we judged which ads appealed to us, and then we traded until we were satisfied that we had distributed the bounty to our mutual satisfaction. And then we called the lucky ladies. Not surprisingly, some of this fair group were not thrilled to learn our selection process. The diner industry loved us until they realized we were taking up booths for just coffee and an English muffin.

We forged ahead, but independently. The three of us met lots of women. We each knew who the other was going to meet and were curious how things would go. One evening I had a date to meet someone new; I already knew she had plans to meet one of my buddies the next night. As we met at the diner, she greeted me by my buddy's name; I told her that his turn was the next night. That evening did not go well.

By the time I reached my sixties, I'd had several multiyear relationships and many that lasted several months. During this period, I was introduced to venues and people I would have missed out on had I remained married. But I was frustrated. Why was I still single five years, ten years, twenty years, thirty years later? My close friends had mostly connected and formed loving long-term relationships. I was left behind. What was wrong with me? What was wrong with the hundreds of other singles I had met who were attractive, intelligent, charming, capable of maintaining a relationship (they had been married), and looking for someone with whom to spend their life? It dawned on me that we probably don't all have something wrong with us; rather, we are part of a new social phenomenon. And I wanted to discover what we all had in common. I haven't figured it out, but my guess is that we all remain single by choice and haven't admitted it to ourselves yet. We like the excitement of new people, new places, the occasional new lover. We like being able to decide what to do when without a long consultation. We like making new friends and being exposed to new things. Seeing different homes is very interesting. Being exposed to different cooking styles and cuisines is delicious. Meeting someone who has passionate interests that I've not known about has greatly increased the fascination of this world. We are singles by choice who still think the key to happiness is marriage. So we keep looking and, on occasion, some of us find ourselves in love—for a while.

I found myself in love a few times, but it never lasted. Usually I left and didn't realize how deeply I felt until the pain of the breakup set in. Once, someone I loved who said she loved me left me. I was devastated because I was sure she was "the One." She wasn't. I was sixty-eight when we met, and for the first time, I thought I had met someone who "got me." The romance lasted four months; then we broke up. I had a planned trip to Japan for a month; we had a warm correspondence while I was away. I thought we were on solid footing when I returned only to find out that she had met someone new. I was devastated, and it took years for me to recover. We still keep in touch and, strangely enough, have become best friends. Another romance that started soon after lasted more than a year until I ended it. I wasn't ready. She wasn't happy. We kept in touch on birthdays and holidays. Eventually, we too became best friends.

I mention these two romances because of the silver lining. These two women are truly my best friends. We talk often and share our lives. We support one another emotionally. It's a by-product of senior dating, making good friends with the opposite sex. Another good thing about my best friends is that I live fifty miles from Manhattan, and before COVID, I would come into the city at least once a week to volunteer and sometimes for dining and theater. I now have a choice of two apartments in the city where I can stay; they even let me use their apartments when they're away. I also have good friendships with a number of other women I have dated. So now, in this late stage of life, I have more women friends than men friends.

Another positive has been that as my daughters got old enough to date, we shared similar situations. Not that we talked about our individual experiences, but it was a commonality that may have contributed to maintaining a very good and close relationship. In fact, my daughters have made friends with some of the women I have dated.

It's good to be single. Currently I'm in a loving, monogamous, two-plus-year relationship enjoying the best and most frequent sexual intimacy of my life. I used to be jealous of my friends with twenty-plus-year relationships because of what they had that I was missing. I am still missing what they have, but what I have is also not to be missed. However, as much as I love my single life with all its benefits, I would rather be in a loving, long-term marriage. Maybe it's just a fantasy, but I still imagine the richness of a lovingly shared intimacy that deepens over the years may still be mine.

An Octogenarian's Adventures in Online Dating

Natasha Josefowitz

"That's really scary," I said to Heather, my personal trainer. "I don't want to do this." But Heather insisted. It was not a new set of exercises she was promoting; it was for me to get on an online dating site. As I resisted, hugely embarrassed, she got onto my computer and signed me up. This was five years after my husband died; I was eighty-eight years old at the time.

A couple of days later, she asked how it was going. What was she talking about? Oh, was I supposed to look? We did together; one ninety-year-old man had found my profile interesting—well, that was a relief. He wanted a photo, which I was reluctant to send. His photo looked a lot younger than his supposed age. I did not reply. A young man in his sixties wrote that he wanted to meet me. I wrote back that he was younger than my children and he replied, "Goodbye, mother," and so ended my online adventure.

The problem is that I don't know any older, single men in my social circle. Neither do my single women friends. This lack of available local options is obviously the reason for this new online way of meeting people. We are a disbursed generation—having often relocated—with distant friends and relatives.

The protocol, as I understand it, is that first you email each other for several weeks, then you talk on the phone for several more weeks, then you meet in a very public coffee shop and decide whether there is a future to this relationship. I'm in my late eighties; I don't have time for all this—it will be one email, one phone call, and then on to the coffee shop.

As I was scanning the various supposed matches, I noticed that eighty-year-old men's cutoff age for women was seventy-five, and their stated preference was for someone in their sixties, thin, and with a good sense of humor. I don't qualify. No one seemed interested in a woman in her late eighties, retired professor, author, warm, friendly and fun, looking for conversation and possibly a long-term relationship. Perhaps I just should sit quietly by the fireplace in my rocking chair with my slippers on, doing my needlepoint, and forget about new adventures . . . but that doesn't sound appealing either.

There are many sites: Plenty of Fish is free while others, such as eharmony, Match, and Jdate require a fee. There are also many senior dating sites. The statistics are that many marriages today began online. This is just a new technology to replace the marriage broker of past generations. My Russian great-grandfather had never met his bride until their wedding day. They were both thirteen. When she lifted her veil, so the story goes, he exclaimed, "She's so ugly!"

This is probably why, to avoid such disasters, photos are posted with the descriptive profiles. From what I have been told, some people use photos of their younger selves and lie about marital status and jobs. According to the *New York Times*, "Men exaggerate their height by two inches and people exaggerate their income by about 20 percent." But as I perused some of the photos, there are many gray-haired men who seem honest, at least at first glance. For all the faults in the traditional method of matchmaking, the shadchans (Yiddish for marriage brokers) of yesterday at least had correct information and could be relied upon (I'm thinking of *Fiddler on the Roof*).

Yes, I still wish for companionship, as do so many widowed people, and I would like to find someone to share thoughts with, someone with whom I can have an ongoing conversation about the latest newspaper article or what we had for dinner. The minutia of daily life is meaningless when not shared and a lot of fun when given a little prominence.

It is now several years later, and I have not tried online dating again. I am in my nineties and may possibly appeal to a centenarian.

NOTE

An earlier version of this essay was published in *La Jolla Village News*, June 13, 2014.

Coping with COVID-19

Phyllis Bogen

I am a ninety-two-year-old recent widow after a marriage of sixty-five years. In 1953, I went from living in my parents' home in New York City to getting married and moving to Washington, DC, with a man I barely knew because we had a long-distance courtship and saw each other infrequently. Luckily, our marriage worked, and three children and six grandchildren later, I am learning how to be a widow and live alone for the first time in my life. (Even my college years were spent at home because I commuted to school by subway.)

I participate in many community activities and social events, and I see my children whenever our schedules permit, which is not as often as I would like. However, I miss the sharing, companionship, and closeness I had with my husband, Bill.

Right now, I am in the position of deciding whether I want another relationship. I have mentioned this to my children, and they support whatever choice I make. I have heard the pros and cons of having a new relationship from other widows, most of whom have opted not to look for another partner. However, even if I were to look for a companion, I would not know how to go about it. A friend who works with senior groups told me that there are many lonely men who would like relationships. Since men typically depend on their wives to provide socialization, they are at a loss as to how to go about it on their own.

I too am at a loss. The COVID-19 pandemic has limited social activities, even with family members and close friends. Introducing a new person into my life at this time would be difficult for several reasons, even if I met one of a suitable age. How to connect safely would be problematic. Furthermore, I have adjusted to being alone and not accountable to another person and am aware of necessary trade-offs. Should the COVID vaccine alter the current reality, I will evaluate the situation and make decisions as the need arises. Meanwhile, I will continue to deal with the status quo.

It's Valentine's Day.
So What!

Erica Manfred

I've aged out of the dating pool.

I had dinner with my COVID-19 pandemic buddy, Julie, this week. She gave me an adorable retro Valentine's Day card with the touching message: *To Erica, a good friend in our "golden" years*, accompanied by a handmade, heart-shaped potholder that is much too lovely to actually use. I almost shed a tear; it had been so long since I'd gotten a non-virtual valentine.

This new friendship is rare and treasured. Julie and I were the only ones we knew willing to get together during the past year. We had a routine. Dinner once a week, outdoor in a park, then outdoor at a restaurant when they opened. We both lived alone. Neither of us had a significant other in our "pod," but we had each other, at least sometimes.

As far as romance, I feel like I aged out of the dating pool quite a while ago. And what's more, I don't care.

When my husband left me at age fifty-nine for a younger woman, one of my biggest fears was having to spend the rest of my life alone. It had been hard enough to find dates in New York City when I was in my thirties. What was I going to do now that I was in my sixties and lived in the boonies of Woodstock, New York?

I didn't realize that the internet had changed the dating scene for us older folks.

141

When I woke up one day, about nine months post getting dumped, and realized I was horny as hell, my friend and internet dating guru, Nancy, told me to try Match, the biggest dating site on the internet. I literally hadn't had any sexual desire for eighteen years, since I started living with my husband. I had married him out of desperation, not attraction, and spent all my energy avoiding sex with him. Except for a brief crush on our carpenter, I had never looked at a man sexually during that time. Now I was long past menopause and supposedly long past my sexual prime. My body didn't know this, however. It started twitching every time an attractive man came into the room. All of the sudden I was evaluating every man I saw as a sexual partner. I was on fire, all the time. Pent-up demand, I guess.

When it came to sex, I found the tables had turned since my youth. Once upon a time, I thought all men wanted was sex. Now that's what I wanted—desperately. Young women still complain about being hit on, but I was praying to be hit on when I went on a date, especially if the man was attractive, but ironically, I found older men were the ones who wanted to get to know me first. Or maybe they had performance anxiety and were afraid they couldn't get it up. I didn't have a hard time finding dates, but I did have trouble finding men who wanted sex as much as I did.

I became obsessed with internet dating. And I fell madly in love—twice.

I knew what I wanted: mad passionate love. I needed to prove I was still alive after years of a loveless marriage. I was searching for what I called my "shaman lover" because I was living in Woodstock—woo-woo land—and was in thrall to various new age gurus. I was convinced only love could save me.

What was I thinking?

I had dates with many duds and even had sex with guys who were not only *not* shamans, but schlemiels. Finally, I met HIM through, what else, Match. Bob was fifty-five, five years younger than me, a short, handsome, boyish-looking tennis pro—a funny, dynamic guy who totally charmed me. To my surprise he found me irresistible as well. Our relationship was explosive for the next three months, including some of the best sex I'd ever had. I even had multiple orgasms for the first time in my life!

I never had this kind of love as an adolescent, and it was a very adolescent kind of love. Unfortunately, the essential characteristic of wild passion is that it is temporary, it's a fantasy that can't go on. Bob, recently divorced, wanted to see other people. I couldn't deal with that and broke up with him. *Poof,* he was gone. The pain was worse than the pain of my divorce. I went through hell when Bob and I broke up, but I don't regret a minute of that relationship. All-consuming passion isn't just the province of the young, and neither is the foolishness that goes with it.

Unfortunately, I'm terrible at relationships with men. I've always been envious of those women who have the "it" factor—you know who they are, the women men flock around. Although men lust after beautiful women, after much observation of the "it" phenomenon, I've concluded that looks have very little to do with it.

My friend Wendy's mom was one of those women. I saw it in action when we took her to a popular watering hole in Woodstock. Wendy and I nursed our drinks while Edna—in her eighties—charmed a bunch of older men who surrounded her. I thought Edna looked ridiculous at her age in too much makeup and too-tight clothes, but maybe that was a female judgement. Men obviously found her attractive. Edna loved the attention, but she had no interest in dating any of these men, much less in having sex with them. I'd witnessed this phenomenon before with another friend, Karen, whom men found irresistible. Despite being dumpy with bad skin and frizzy hair, she also instantly became the center of attention of the men at any gathering.

What is the "it" factor? It's total confidence in one's attractiveness, combined with a nonthreatening friendliness that encourages men to flirt. I'm neither confident nor friendly—insecure and suspicious is more like it.

After Bob, I met someone else and fell in love again before I gave up dating. Jamie would have been perfect for me. A handsome, sweet, funny, retired teacher with a good heart and similar interests to mine, he was sexy and adorable. But he, too, was recently divorced and wasn't ready to settle down again. He, too, was dating someone else. I turned into a nutcase—clingy, desperate, and demanding. I was unbearable. Unsurprisingly, he left me and wound up marrying the other woman he was dating. I couldn't blame him. I will never be Edna or Karen. Relationships with men brought out the worst in me. I was dating with a huge handicap—zero confidence in my desirability as a woman.

After Jamie, I made a desultory attempt at more internet dating, but it was too cruel for my delicate ego. I'm not thin, which seems to be a bottom-line requirement for dating, young or old. As a lifelong fat girl, I was sick of being judged by my size. And late-life internet dating is particularly cruel because judging potential partners by their looks never ends. What does end is good looks. Women are as guilty of this as men. Who still looks good in their seventies or older? Not many of us.

Then a miracle happened. No, I didn't find Mr. Right. Instead, I totally lost interest in men and sex around age seventy. I have no idea why. My hormones were long gone. What I do know is that it was an enormous relief.

I don't miss those hormones or the anguish of longing for love. Yes, I do miss sex, mostly the huggy, kissy part, and I miss close companionship the most. I may have aged out of the dating pool, but I haven't become miraculously self-sufficient. I envy friends with long marriages who are still friends with their husbands. I'd love to have someone to curl up with and watch Netflix and share a pizza. But a long marriage is no longer an option for me. And the alternative, dating, is too stressful to even contemplate at this age.

Don't tell me it's never too late to find love. Yes, it *is* too late—and that's okay. Maybe I'll find my soul mate in my next life.

What's Sex Got to Do with It?

Judith Ugelow Blak

When I was finally ready to consider a romantic partner after being married for sixteen years, separated for ten, and divorced for three, at the ripe age of sixty-two, I became a little girl again, hiding behind her father's legs, peering between them, totally fearful of what might lie or not lie ahead. The little amount of flirting I did during those first divorced years had amounted to nothing. Nothing. I had had no takers—there were no affairs. One might say I was still stuck in my marriage, but others might say it was just bad luck. On one date, after I formally got into the online dating game, with an online profile and several rounds of corresponding before meeting, the man, who I was actually very interested in, asked me, as we walked around a beautiful, iced-over lake in an equally iced-over forest near the center of Copenhagen, how it was I still was single. I didn't know, I said. That perplexed him; it perplexed me too. And evidently it wasn't enough of an answer—he feigned continued interest for the rest of the date but blocked further calls from me.

I could have claimed my lack of success on my rusty dating technique—I should have had better answers than "I don't know," but that would have assumed I had had a technique to start with. I didn't. I was probably the dating queen in my time, but truly, my dating skills, even when younger, were severely lacking—I knew only how to coax a man into bed. It's not that I had any finesse about it, and it's not like I succeeded each time, but my body and my dress signaled I wouldn't mind getting laid. I wore clingy clothing with no bra. The necklines didn't plunge—my breasts were too small to even pump up—but I had a dancer's body with legs more developed than the rest of my body. We used to joke in my family that when God asked about legs, we thought She said kegs, so we asked for two big ones.

Mind you, I didn't dress like this by design. In fact, I didn't realize I had this petite frame with advertised nipples until rather recently, when I looked at photos from that time. Really? I walked around like that? Oblivious to the provocativeness of my dress, I claimed it as my style, given my comfort with leotards and other accessories I used in dance classes. Clingy clothes felt natural. And while my goal was presumably not to get laid, it seemed the most expedient path to my ultimate goal of bagging an ambassador husband and a penthouse apartment with a sunken living room. Meeting a guy and having sex seemed infinitely easier than going the dating route.

My problem was, then, if the sex was good, I always mistook that for more interest, and it almost always wasn't. Even if any of these encounters might have developed further, I delivered the death blow to each with my demands for an overwhelming commitment from the start, since each episode of lovemaking felt like the route to salvation, and I needed that badly. I was devastated with each over-the-top rejection that was necessary to keep me at bay. It was like being left at the altar over and over again—an altar I never thought I would get anywhere close to.

But I did get to the altar, though truly only because I asked a guy I knew, a guy I had researched thoroughly, to father my child. I was thirty-eight, still single, and desperate to have a baby. I knew the time it would take to get to know a man would tax my biological clock. That is, if I ever did find a man. So, I lied to this man when I said he didn't have to be anything other than a sperm donor—using traditional lovemaking, of course. But lucky me never had to confront this lie because the two of us, spending time in bed and then expanding our trysts to include movie and dinner dates, and walks in the woods, fell in love. The irony of this arrangement was that we couldn't produce a biological child. We eventually adopted two fabulous though challenging boys, but more relevant here was our inability to have both good fights *and* good sex. We wore each other down with our mutual complaints and demands, neither side learning nor conceding nor compromising. Thus, divorce.

So, at sixty-two, the only skill I had was to resurrect was my inefficient dating modus operandi: the sex card. The body part wasn't a problem. I still had the youngish face that got me carded into my thirties, fewer wrinkles than most at sixty-two, now many more at sixty-eight. I still had my petite body, though with saggy thighs that were still attractive enough in a bathing suit, and fairly firm breasts, probably because I never bore children. I was still then, though less now, energetic, able to take long walks without a knee or hip or foot hurting; I had my mind, not yet in the category of even forgetting those small things. I felt like a fit specimen, and if I clothed myself in anything other than sweatpants, if I were to comb my hair and exercise just a little bit, I could count myself among the cohort of attractive older women; thus, my perplexity about why I remained single.

Minor success in finding a romantic partner at sixty-two might have come more easily if I still had my libido, which I wasn't yet ready to admit was lost. My memories of great sex pre-marriage left me with an intense desire to have that again. I missed it so much. I loved the touching and the daring to touch in public and the taste of another's body and the aliveness this all produced. My friend told me that when I met a man I liked, my body would respond again, not to worry. But I was stuck in a catch-22, for I couldn't anymore feel the chemistry to get me to the point of wanting to even kiss a man. When I was younger, my skin and breasts would perk up, my vagina would ooze, and I swear my lips would swell. I would have an impulse to reach out and kiss, touch, grind. That didn't happen anymore. I couldn't get to that place where I wished that closeness. As far as I could tell, my body had shut down.

And so, when I met a man in his fifties who thought I was just who I thought I could be, that is, if I hadn't lost my libido, I made an extra effort to find that physical connection. Let's call him Jørgen. We went to see a romantic film, something I hoped would titillate me. That didn't quite happen, even when he kissed me as my bus home was arriving. Something compelled me to keep on trying with him, so I invited him disco dancing, because with the right partner, disco dancing becomes virtually sex in action. Jørgen gladly accepted my invitation, and I hoped he would be able to hear the rhythms and translate them into nonstandard creative moves, engaging me in the story his body wanted to tell. Jørgen wasn't bad at this dance bit—his focus was clearly on me, and he wanted badly to follow my lead. And so I led, pulling him close, putting my arms up over his head and around his neck, dropping one hand to take one of his in mine, placing it around my back, placing my hand back on his neck, dropping my other hand to take his other hand to place it on my back, placing my hand on his neck again, pulling him smack up against me, feeling the firmness of his penis against me, moving him away and around, turning him around, back to me again. I continued to manipulate his body and he loved it. Though I preferred a man who would lead me, it tickled me that he was so game to move so organically with me. Yet I couldn't feel the pull within me to get close to him. He got only another kiss when the bus came. Forty years earlier, we would have been rolling in bed if not on the dance floor by this time. But that familiar spark, it just wasn't in my body anymore.

I was far from in love with this guy, which is what getting turned on required when I was younger, but I wanted to test out my friend's belief that with the right man, which Jørgen was close enough to being, I might get turned on. So, I continued, though it took me a few weeks to call him. I invited him for dinner at my house, figuring that if we were to have sex, it was to be on my territory. "No problem," he said. "I'll be there." I had never met a man in my youth who could control his libido the way it seemed Jørgen was able to control his. After all, this was our third date.

I wasn't used to this and worried that perhaps I should be suspicious of something not right. Turns out there was nothing to be suspicious of; it was just me in unfamiliar territory.

My two teenage sons were home for dinner that night before running out for the evening with friends. They could have cared less that a date was at our house. While there was no official test to pass, Jørgen truly impressed me with his sweet and funny interaction with them, thus checking off some boxes on the internal list I kept. After dinner, he helped me with the dishes, casually picking up the dish towel, drying dishes I had washed, while we talked. I remember not what we said, only the feeling it was all so easy, checking off another box on my internal list.

Still, while my brain said "I can't believe this younger, handsome guy is into me," I couldn't get my body to react. So now alone, I plied him and me with more wine and followed that with a joint—it was all stops out to get me in the mood. I led him upstairs to my bedroom, and I think from that point on, until he left two hours later, my eyes were closed. He asked permission before taking off my T-shirt, before taking off my bra, before undressing me completely and pleasuring me. And I mean, he pleasured me. He touched my body so delicately and used his mouth and tongue so delicately, I thought I would swoon from ecstasy. I offered no pleasure in kind. I felt no inclination to, and he didn't ask.

Yet, my vagina was so tight, probably not even the thinnest of vibrators could penetrate. I was too stoned to care. Jørgen didn't react. I think we lay together and talked about how I might practice with a vibrator for next time. So, I promised to practice. But without the heat Jørgen created, practicing was not fun. Shit, solo sex was no longer fun, and I had to admit that partner sex no longer measured up to what I remembered it being. Hell, I didn't offer this partner anything. Perhaps my mother would have said, "Judith, he's a nice guy, go for it." But in my head, the sex was all I could connect to. No sex, no connection. That was the end of my trial with Jørgen.

That left me in a lurch—as a novice in a pursuit of something I was never really good at to begin with—the relationship. I have news for you; it took me some time to realize, but I am ecstatic about this: if the sex had succeeded, I might still be stuck thinking sex is my path to love. At least now, I have no choice but to tackle the real stuff. I am excited that I might finally get to a place of loving myself and making room for the man who will complement that.

Gray Love en Noir

AFRICAN AMERICAN WOMEN FLYING SOLO
BY CHOICE AND BY CHANCE

Linda Wright Moore

For African American women who find themselves alone post age sixty, making peace with solitude may be a more practical solution than searching soul-crushing online dating websites for what is in truly short supply: healthy, educated, interesting, decent-looking, solvent, and age-appropriate Black men. The search for "gray love" *en noir* can be a daunting and frequently disappointing endeavor.

I am reminded of a *Newsweek* cover story back in 1986[1] on the so-called "marriage crunch" facing women like me: the most educated and "liberated" generation of women in American history at that time, we were baby boomers who had career success to go with our advanced degrees. But unlike past generations of American women, many of us hit our thirties without husbands or children—as the biological clock began its inexorable countdown to the end of fertility. I've always remembered the image on the cover of the magazine: a chart with a precipitous plunge from high to low—reminiscent of the 1929 stock market crash that ended the Roaring Twenties and ushered in the Great Depression. However, the decline in this chart wasn't about the economy—rather, it illustrated the dwindling chances of marriage for college-educated women. According to the *Newsweek* report, white, college-educated women born in the mid-1950s who were still single at age thirty had only a 20 percent chance of marrying.

By the age of thirty-five, the odds dropped to 5 percent. And this line I'll never forget: "Forty-year-olds are more likely to be killed by a terrorist" than to marry! Their probability of tying the knot was calculated to be just 2.6 percent. And the kicker: "Black women face an even larger gap, since there are far fewer college-educated black males than females." I read this ominous analysis after my divorce, when I was dating the (Black) man who would become my second husband. I was already thirty-five and after seeing that story, I felt as if I'd escaped the horrible fate of living life alone, but just barely.

Fast-forward, and here I am today, widowed at age seventy. I am alone after all—the so-called golden years stretching out before me, without a soul mate to share them with. Marriage was supposed to shield me from this fate, but ill health flipped the script. I had wanted us to emulate my parents, whose loving union lasted more than seven decades. They survived together happily into their nineties, and their years were golden indeed!

I still want some of that, as do many widowed, divorced, and single Black women. However, the odds—and demographics—are against us. By the numbers, the mature Black woman's quest to find love in the twenty-first century will be arduous. And there's no denying that the numbers still are not on our side.

My friend Anne[2] is sixty-four, long divorced, and childless by choice. She's engaged in online dating for years with mixed results. A Brooklyn-based professional science writer, she deals with hard facts and statistics for a living. She asserts that educated African American women face a shortage of educated eligible Black men at every stage of their lives. "[Black men] are least likely to go to college. They are most likely to marry outside their race, and most likely to be in jail after high school," she says. "Everywhere you look, we're going one way and they're going another . . . The challenges are the same across the life span—and are exacerbated by age."

Census data backs up much of what Anne says. Among Black Americans twenty-five and older, 33 percent of women have associate's, bachelor's,

graduate, or professional degrees, compared to 25 percent of men. And
a snapshot of Black marriage in 2017 showed 9 percent of Black men
(409,000) had white wives, while 4 percent of Black women (172,000) married white husbands.

But a bigger factor than interracial marriage in the decline of matri-
mony among African Americans is mass incarceration. According to an
analysis by BlackDemographics.com,[3] until 1970, Black women were more
likely to be married than white women. Yes—you read that right. Further,
until 1960, Black men were more likely to be married than white men. African Americans thirty-five and older were more likely to be married than
white Americans from 1890 until the 1960s. What happened? Starting with
the declaration of the War on Drugs in 1971, the number of never-married
African Americans began a steep climb,[4] which coincided with the sharp
increase in incarceration of Black men, driven by enactment of the 1984
Sentencing Reform Act and the Anti-Drug Abuse Act of 1986. While these
trends do not prove causation, one need not be an expert in statistics to
recognize that being locked up is not conducive to romance and wedlock.

As of 2016, half of African Americans have never been married, compared to 34 percent of all Americans. Add the fact that Black folks—
particularly men—live sicker and die sooner than white people, and gray
love *en noir* can be a long shot. "At this point, half of us are dead," says
Dana, a retired, California-based health professional in her seventies, who
easily could pass for fifty if not for her silver-streaked mane of hair. "You
can take twenty years off life expectancy for Black men. I know two widowers and thirty widows!"

The deck is stacked, and clearly not in our favor. However, it is also true
that like any lottery, you can't win if you don't play—and I found several
friends who think long odds are no reason not to try their hand at the
twenty-first century dating game.

The 1986 "marriage crunch" article included a sidebar, "The New Mating Game," which described the end of "singles' bars" due to AIDS and
aging. It hailed the rise of matchmaking services and singles' ads, which

have evolved into the online dating culture of today. The half dozen African American friends I interviewed all expressed frustration with online dating, ranging from mild discomfort to flat-out refusal to pursue relationships in cyberspace.

———

At seventy-one, Carol, who curtailed her career to become a corporate wife and mother before her marriage ended in divorce twenty years ago, considers online dating a nonstarter. "It's kind of a waste of time to try to find a person online. If you're looking for deeper, richer relationships, you have to develop better strategies," and perhaps change your objectives, as Carol clearly has. "I want to spend time with men who are heterosexual, single, and solvent. I'm not looking for a romantic relationship, I'm looking for friendship," she says. Wary of the "nurse or the purse" trap, in which older men seek a caregiver or someone to provide financial support, Carol believes that with age comes self-awareness and honesty about oneself and others. "In your seventies, you're more concerned about a person's character, and did they take care of themselves—physically and financially—so they are functioning, independent human beings," she says. Carol is content with her posse of male buddies—the "Fab Four"—which includes a jazz singer and three other music-loving retirees. "You have to have clarity about who you are and what you seek," she says. "Others judge the book by its cover. I don't do that."

Anne, the science writer, reports having a five-year relationship with man she met online, a nice guy who became financially dependent on her. She warns that older women need to be aware they are competing with thirty-year-olds. "Make your life easier by trying sites like *Our Time* for folks over fifty or Chocolate Singles," she says. "It's best to use an app where men have already opted for someone of their age and their race." She cautions that even when a guy checks all the boxes—he may not be what he seems.

When Sarah, a retired secondary school teacher in Southern California, first tried online dating five years ago, she quickly realized that sixty-
year-old men were going after forty-year-old women. "I found online
dating sites exciting at first, but then I cried and cried. I thought, 'Is that
all there is? Rejection—and knowing that the older we get the fewer [men]
there are [interested in us]?'" For Sarah, seventy is just a number; she still
does a mean tango. Her last relationship, which ended after six months,
highlights how age and performance issues can undermine silver relationships. She says the nice man she was dating dealt with his erectile dys-
function by breaking up with her on her seventieth birthday. "I'm grateful
for what was a nice six months—I have no regrets," she says, though she
is dejected. "[Men] can swipe right and get another date every night. We
can swipe and swipe, but nothing may come our way. It seems that almost
totally—nearly 100 percent—the advantage is theirs."

Barbara, sixty-nine, a professional woman who left her three-decade-
long marriage several years ago, is, like Carol, wary of online dating. "One
reason I don't do it is because I'm suspicious of the information people put
out there," she says. "On dating apps, who are you going to meet? Older
folks don't do that sort of thing." Barbara says it's not that she wouldn't
like a relationship with "someone who is happy to be in my presence, shares
my interests. We go places together; we respect each other. No games, honesty, and great sex too. I'm not looking for someone to marry—or even to
live with. I might change my mind, but I don't think so . . . It's not that
I feel burned; I'm just not interested. I've moved on. If you're financially
independent, who needs a man?"

Megan, a fifty-eight-years-young friend, is a senior executive for a
major media company. She came of age in the era of dating apps, as she
built a career that has carried her around the globe. When I call her to
talk about post-sixties dating—she howled, "But I'm not THERE YET!" and
then shared her story. She talked of laughing and even playing dress-
up with girlfriends, to figure out the perfect profile picture. (You won't

be surprised to learn that men look at pictures and women read profiles.) "We spend an inordinate amount of time trying to put together the ideal photographic image . . . then spend weeks/months/years wondering if the profile and the photo are good enough that someone will swipe left or right, depending on what app you're on," she laments. "Not everyone has the ability to portray themselves in a way that's honest and sincere, so you just keep reading and reading . . . searching for authenticity."

Megan thought she'd hit pay dirt when she found Robert, her "one fabulous one," a few years ago. "Robert worked in tech, had the degrees, the humor, was handsome, loved the same music and even the same sports teams that I do. And he danced around like I danced around! He even looks like his photograph," Megan recalled. But when it came time to get beyond great dinners, sporting events, and conversations—time to consummate the relationship—things veered off the rails. "He started reminiscing about sinewy bodies he recalled from Brazil. *And they were not female bodies.* So, he was trying to work out issues about his sexuality." Megan sighs and goes on, "And that was on [the dating app] Black People Meet! You just don't know what you're going to get. I'd love to get rid of this cyberdance of trying to suss out between written words and photographs whether this person is legit."

When I called my friend Dana to present my premise about how Black women need to make peace with solitude rather than engaging in a hopeless search for intraracial romance in our senior years, she started laughing—loud, happy cackles. "Why are you laughing?" I asked.

"Because, well, what else is there to say? I mean, really . . . However, if love finds me, I ain't judging the package!" She giggled again. "But it is really difficult." Dana, who never married, did adopt and raise two sons alone. Now retired, she fills her time with travel—lots of it—as well as her post-retirement avocations, writing and acting. "I've been okay with solitude. For me, it's always been clear I'd rather be alone than be in a situation where I cannot be myself," she says. "Dealing with dating apps really *is* soul-crushing—and not the way we're used to relating to people. It is impersonal; you cannot trust what you see."

———

There's a postscript to the famous 1986 "marriage crunch" story in *Newsweek*: The "research study" upon which it was based hadn't been published when the long, alarmist cover story appeared. Twenty years later, the findings had been so thoroughly debunked that *Newsweek* retracted the story in 2006.[5]

In the bright light of a new century, the article that frightened a generation seems almost quaint. At the beginning of the article, an illustration beneath the headline "Too Late for Prince Charming?" featured a forlorn, thirty-something woman sitting on a neatly made bed. She carelessly held a slim book (*Sonnets from the Portuguese* by Elizabeth Barrett Browning, perhaps?) while staring vacantly off into the distance with a teddy bear propped against the obviously unused and unwrinkled pillow next to her. Funny thing, though: looking at the image now, while we are all dealing with COVID-19—she appears more like a busy professional winding down after a long week of back-to-back Zoom meetings, relaxing pandemic-style in sweatpants and a tank top without a bra. She is alone, yes . . . but solitude isn't the same thing as loneliness.

"It takes a really, really long time to be successful and comfortable in your skin and to appreciate that there is absolutely nothing wrong with enjoying solitude. But it's not easy—especially when you are bombarded by images of couples and still go to the *New York Times* style section to read the wedding announcements . . . and you've searched the websites to find the prince among all those frogs." Megan is not ready to give up on finding love and companionship, even though there are no guarantees. "Maybe after the pandemic there will be new energy and possibilities," she says. "Because I still grab the frickin' style section and keep reading those announcements and wonder what if there's someone out there for me."

———

My own forays into online dating have been tentative. Even writing about myself and selecting photos for a profile felt a bit like stripping naked and shouting, "Hey, look at me! Like me—PLEASE!" And the likes have come— but rarely from anyone I could imagine liking in return. I try to find educated Black men who are widowed or divorced, but a torrent of never-married frogs of all races continues to flow my way. Here are a couple of examples of my dating app misadventures.

There was "Michael" from Tennessee, who loves traveling, beaches, all kinds of music, and has a graduate degree. Sounds good, but two red flags: he said he's reading *Fifty Shades of Grey*, plus he's never been married. He is a near-elderly guy reading a novel featuring bondage and still looking for "a lady with total passion for life." *No thanks, Michael!* Another mismatch was "CountryBoy," a sixty-two-year-old from rural Pennsylvania who attends horse shows and auctions for fun. I wonder: how could a white country guy like a very urban Black woman, eight years his senior, who prefers art galleries and live jazz to horse-focused events?

The dead ends occur in both directions. I've sent out occasional likes myself. Usually, I get no response, but the real downer is receiving a virtual brush-off: "Thanks for your note. Good luck in your search." *Ouch!* The pattern of likes from men who don't meet my expectations and rejections from those who do prove the obvious: that the sort of guys I prefer are in short supply and high demand, with a big pool of women younger than me to choose from. There are plenty of fish for them—but alas, not for me.

So, I'm no fan of digital matchmaking and have been, at best, a reluctant participant in the online dating sweepstakes. Frankly, it seems pointless. Once or twice a week, I do check the latest possibilities sent my way on the popular app I subscribe to and consistently find myself amused and occasionally appalled.

There is one exception: Steve, a gentleman I found two years ago, early in my online dating adventure. I sent him a message with great trepidation. He responded, and after a few emails, we "met" by phone a couple times. Our first date was a movie and drinks after. Another dinner followed. We then agreed that while there were no sparks, we liked each other, and became friends. That works. We've stayed in touch, gotten together for cocktails and lunch, and checked in with each other during the era of coronavirus. As a friend, Steve is a keeper, and that seems enough for now. For me, solitude and flying solo make sense—though the romantic in me still believes a charming companion may be just around the bend.

So, I'll keep my eyes open. And, in the meantime, I'll kick back with a glass of wine, read a little poetry, and enjoy my life.

NOTES

1. "The Marriage Crunch," cover story, *Newsweek*, June 2, 1986.
2. Pseudonyms have been used for all the women interviewed.
3. U.S. Decennial Census (1890–2000); American Community Survey (2010).
4. U.S. Department of Justice Bureau of Justice Statistics, Prisoners in 2010; Historical Corrections Statistics in the United States, 1850–1985, and International Centre for Prison Studies King's College London.
5. Megan Garber, "When '*Newsweek* Struck Terror in the Hearts of Single Women,'" *The Atlantic*, June 2, 2006, https://www.theatlantic.com/entertainment/archive/2016/06/more-likely-to-be-killed-by-a-terrorist-than-to-get-married/485171/.

Passion and Prejudice

Jean Y. Leung

"Where are you from?" I frown—this is a touchy question. I sigh and try not to take it so hard. After all, most people don't read the bios in dating profiles, I've been told—it's the pictures that capture them. If this is the case, he wouldn't have seen that almost at the top of my profile, I proclaim that I am a native New Yorker. On a universal level, I should still be annoyed. After all, how much time and effort have I put into formulating the words in my profile? I think anyone would say they prefer someone who also put some effort into getting to know the person they want to meet. But on a personal level, this question goes deep. Because behind it is a belief that someone who looks like me could only be a foreigner in the United States.

This idea has helped fuel and excuse anti-Asian sentiment throughout the history of Asians in America. Chinese people are, and remain, the only group singled out by nationality for immigration exclusion. And while the U.S. fought Germany and Japan during World War II, only Japanese people, native-born or not, were herded into "internment camps." When the COVID-19 pandemic hit the U.S., President Trump made it worse by labeling it the "Chinese virus." This name has skyrocketed the number of anti-Asian incidents to 150 percent above pre-pandemic levels. And these are only the reported cases. Who knows how many cases have not been reported because of fear, shame, disbelief, and other factors?

When I was growing up in the 1950s and 1960s, the Asian American community was too tiny and fragmented to effectively fight harassment, bias, and discrimination. Thankfully, as recent events have shown, the community now has its own resources—lawyers, activists, and yes, even politicians—to defend and protect itself. Yet what endures are the prejudices and stereotypes of previous eras.

Dating when you have passed the half-century mark is tough enough, but when one is trying to climb out of the cave of widowhood during a pandemic, being a minority in a prejudiced country adds a complicated layer.

I don't discriminate in the dating arena. I didn't the first time around, which opened the opportunity for my marriage to a white Jewish man. It is true that sometimes our relationship was a comedy of errors because of misperceptions on both our parts due to our different cultures and upbringing. But I like to think we not only proved to be an education for each other but for our overall community as well. Yet the reality is, that because I was part of a minority, I assimilated more into his world than he into mine.

There are those who would say, "Then why don't you stick to your own kind?" But that creates another question. What exactly is "my own kind?"

Whether it is acknowledged or not, there is a mating hierarchy. On the top are those with pale skin; on the bottom are those with dark skin. Somewhere in the middle are Asians. Most of us have pale skin, but most of us also have the "incorrect" eyes. As with any upward striving (which has been glorified as the "American way"), one aims for the rung above, not the rung below. This can be overlooked if you bring the exotic factor into play. Being exotic is limiting; however, it makes one less human.

Of course, there's also a factor that is more benign because it has nothing to do with race or prejudice but everything to do with age. Many people become more rigid with age. After a lifetime of change, they want the tranquility of familiarity. One can't make it to the half-century mark without being shaped by the life you have lived. For a lot of us, this makes us unique.

You can't quantify who we are because that leaves the quality of our life out.

An Asian man might find me too "white" because I was married to a white man and live in a predominantly white neighborhood. Or he could find me not "white" enough because I try to live a culturally Asian life. This could make me too Asian for him. And just as you can't lump all white or Black people together since they vary by nationality and religion, the same is true of Asians. A non-Chinese Asian might feel that I don't blend in with his nationality in ways such as language, food, and traditions. Even though I was married to a white man, white men might think that I won't blend in with their family and friends. A Black man might feel the same way. He may feel that since I am so comfortable in the white world, I would never be comfortable in the non-white, non-Asian world.

There are also many stereotypes surrounding Asian women. Think of how popular culture as painted us in movies such as *The World of Susie Wong* or even in an opera such as *Madama Butterfly*. The many wars America fought in Asia made the perception of Asian women worse, since soldiers mostly had contact with Asian women as bar hostesses and prostitutes. That shaped their perceptions of us. We are the exotic erotic, the wooden China dolls, the submissive permissive, the dragon ladies, etc. Even before the twentieth century, Asian women were subject to sexual stereotyping. They were the first immigrant group, under the federal Page Act of 1875, forced to carry photographic identifications, supposedly to confirm their moral character.

Personally, I cringe at any hint that this history might be on the mind of someone I meet. And who knows how the media's exploitation of these stereotypes might be planting these ideas in some minds, even as it may also seek to dismantle them.

In addition, online dating is plagued with scammers and people who exploit lonely hearts. If you are part of a vulnerable segment of the population, you could be targeted more for abuse. On one dating site, practically every Asian male profile I encountered seemed to be that of a scammer. These profiles had pictures of Asian men and sometimes even had Asian-sounding names. There were even ethnic communities cited as their residences such as Chinatown, New York. But under scrutiny, their stories fell apart. Nonexistent universities were named, geographic perplexities existed, and cultural inaccuracies were rife in their profiles. I have tried looking for sites that cater to senior Asian Americans but have been unable to find one worth investing in. Friends who have used some of these sites say that they, too, have encountered scammers. So, for now, I use sites that have the largest clientele, on the theory that the more people you can be exposed to, the more likely you are to find someone. Perhaps, though, the scammers just target every possible segment of the dating market.

For Asians, the query, "Where are you from?" is a familiar and painful one. It reminds us that we are still not accepted as part of mainstream America, that we are perceived as not belonging. Many non-Asians can't understand this. They think that we are ashamed of being Asian. After all, they are proud of where their ancestors came from. They don't realize that the inquiry is about who *we* are, not who our ancestors are. Those of non-Asian ancestry are almost never told to "go back to where you came from."

The question I like to pose in return is, "Where is your question coming from?" This often elicits a defensiveness. In the dating world, just asking this question could be the death of a possibility. Yet I think it's a necessary one. If a relationship is to be an equal one, then all the sources of inequality need to be laid out on the table and examined.

Finding a partner when you are part of a minority with a legacy of exclusion, exploitation, and prejudice is beyond hard. But I persevere because while I can't forget the past or allow anyone to trivialize it, I won't let all that has come before stop me from believing in a future that is better. It's not where you've come from; it's where you are going that matters.

The Complications and Pleasures of Elder Relationships

Checking a Different Box

Jan Jacobson

I'd contemplated it for a year or so, and on this particular day I did it. A simple click. Looking for: Female.

"Male" had been checked on my online dating profile for the fifteen years since my divorce. I was sixty-one years old and until that day had only dated men.

Looking for: Female.

Had I been yearning to do this my whole life? The simple answer is no.

As a teenager growing up in the South in the late sixties, I'd had crushes on boys like all the other girls I knew. I'd had boyfriends, was even chosen as a "sweetheart" for the fraternity of the boys in our Jewish crowd, an honor I politely declined in keeping with my budding feminism. I'd had boyfriends in college and in the years after, and at age twenty-seven I married Ron, a man I loved. We were together for nineteen years and had three fine kids. He was and is a good man, but we didn't communicate deeply, and a reedy marsh grew between us.

One night, soon after my divorce, I dreamt of my younger self on my wedding day. She danced with abandon in a coral wedding dress, her skirt billowing, full of youthful hopes for what married life would bring. Suddenly, she stopped, reached both hands down to the hem of her dress, and pulled its silky softness over her head. She walked across the room to where a trunk was waiting and folded the dress, straightened its tiny pleats, and placed the dress inside. When she closed the trunk, I felt her giving up hope of ever finding the kind of love she wanted.

Nonetheless, a year later, I started dating men again. The men I met, though, didn't interest me. They certainly didn't justify the anguish of the divorce I'd put myself, Ron, and my children through. Why had I endured all that if not to find a deeper love?

More than a decade of disappointing dates and a few short relationships later, I went on a walk with a friend. She and I bemoaned our dating prospects under a sunless sky, my mood becoming as bleak as the day. I had no illusions left about finding the kind of man I'd been seeking. I mentioned (for the first time out loud) that I had recently thought about dating women. I told her I was sure there were far more interesting women looking for a partner than the men I'd been meeting. After the walk, though, the thought remained just that for almost a year.

Why did it take me so long to act?

I did not believe, as many do, that there was anything wrong with same-sex relationships. I had been a social activist supporting civil rights, including gay rights, since college. In the sixty years of my lifetime, the LGBTQ+ movement had made huge gains, and the stigma so prevalent in my youth had lifted. And though I wondered what it would be like to bring a woman to family gatherings at my eighty-three-year-old mother's house in Memphis, I knew it would be fine. So what held me back?

I could not remember ever being attracted to other girls when I was growing up in Memphis in the fifties and sixties. Did this mean that I wouldn't be attracted to women now? I wanted the closeness, but could I touch another woman in that way? And what way was that, anyhow?

Short inventory. What did I know?

In college, the book *Rubyfruit Jungle*, a groundbreaking lesbian coming-of-age novel, had an impact on me, unarticulated but felt. Courageous, I'd thought.

When my ex and I had watched erotic movies, my body responded to the images of both the men and the women. Wasn't that true for everyone?

I once saw a Chilean film about a fifty-eight-year-old divorced woman who decides she doesn't want to spend the rest of her life alone. At one point the woman drops her robe and stands naked before a man, who turns away. "Damn him," I thought, aroused by her offering, "I'd make love with you."

But I couldn't actually imagine touching a woman's body. What would that feel like?

Months later, I went out to dinner with two friends of mine from work, a lesbian couple. As Terri spoke to me, her eyes also communicated with Mary Ellen. I noticed how much was conveyed between them without words, how utterly connected they were. I thought, "That's what I want."

Finally, I checked that other box.

Over the next few months, I had initial meetings with three women. The first had come out as a lesbian in her twenties. When I told her I had three children, she asked if there was a sperm donor, assuming I'd been with other women as long as she had. I had lived in a straight culture, she in a lesbian one, and I felt the gulf between us. I could not sense in myself even a quiver of physical attraction.

The next woman I met admitted that she had lied about her age online, just so she would come up in the searches. She sounded righteous for revealing this to me at the beginning of the evening, but I felt just as manipulated by her as by the men I'd met who'd lied about their ages. As for my body—nada.

The third woman was more like me. She'd gone through a divorce some time before, and I was the first woman she'd met online. I imagined us in bed together, awkward and equally mystified as to what we were supposed to be doing. We parted with a friendly, unlikely-to-follow-up goodbye.

Was I learning that my body simply wasn't wired this way? Too early to know, I decided.

One night I looked online again and saw the profile of a woman named Suzanne, who lived in Connecticut, a two-hour drive from my home in Boston. She wrote about wanting not just a physically intimate relationship with another woman but also a deep emotional connection. (I had once written something similar when my box said "Male." I had deleted it when a guy friend shook his head, saying any man he knew would run from those words. Later, Suzanne confided that she had wondered why all I talked about in my profile was hiking and writing.)

Intrigued, I contacted Suzanne, and we met in a town halfway between us. I was sixty-two, Suzanne sixty-six. She was intelligent, Jewish like me, and adept in expressing her feelings and listening to mine. She was vibrant and confident. For the first time, this thought came—I could be interested in this woman. My body remained quiescent, but I was drawn to her.

We continued to talk on Skype and share our stories. Suzanne had been married to a man for thirty years and had a son, but she'd also been with other women. Over time our connection grew. One evening Suzanne told me, her image vivid on my screen, that her back would arch when she thought of me, and there it was. I felt it for the first time. That unmistakable current.

Another evening on Skype, at the end of a long conversation, Suzanne asked me if I felt attraction for her "in my body." I answered her later that night in an email, "I long to touch you." I couldn't believe how natural it felt to write this or my boldness in telling her.

I liked her, this earthy creature rising within me. Her daring was in striking contrast to my training as a Southern woman not to be forward. Where had she been all these years?

Suzanne and I kept talking over Skype, and the current intensified. I drove from Boston to her home in Connecticut for our second in-person meeting. By the time I walked in her door, we couldn't wait to touch, but I still didn't know what it would be like, this unfamiliar intimacy with another woman. Would I feel that heightening of senses, that quickening of pulse, those surging rapids?

Suzanne took my coat, set it aside, and walked me to her bedroom.

Three hours later, lying next to each other in bed, Suzanne asked, "Are you sure you've never been with a woman?"

I hadn't been, but I had the sense that this newfound woman inside me had been waiting for this since forever, or at least since she'd read *Ruby-fruit Jungle* all those years before.

Yet later that night, I took a breath and said, in the most unoriginal way, "I can't do this. I think you're great, but I only want to be friends." I felt a panic I couldn't explain to her or myself, just an overwhelming urge to stop what we had started. We slept in separate beds that night, and as I was packing up the next morning, she said, "I'm offering you the whole package and you're walking away." I looked at her for a long moment, apologized, and left.

Back home, my spirits sank. The buoyant energy that had whirled within me vanished. When Suzanne had said she was offering the whole package, it had felt for one long moment like it really was all possible—someone loving you and you loving them every day, nurturing each other, erotically connecting, grappling together with life, and being willing always to talk about what was going on between the two of you. And I had pushed it away.

Weeks later, I found myself crying not once but three times in a single day. I wrote Suzanne to ask for a second chance. It turned out she wanted this too. We set a date to meet again.

This time I wanted to be sure I didn't push Suzanne away. What had I been so afraid of? When I asked myself this question in a therapy session, an unexpected image came. That first night at Suzanne's, I'd looked at her soft, vulnerable eyes, and thought, *If I let myself love this woman and then decide to leave, I could really hurt her.* And then, a second image came. I saw Ron's face in the days after I told him I wanted a divorce. I felt like I was drowning in his pain. It hurt so bad to hurt him.

But did that mean I should never love again? And who was I to decide what risks Suzanne was willing to take?

We started to see each other regularly after that, usually at her cozy house in the Connecticut woods. When we were apart, waves of desire swept through me. These urges were so organic and powerful, I marveled at their presence in this body on the cusp of its seventh decade.

One night, we watched a documentary about two women, Edie and Thea, and their decades of love for each other. I was calmly watching one moment and sobbing the next, thoroughly unglued. Though my mind couldn't make sense of this reaction, I somehow knew it was grief that had unraveled me, grief for the aloneness I'd inhabited before I met Suzanne.

Another night, I took a risk and shared with Suzanne that particularly painful dream of the disappointed young bride who packed away her hopes after the divorce. The telling brought to the surface the sadness of that younger self who'd had high hopes for her marriage and then lost faith in love itself.

Afterward, Suzanne observed, "You seem different—softer, fuller, more present somehow." I felt like I was offering and she was seeing a part of me that had long been invisible to others, like a seedling under snow, shy to its new world, warmed by its first brushstrokes from the sun.

On the day I checked that different box, I had no idea what that click of a mouse might bring. Now, as I prepare our coffee each morning in the house we bought together in Asheville, North Carolina, I know.

Weume

Stephanie Speer and David Levy

Over the years, when we were asked, "How did you meet?" we would look at one another, laugh a little, and happily tell our tale. Each time in our telling, we would find ourselves highlighting the same sequence of events in our journey, from first encounters to life partners where a she and he, a you and a me, gave birth to a third entity we christened a Weume. We have chosen to tell our love story from the vantage points of our individual memories, perspectives, voicemail recordings, and journal entries, keeping our writings private from one another until completion in part to protect our individual narratives and in part to enjoy the pleasure, and surprise, of the final reveal to one another.

DEATH CAFÉ

Stephanie

My first chance encounter with David took place on a warm, sunny summer's afternoon in 2014, when, at the age of sixty-seven, I attended a Death Café, held in an open-air pavilion at a nearby park. This was not my first visit to a Death Café. During the past year, I had attended several of these pop-up cafés at a variety of venues in the county. There, people gather to drink and eat and to discuss death and dying. The aim is to increase awareness of death in order to help people appreciate their lives more.

I appreciated having these opportunities to gather with strangers to enjoy the connection and intimacy I find in in-depth discussions on what I view as important and meaningful topics. These connections were especially important to me since I had recently experienced a sudden and surprising ending of a sixteen-year-long relationship.

While adjusting to this loss, I had come to believe that at this age and stage of my life, I would most likely be living the rest of my days, years, perhaps even decades, without romance or a loving partner. And although there was a sadness that still seeped into this acceptance, I was committed to ensuring that I would continue to develop a variety of meaningful connections with others and abstain from seeking a life partner.

On this summer's day, while standing in the shade of the open-air pavilion waiting for the conversation on dying and death to begin, I introduced myself to a woman standing nearby. Before taking our seats, we, Ann and I, began sharing a bit about ourselves with one another. She mentioned her marriage. I told of the recent ending of my long-term relationship.

As the event began, we were instructed to take a seat at one of the picnic tables set aside for the event. Ann and I chose to sit together. After we were greeted by the volunteers and told a bit about the Death Cafés, their history, mission, and format, we were asked to contemplate and answer the question, "Why are you here?" As we took our turns to speak, I was particularly touched by the story told by a man named David. He spoke with great tenderness and eloquence of the recent death of his life partner: her cancer, her body lying in wake in their living room, his grief, and his love. One thing that impacted me was his expression of never-ending love for his partner, and that though she was no longer in her body, his relationship with her had not ended. It was now being lived in a new form, in another dimension.

As the event ended, Ann and I turned to one another and asked, "What did you think?" During this conversation, knowing that I was now single, Ann smiled and said, "David is interesting, smart, and good-looking!"

I scoffed. "His partner just died!"

David

Entering a new relationship at this stage of my life has been a bit like being on a long life journey, like taking an adventure—an unexpected and unplanned detour filled with delightful and challenging experiences. I had been in a special relationship for fifteen years. My partner died in 2013 (when she was fifty-eight and I sixty-five) after dealing with cancer for six years. These final years were difficult and full of opportunities for me to be a supportive caregiver. I said my goodbyes at home during a three-day vigil, her body resting in our living room, a room that had been filled with flowers and visiting guests. At night, I would sit by her body and read children's stories, sing, and cry. Grieving was a slow process, filled with tears of sadness and a lot of walking. Eventually, fond memories began to surface and comfort me.

As I walked the sidewalks that Monica and I had walked together, signs of new life began to encourage me to raise my head and gather in the sights and sounds of another new day. I first heard about Death Cafés from a local oncology support program during Monica's illness, but I chose to attend a caregivers' support group instead. After Monica died, I continued to seek support and companionship with men going through similar experiences.

One of the many gifts Monica gave was my acceptance of this mystery of her being ill, struggling to live, and dying with stubborn grace. I say stubborn because Monica chose not to focus on dying and death; she was too busy living and planning her life projects. I had been invited to accompany Monica on her navigation of these seas. How did other people navigate? After her death, I volunteered at our local hospital, where I played Native American–style flutes in patients' rooms. My experiences with Monica suggested to me that something special had happened, something unique, and I dare say, full of spirit.

I was now ready to attend a Death Café, to share this very human experience of living and dying with fellow humans, and to enter this new neighborhood of life and death. I don't remember if the Death Café in the park was actually my first Death Café experience. This was still a time of grieving for me, and time had shifted into a slower, overcast weathering of days and nights.

I do remember the café in the park, sitting at a picnic table with a group of people. I remember a man sitting across from me who was struggling with the demands of being a caregiver. Much further down the road of days, Stephanie told me that she was also sitting at the table with us. What I do remember is that the mood around our table was tender, attentive, and thoughtful and that I felt safe enough to talk about Monica's death.

SANGHA

Stephanie

In December 2015, a year and half after my visit to the Death Café in the park, I drove to the first meeting of a new Sangha being held at a friend's home nestled in the hillside at the end of Hidden Valley Road. A Sangha is a group of people who, in the Buddhist tradition, come together to meditate and study the teachings of the Buddha. During the past thirty years, I had been a member of several Sanghas, including one that had recently disbanded after a decade of monthly meetings.

Upon arrival, on this winter's day, I entered the house, removed my shoes, and walked into the living room to join the new group. There were several women from our recently disbanded Sangha, plus several men, one of whom, to my surprise, was David from the Death Café.

During the year and half since I met David at the café, I saw him now and again at our local library. Although I was curious about how he was doing, I said nothing. If there had been some eye contact, a hint of recognition, perhaps I would have spoken to him. Instead, I chose to be silent and not intrude. Seeing him at our new Sangha, I made no mention of the Death Café or the library.

Winter turned to spring. Our Sangha continued to come together each month to meditate, to discuss the teachings of the Buddha, and to share our life experiences. During these times together, I learned more about David. He appeared to be a person who held firmly to his beliefs and lived his life in alignment with a personal set of principled core values. I also discovered a person who could become playful and downright silly, as when he ended one of our meetings by performing the "William Tell Overture" on his cheeks.

After several months, David announced to the group that he would soon take a journey to the Middle East to perform at an international music festival and to attend a Nonviolent Communication Training in the desert. His journey would also include playing his flutes for young children in their schools. He also mentioned that he did not know when, or if, he would be returning. We wished him well.

David

A couple of years after Monica's death, I learned about a poetry reading group at our local library. I tend to avoid such gatherings, as I find extended discussions about a poem not my cup of tea. During one visit to the library, I noticed that the poetry group was meeting on that very day. I put aside my caution and walked into their cozy room. Although I only attended a few meetings, I was invited by one of the group members to join a meditation group, or Sangha.

Life has its peculiar directives. Upon joining the meditation group, I discovered that one of the members had taught at a music school for young people in Palestine, the same school that I would be visiting during my upcoming trip there. In addition to this fellow musician, the Sangha also contained a member by the name of Stephanie. I remembered her striking white hair and quiet, thoughtful manner.

I left for Palestine in March 2016. I had no idea if I would be there for a month, as originally planned, or possibly much longer. This journey turned out to be an amazing opportunity. It provided me a sweet introduction to the Palestinian people and a fine excursion into Israel. After a month of traveling, I was more than ready to return to my quiet apartment in the woods in High Falls, New York.

SAGE ARTS

Stephanie

The next time I saw David was April 2016 at a concert to celebrate the lives of the elder farmers living in our community. While waiting in the lobby, I noticed David standing alone in the crowd. This was the first time I had seen him since his return from the Middle East. I walked over and welcomed him back. "How was your journey?" I asked. As he began to tell me tales of his travels, the doors opened. "Would you like to sit together?" he asked. I answered, "Yes."

During pauses in the program, sitting side by side, we shared easy conversation and laughter. At the end of the concert, we rose from our seats and hugged goodbye before separately making our way to the aisle. A friend of mine, who happened to be sitting nearby, asked, "Who was that?" I explained that he was a friend from my Sangha. She said, "By the way he hugged you, I think you're more than a friend to him!"

David

Soon after returning home from my journey, I attended a Sage Arts concert celebrating elders in our community with songs about their lives. During intermission, I seem to recall, memory being a tricky storyteller, that I met Stephanie, the woman from the Sangha, on my return from the bathroom. We talked in the hallway and decided to sit together for the remainder of the concert. I do vividly recall how we shared a mutual concern that the celebrants, people in their seventies and eighties, were being asked to climb stairs to receive flowers and applause. Being in our late sixties, we were both concerned about asking these elders to navigate stairs, especially stairs without railings. I appreciated our shared concern for people's safety.

The Storytelling Table

Stephanie

Not long after the concert, I received a voice mail from David. "Hello Stephanie. I'm calling to say hello and, um, would like to invite you to tea and coffee at my storytelling table." I accepted his invitation. A week later, on a chilly, rainy afternoon, I arrived at his small apartment on the second story of an old farmhouse atop a hill. We spent the afternoon sitting at his table, sipping tea from small ceramic cups he had made during his years as a potter. I listened while he shared a detailed account of his adventures in the Middle East.

Before ending our visit, he showed me his collection of Native American–style flutes. He played a few, briefly. We also stood at his living room window as he recited a poem that he speaks aloud each morning while gazing out the window at his beloved tree. We ended the visit with a hug. This time I noticed that the embrace was strong and long.

I was weary as I left and walked to my car, in part from a lot of listening, low blood sugar, and the throbbing pain in my mouth from a recent visit to the dentist. The following morning, I wrote in my journal, "Yesterday with David, interesting. I hoped for connection and laughter, but the long stories finally wore me out. Blood sugar plummet, deep fatigue."

David

Nine months after Monica's death, I moved into a small apartment in the woods near High Falls. Settling into my new home, I needed a kitchen table—not just any table, but one that had a certain character. I began to look for one that inspired laughter and curiosity. I ended up asking a woodworking friend to create a table that would be unique in size and shape. This creation was to be my storytelling table; a place where I could sit with others, drink tea, and share stories. I believed that this special table would call forth inspiring stories of each of our life's possibilities. One of my guests was Stephanie. I invited her for tea and talk at the table. Although

I have little memory of the details of that day, I remember that I appreciated her willingness to visit the table. Pleasant images of our tea and talk remain.

THE FALLS

Stephanie

Several days after my visit to David's storytelling table, I received a voicemail. "Good morning, Stephanie. This is David. It's Sunday morning. I was taking a chance to say hello and wondering if you'd be interested in a walk sometime today?" Walks and talks are some of my favorite activities. I called back and said, "Yes!" We agreed to meet midway between our homes at a small parking lot at the top of the local waterfall.

Before leaving home, I wrote in my journal, "Spring has popped. There are blue skies. And a walk with David—Surprise." Upon my arrival, I found David standing near the falls. We stood there for a moment, side by side, in silence, while listening to the roar of the water. He then turned to me and asked, "Would you consider dating an older man?" I felt as though, as the expression goes, you could have knocked me over with a feather, and I told him so. With a moment of hesitation, taking a deep breath, I answered, "Yes." I also shared that I found his question to be unsettling. "What does dating mean?" I asked. He answered, "Anything you want it to mean." I exhaled. Relaxed a little. We laughed and took a two-hour walk in the forest, realizing that we had begun a journey together, destination unknown.

David

Soon after our tea and talk, we shared a few walks in the woods. Before one of these walks, we arranged to meet at a local park above the falls. At that time in my life, I was exploring putting my foot in my mouth; speaking what truly was going on in my head and heart. As the waters roared over the falls, I decided that I would ask Stephanie if she would consider dating an older man. Upon her arrival, I asked the question. She paused, wondering what dating implied. My response was, "Whatever we wished it to be; we could create a meaning." Thus, we began a new chapter in both of our separate elderly lives. (We discovered later that Stephanie, at age sixty-nine, was a year older than me.)

LIVING AND LOVING IN THE TIME OF COVID-19
Stephanie

Not long after we began dating, I needed to return to the dentist for more surgery. David offered to care for me and my beloved cat, Figaro, during my recovery. I declined his offer. In this stage of a new romance, I must admit, I was unwilling to let him see my bruised and swollen face.

In the early morning, prior to my surgery, I sent David an email, "By the time you read this message, I will most likely be at home, taking drugs, applying ice packs, while gazing at your beautiful bouquet of flowers, and then, hopefully slipping into a very deep sleep." By early afternoon, he had called to see how I was doing. "Do you need anything?" Nothing needed, but I was grateful for his call. He then asked if he could read to me. As I slipped in and out of sleep, and held ice packs to my cheek, I rested my phone on the pillow beside me and listened. After having read a poem or two, he would ask, "One more?" As the hours passed by, he continued to read, soothing me with his voice, comforting me with his tender loving care and attention. I was besotted. His kindness had opened my heart wide.

Weeks later, we came to realize that although I remembered him from the Death Café, he did not remember me. We smiled. It has now been five years since we began this journey together. Our dating quickly and easily transitioned into a loving life partnership. During the week, we continue to live in our separate homes; I, savoring the solitude and silence; he savoring the time and space for music and creative pursuits. We text a lot, enjoying the pleasure of connection. On weekends, David comes to my home. We begin our time together with a long walk and talk, sharing our stories from the past week: the details, delights, insights, and ponderings from the week gone by. Our weekends are filled with a series of simple and beloved rituals, including sitting side by side on the couch sipping coffee and watching the dawn's early light brighten the distant hillside, reading poems aloud before each meal as our blessing, and he serenading me with his penny whistles while I take my morning shower.

Through these years, I continue to be surprised by a giddiness that spontaneously erupts from deep within me when I am with David. These seemingly unprovoked bouts of giggles overtake my body. Early in our relationship, I wondered why this was happening. As time has gone by, I have come to believe that this laughter is the uncensored release of pure joy, delight, and gratitude for him, for me, for this gift of Weume.

David

Stephanie and I have lived satisfying lives in solitude. We each have a home, a nest. We have chosen to maintain this living arrangement. Weekends we share together. Weekdays we continue living quiet lives of solitude. Stephanie enters the front door of Love's house. I am more like a stranger who keeps knocking on the servants' back door. Love, the key to the front door to one's heart, is recognized and named more easily by Stephanie. We both seek to enter this house, this relationship, though through different doorways.

During our time together, my need for hearing aids became apparent. The combination of my hearing loss and Stephanie's soft speaking voice began to interfere with our communication. Now, with the purchase of the hearing aids and when I remember to wear them, our communication has improved.

Stephanie has designed a life in which she moves softly, quietly, thoughtfully, and kindly through her days. These qualities have served her well as a skilled teacher and trainer. I enjoy exploring the production of sounds, music, and participating in nature's orchestral presentations. On our walks, Stephanie can be fully present, where I can easily be drawn into a frog's croak or the powerful scent of a skunk. I find that all these environmental sounds and scents make up a dynamic fabric of experience, each calling for its own attention. I tend to wander a bit more, led by the lovely cacophony around us.

The current pandemic continues to shape our lives as individuals and as a couple. Our solitary lifestyles have prepared us, in some ways, for the restrictions and isolation required when living in the time of COVID-19. We continue being with one another on the weekends, forming our very own couple pod. As elders, a year into the pandemic and not yet vaccinated, we do not spend time with other people. We are very careful about grocery shopping, visits to the library, and trips to the post office.

I sense that Stephanie provides a grounding for me, a reminder that she—as well as other people—is present in my life. Stephanie is a steady light beaming out in the dark. She seems filled with a desire to cultivate kindness and can be very attentive to the perceived needs of another person. I am often exploring and searching for mysterious treasures, images, and sounds. This life, this love, curious this!

Begin Again?

Sandi Goldie and Jim Bronson

JIM'S STORY: Sandi gave me a call one Sunday a year and a half after my wife died in a single car crash. That afternoon I had been binge-listening to NPR and had just turned the radio off after a TED Radio Hour episode about ways of dealing with trauma, none of which held any promise for me.

"Hi Jim," Sandi began. "I've got a family reunion in Salem in July, and I'll be coming down with my sister; I wonder if you'd like to do a bit of a road trip after that? How about picking me up on Sunday the sixteenth? From there on it's your choice."

Widowhood had come to us each within the first three months of 2016. In one sense, it felt like our lives were stripped of their meaning. But this was more than a year after the initial loss, and we realized we were free to experiment with life. My favorite hot springs resort, Breitenbush, is an hour east of Salem in the Oregon Cascades. I started imagining Sandi and me skinny-dipping after dark in the tubs by the river. "How are you with skinny-dipping in hot tubs after dark?" I inquired.

"Well, um, if it's really dark, I guess," she said.

"Well, then," I said, stretching out the silence when I should be saying something decisive. I pictured Sandi, my dear friend of fifty years—blonde, tall, willowy, and full of fun; now age seventy-one, and me, seventy-two. She and I had met at the University of Washington, where we shared meals in the dorm dining room and talked about heartfelt matters. She was the first woman I had met who triggered the thought, *I could marry this person!* She wasn't available then, having found her first true love in Konrad, a U.S. Navy man who was soon to get an early release, avoiding Vietnam.

Sandi got who I was like nobody else had. Shortly after gently letting me know she was not going to be mine, she introduced me to her best friend from high school, Merrily. I fell deeply in love with Mer, and two weeks after Sandi married Konrad, I proposed. Merrily and I had our wedding in the spring, and the four of us sparkled with the excitement of starting marriages and families. We had our dream life partners and stayed close friends, sharing family vacations together over the years even though we lived far apart.

Konrad died in 1991 of sarcoidosis, a lung disease he may have contracted years earlier while he was a poultry consultant in India with the Peace Corps. When Kon died, Merrily was just beginning a fight for her life with breast cancer.

Two years later, Sandi met a dear Canadian man named Jeff, and they visited us together. We liked Jeff. When Mer and Sandi went for a walk, Mer confided how happy she was Sandi had Jeff in her life but admitted that she had secretly been hoping Sandi could be my wife should Mer not survive the cancer. Three months later, in January 1995, Mer was gone, after a valiant effort to have one last Christmas with our two boys and me. The following summer, Sandi and Jeff were married.

A lot died in me with Mer's death. Yet something kept me going. I poured myself into a mindfulness meditation practice, changed my career to grief counseling, and hunkered down for the duration—of what, I didn't know. I eventually dated, but without enthusiasm. I came alive a bit when I was challenging myself in wilderness adventures, but I knew few women I could share them with.

Then I met Jan. She was an extraordinary hiker, loved mountains, and had two wonderful kids. Jan was in a disastrous marriage and had made the tough choice to let go of her remaining financial resources in order to get out of it. While the drama raged, Jan and I found a common love of the outdoors in California's Coast Ranges and the Sierras. We were married in 2004 and had a reception on Bainbridge Island with dear friends from my UW days, including Sandi, who came down from British Columbia to celebrate with us.

Jan was diagnosed with breast cancer in 2012. She had two years of grueling treatments and struggled with loss of energy and mood swings. In the end, there was nothing for her except Tamoxifen, a hormone blocker with devastating physical and emotional side effects. Jan struggled to keep hiking, then gave it up and became mostly a couch potato.

One icy night in January, she stayed up late after I kissed her and went off to bed. When I awoke the next morning, our car was gone, and she was nowhere to be found. I called anyone who might have heard from her and fought mounting panic. By evening the police had initiated a nationwide search, and friends and family began pouring into town. Three days later, my son and I found her in our crumpled SUV at the bottom of a steep cliff. Car tracks in the snow showed that the car left the road on a tight curve and was unable to stop, crashing into an oak tree by a stream. The coroner's report said she might have had a transient ischemic attack (TIA)—sometimes called a mini stroke—or swerved to avoid an animal in the road.

———

SANDI'S STORY: I remember the exact moment I got Jim's email telling me of Jan's death. I burst into tears, read it to Jeff, and immediately wrote back to Jim my great sorrow at his second loss of a beloved partner. He had said in his message, "I hope you and Jeff are doing well." I had to tell him, "Actually, Jeff has brain cancer and doesn't have much more time." Jim and I hadn't been in touch for more than a year, unaware we were each struggling with our partners' illnesses, he in Oregon and me in British Columbia. When he got my email about Jeff's cancer, Jim sent us a beautiful fruit basket. Jeff died three months later, and Jim and I were grief buddies for the fourth time.

We talked on the phone occasionally and exchanged emails as we each struggled with this second wave of enormous loss. One day Jim told me he and his son James and James's family were traveling to Vancouver for a Disney cruise to Alaska, so I invited them all to stay with me. I would show them around the city before the cruise. The close friendship Jim and I had formed in college was still alive, but we hadn't actually seen one another since we were in our late fifties. It was just three months after Jeff died, and I was starting to find my footing. Since losing Konrad twenty-five years earlier, I had made it through the grief and created a new loving partnership with Jeff, so I knew I would have the resilience to somehow survive and adjust once again.

As I anticipated having my dear friend Jim visit, I suddenly had a crazy idea, and called him, "Jim, since you're driving up for the cruise, and we're both grieving right now anyway, how about if we go on a road trip when you get back? Separate rooms wherever we stay, but I would love a change of scene and just time to talk!"

Not being so quick to do crazy things, Jim said, "Let me think about it." A couple of days later, he agreed, and we decided to drive down the coast, visiting family and friends along the way, and we would end up at his home in Ashland, Oregon. That was a very strange trip, with both of us crying a lot, but also talking nonstop about our relationships and how the losses had affected us. When we got to Ashland, we went to the Fourth of July town parade, and the next day I think Jim was relieved to put me on a train back to Vancouver.

Fast-forward nearly a year: Jim and I had been exchanging emails and talking on the phone at least weekly. Our deep friendship was fully revived. After twenty-one years of a rich and loving relationship with Jeff, I was open to the possibility of beginning again with another life partner, but I hadn't met anyone of interest in Vancouver. One day it dawned on me that perhaps . . . just perhaps . . . there was another relationship possible with this dear man I had always considered one of my closest friends. And it struck me that with Jim's love of hiking, backpacking, dancing, and going to plays and symphony concerts, he was one of Ashland's most eligible bachelors in the seniors set, and if I didn't let him know what I was thinking, he would likely be partnered up very soon.

I wrote a very honest email to him and proposed we do another road trip, get a B&B for a week, and explore this intriguing possibility.

I didn't send it. I talked it over with the close friends in my women's group, and they cautioned me against going too fast and scaring Jim.

But this was Jim, and I felt safe telling him anything! After much soul searching, I told him what I was thinking in a phone call. I think he really was a bit stunned, but after much soul searching on his part and wondering if we might be risking losing the friendship we both so treasured, he agreed to join in my experiment. We booked a cozy house on the beach in Anacortes, Washington, and in April 2017, I picked him up at the train in Bellingham.

Throwing himself fully into the exploration, I remember Jim taking me by surprise with a session on the couch that I can only describe as a making out, kissing frenzy, the likes of which I remember from my teenage years. Our sharing of a bed was much slower and more tentative, especially after I found out he was already in a relationship back in Ashland. I didn't want to interfere, and I was definitely not open to being one of two women in his life.

During that week, we had magical moments of walking on the beach in the spring sunshine and reading poetry, and painful times of him dipping deep into the grief of his complicated losses. When I saw him off at the train station a week later, I felt totally confused. We kissed and he said, "I love you." I thought to myself, *What do you really mean by that? We have always loved one another, but what kind of love is this?*

Two days later, he called and said, "I have something personal to share with you. I told my girlfriend in Ashland that you and I are exploring a new relationship, so from now on, she and I will just be friends. She thanked me for my honesty and said she had loved the year we spent together." I breathed a sigh of relief; now we could begin to figure out if this might be the third great love of our lives.

———

JIM'S STORY: Sandi's call about the Breitenbush road trip (our third!) coincided with one of my grief spasms. I had been turning down offers from friends and family for me to get out with them, go to a movie, have a meal together. I felt most comfortable when I turtled up in a blanket by my wood stove and fed the fire all day long while listening to NPR. Sandi's suggestion of going on another road trip, just the two of us, sounded risky; maybe hot, maybe not. I thought, *I have loved Sandi as a dear friend for half a century. We both have just experienced the deaths of our second spouses. She's inviting me to be on the road together again. What will we talk about? Who are we after so many years? What about sleeping together?* I couldn't imagine being comfortable sleeping with my beloved Sandi. By the calendar, I was two months farther along in my grief process than she was. But by any emotional adjustment measure she was light-years ahead of me.

"Okay," I said. "I'll pick you up in Salem. I'll reserve cabins for us at Breitenbush. You don't need to bring your swimsuit . . . unless you want to."

"I'm bringing my swimsuit," she said. "And let's save the money from the second cabin."

Our rustic cabin was fragrant with moist cedar siding and paneling. The screen door squeaked, the sink had an iron stain by the drain, the double bed sagged in the middle, and it looked altogether like it was already a has-been in the 1940s.

Dinner in the lodge dining room was chaotic. Breitenbush was hosting a family conference, and kids and noise were unavoidable. We filled our plates and found the most secluded spot. After dinner, next on the agenda was hot-tubbing. My nervousness was such that I forgot to check if she was at all concerned about the clothing-optional group tubs. As we approached the hot springs, I could see we were early and nearly alone. I stripped my clothes off and waited, shifting from foot to foot in the chilly evening air, as Sandi slowly peeled down to her swimsuit. When her last sock was carefully placed in her shoe, she turned to face me and said, "Well, there you are."

She kindly took me by the hand to the tepid tub which, thankfully, was without companions. The underwater benches held us, so the surface was at chin level. Modesty seemed to fade between us. The warm fluid and its touch on our skin was soothing, enfolding. I was just getting comfortably settled when Sandi took her swimsuit off and placed it carefully on the edge of the tub. I managed to say, "Well, there it is."

Sandi asked, "Are you glad?"

"Yes. It doesn't have to mean something, right?"

Sandi gave my hand a squeeze and said, "Right. Let's just be quiet and feel the night coming around us."

In the silence, I recited a line from the Grace Paley poem "In the Bus," where a girl says, "you'll see/it's easy begin again," that seemed so effective in soothing my grieving nervous system.[1] After a long pause I said, "Begin again? My sweet Sandi, friend of fifty years, now is it time for *us* to begin again? After so much that has happened in our friendship and in our separate lives, so many beginnings with others, can we begin again?" I looked at the soggy bathing suit on the edge of the hot tub. I looked at Sandi, glowing brightly in the half-light of early evening. I thought, "If we can do it anywhere, it must start here, and pretty much now."

The next years have unfolded nicely, quite like that road trip to Breitenbush. Now we take road trips in the electric car we bought together. We are about to build a home together on the Willamette River just northwest of Eugene, Oregon, where we will have extra bedrooms for long visits from our five kids and six grandkids.

I am honored to give Sandi, my sweetie of fifty-four years, the last words.

———

SANDI'S STORY: Now at seventy-five and seventy-six, Jim and I are excited to be planning our new life in Eugene. We live in daily gratitude for the

joy of simply being together. I sometimes pinch myself that I have
the opportunity for a third kick at the can, with someone who has been
a true friend for over half a century. There is nothing like a poem in a hot
tub as the sun sets in the west and the pines whisper, "Begin again. Begin
again."

NOTE

1. Grace Paley, "In the Bus," *Begin Again: Collected Poems* (New York: Farrar,
Straus & Giroux, 2000).

The Wizard of Algo

Vincent Valenti

After my late-blooming eighteen-year relationship crashed on the rocks, I found myself in my early fifties and not about to give up on the dream. I was determined to make another go of it, this time with kids, if possible, and follow it to the end, no matter where I might end up. Life was about to get more complicated.

I got married to a much younger woman, changed my style, and hung out with her friends who occasionally called me sir. That marriage lasted seven years and cost me more than my dignity; it left me in a wasteland with no landmarks. I had a young man's dreams informing an older middle-aged body with wrinkles and thinning hair and clothes that made me look even more like that lonely guy we all see—rudderless, disillusioned, and desperate.

So, I lurched in the other direction. I started accepting my age for what it was . . . I was doomed to be alone. I became, as a close friend kindly told me, an urban monk. It took quite a while to come to terms with this new phase of my life, but I took it on as a badge of courage and wore it like a purple heart. I was through with the dream of love and romance. I was through with the hunt for a partner. I was through with sexual relations. I was through with the fantasy of companionship and finding a fellow traveler. I was an urban monk, goddamn it, and I was going to suffer for the sins of my youth until I was dirt.

My younger friends abandoned me. I interpreted this as a sign of my impending doom. As I watched the trees drop their leaves at the summer's end, I removed the hair from the drain of my shower and, like any monk, meditated on the significance of my oneness with loss.

I was gray, invisible, a spirit in the night. I fell back on the things that I thought I could control. I read a lot, I ended my cable subscription, I mined Bitcoin. I started wearing strange hats and colored Converse sneakers. I became part of the millennial music scene in Williamsburg and Bushwick, playing my sad songs on the Tuesday and Thursday late-night open mics. I got laid a few times by women who didn't want to know me afterward. And I was dying. I was left alone with myself and a bunch of really terrible music.

Who would have thought that an algorithm could reach into the dark recesses of the unconscious mind of a man as disillusioned as I and produce an introduction to the woman who would make me right with the world? I had tried dating sites and could write a book of funny stories if the realities of those interactions weren't so terrible. I had no interest in anything any algorithm had to say. I don't need no stinking algorithm to tell me that there's nobody for me. I already knew that. End of story.

But one evening, my upstairs neighbor, Eddie, a young, bright, amazing man, was visiting and conferring with the monk with all the answers who lived downstairs, and he looked me in the eye and said, "You have so much to give." And I scrunched up my face and tried to find a reason why he was wrong. And he said, "There's a great woman out there who's looking for you, who also has a lot to give." I wanted to kill him. He added, "Try OkCupid. They have the best algo."

I didn't want to go to jail, so I begrudgingly thanked Eddie and finally tried it after he prodded me a few more times. I talked myself into it in the way I would have tried coaxing a partner into bed. I was almost ready to lift the robes, but before I pushed the button, I resolved that I didn't want to duplicate the errors of the past; I wanted to make new ones.

My plan was to consider all the things I honestly wanted in a partner. That culminated in a list with twenty-eight aspects. Now I had a job to do. I wrote the most honest profile I could. I pushed the send button and off it went to the Wizard of Algo. I was sixty-seven years old.

THE 28

Around my age.

Someone I can tell about my Hep (compassionate, nonjudgmental).

Health-conscious eater. No GMO. No processed food. No industrial food.

Socialist leaning to anarchist, anti-corporate.

Smart, curious, open-minded. Well read, willing to learn.

Likes the details, getting it right, tenacious.

Strong political beliefs (anti-fascist, anti-Republican, Progressive
    or Liberal).

A giver, a lover.

Likes animals.

Has great friends (kids would be nice).

Likes exercise (cycler, runner, or some other physical challenge).

Happy in NYC, but open to move.

Not looking for perfection. Realist.

Great sense of humor, sarcasm.

Sexual, romantic, likes to kiss, somewhat old-fashioned.

Sees life ahead of her.

Non-religious or atheist, not superstitious; Jewish upbringing would
    be nice.

Musician or likes music (old-school, classical and/or from folk
    to current).

Has a cause (personal health, kids, animals, Mother Nature, etc.).

Not into TV. Movie person would be convenient.

Anti-drugs or casual marijuana user. Not a heavy drinker or willing
    to quit.

Not a super neatnik, but clean living.

Doesn't make fun of people, not too judgmental.

Into monogamy, maybe living together.

Has a forgiving nature. Empathic.

Needs a man who needs her.

Can tolerate my imperfections or help me correct them.

Laughs a lot.

THE PROFILE

Athletic, artistic realist in an unglued world seeking partner. I'm looking for a strong connection with an enlightened and down-to-earth female.

Traits:

Being open and compassionate is central to my life.

I take care of my body with exercise and good food, my mind by reading and being open and curious.

I have an agnostic view of spiritualism, mysticism, and the other worlds outside of our physics.

I suppose I'm more of a Mother Earth worshipper.

I love summer, the heat, the sultry nights, and thick atmospheres laden with possibility.

I am on my bike most mornings getting some miles under me. I like tennis.

I enjoy playing the guitar for the mourning doves that congregate on the sill in my kitchen. Sometimes a few sparrows show up and I've had the occasional pigeon.

I have always been a writer of something, spent many hours writing, rewriting, or adapting screenplays and scratching out a living. I wasn't much for the Los Angeles lifestyle, so I commuted from here.

I'm a dog, cat, and bird person. I like to cook, I like to repair what's broken, and I build my own guitars.

   I am really enjoying this period in my life, but it would certainly be
richer sharing it with a co-conspirator.

———

I answered more than three hundred questions the site presented to me
and browsed the pages and pages of prospects: beautiful, deserving, amazing women, who were likely in a similar position as I was. All of them
were 85 to 98 percent matches for me, and I got a lot of likes and "hi"s the
first few days, as I was the new guy on the old block. I "hi"d them back
but just stayed in a holding pattern over the sea of loneliness that is the
seniors' dating scene and waited for disaster to strike.

   I finally responded to the profile with the highest rating. We met on a
sunny day and after two hours of getting to know each other, as we were
saying goodbye, she told me she only dated younger men, but that she liked
me and that if I were younger, she would have been interested. She apologized for being shallow, but I thought it was a pretty clever way of blam-
ing our mismatch on my age. We were at a café on the East River, and after
she left, I didn't even want to jump in.

   I had a few other prospects I thought might be possible matches, but
one stuck out. I looked at her every evening. Her profile and picture and
answers to the survey questions were frighteningly interesting to me.
Something about her lingered in my consciousness for some reason only
the algorithm would understand.

   Not long after not jumping in the East River, I got an email from that
same woman. How did OkCupid know I was reading her profile every
night? Her name was June. She was sixty-three, unmarried, with a
grown daughter and beautiful eyes that smiled. We met the next week on
a bench across from the Strand bookstore and talked for two hours. I really
liked her. I couldn't put my finger on what it was about her at the time,
but now I think it was her vulnerability, her gentleness coupled with her
directness and candor. We had a date four or five days later that went

great, not too much, not too little, just right. We had both found the safe sweet spot.

I had no desk to clear of candidates who I had any communication with, but she had plenty, and it took a couple of weeks to ask her if she had closed her OkCupid account. I had already closed mine. When she said she had, it was our first milestone.

It is noteworthy to point out that, at least with us, falling in love later in life felt quite a bit like falling in love as a preteen. The process felt new and dangerous with high stakes and massive rewards if it worked out. There was a sense of wonder and excitement, of newness accompanied by a giddy feeling. All were signs that maybe this was going to work for both of us.

Over the next few months, we found out quite a bit about each other. I had met a great person—she ticked off almost all my twenty-eight points of interest. I had been ten years in the darkness, and she was a woman who had had a few failures recently and was wary of my enthusiasm. But as the months passed, she let her guard down, and we became more confident that we were a good match for each other. It took her over a year to agree completely, and she tested me, probably unknowingly, looking at me with occasional skepticism as she pushed to see if I was real or just a lonely guy who needed attention. The truth is that I was that guy, but the attention I needed was hers.

We've been together four years, and we've gone through some pretty trying times, but we never give up hope that we can work it out no matter what. We used our lived experience to help us talk things through. We've set some ground rules, and for the most part our good days are great, and our down days are worked through and then put aside. To this point we have proven that always being as honest as we can, communicating clearly, and giving each other the benefit of the doubt can work wonders. We're committed to the relationship because we like being together. We trust each other because there's no reason not to, but we are realistic. Things change, and every day is a chance to make it better.

I remarked to June the other day that we are in a relationship, but what we really have is a true romance.

Date, Marry, Repeat

Stacey Parkins Millett

Dating bookends my sixty-five years of life on earth. I began with teen flings during the sixties and seventies, followed by revolutionary free love in my youthful twenties. Traditional dating eluded me as a teenager growing up in Manhattan, New York, where it was socially "in" to hang out in gender-mixed groups without the peer pressure to pair up after school and on weekends. Plus, I knew that as a middle-class Black child in a progressive private school my "unit pair" dating options were limited.

I acquired a first husband in my thirties. I believed the love was right and felt now-or-never social and biological pressures. I ventured to that husband's Midwest home, after he assured me that we'd be fine as an inter-racial couple and agreed to let me have children (my first, his seconds, he was eight years older and had a previous family). I assumed my dating days were done. Wrong! After we divorced when I was in my fifties, I regressed to pseudo-dating in mixed-gender groups before learning how to succeed at traditional dating. In my sixties I finally found the "one for all times," so keep reading.

I had steeped myself in working motherhood and domesticity and ulti-mately sublimated my soul and aspirations for the sake of all around me, except for my decision to run a marathon. Just one-and-done, I vowed to my family. My father had introduced me to running at age eleven when he started taking me with him to our local track while striving to regain his college running fitness. Those weekday mornings were rare solo father/ daughter times. Over the years, running became my joy and refuge as well as a competitive space to push myself toward excelling at something, anything.

Two years shy of my twentieth wedding anniversary and twenty marathons later, I acknowledged to myself the toll a now-empty marriage had taken on me, manifested in profound loneliness and diminished self-worth. I had lost my sense of self and yet was determined to fix everything by myself without talk therapy or talk shows or talk-to-your-self-help books. Out of the blue over breakfast one morning, a good friend happened to share their own marriage hard-times story. Uncharacteristically of me, I found myself asking for advice on how to get help. I started seeing a therapist, who guided me toward understanding and validating my individuality and worth. A talk show line resonated with me, something like, "You can't live the life you've planned; you have to live the one that's waiting for you." I surrendered to purchasing a bestselling book for the relationship-perplexed called *Too Good to Leave, Too Bad to Stay*.[1] The book propelled me to finally act. My responses to the thirty-eight questions, simple yes or no questions, revealed which way to go. I hired a savvy, sanguine divorce lawyer, and one year later I was on my own as an older single parent poised to rediscover myself and, for the first time in my life, to begin loving myself.

Premarriage I had a few longer-term, monogamous boyfriends, including a live-in, but my approach to male companionship at the time was typically "carpe diem, c'est la vie, come what may." Postmarriage I entered the still-vague dating arena as a middle-aged Black woman and tried to bypass the habitual relationship pitfalls. Race or ethnicity didn't influence my choices, either. People-are-people-are-people is a basic belief of mine that I always strive to uphold. Thus, my partners have spanned hues of skin color. Early postmarriage I skeptically flirted with online dating platforms (eharmony, Match, Fitness Singles, BlackSingles, OurTime) as a way to broaden my circle beyond couples only; a pod in which I no longer fit. Online I sought male companionship for occasional social stuff, not for sticking together forever. When meeting men through these online sites, I was perplexed when they said, "you actually look like your picture," because I didn't know that people posted ancient photos or fibbed about their age. I cringed at first coffee conversations when older men poured out the sad sagas of their last marriages. I had no interest in being a cougar companion to the younger men who winked and invited me out, although admittedly I was flattered.

Venturing down memory lane became a sanctuary where I rekindled memories of how I attracted the appeal and attention of others, especially my first boyfriend. We'd met at a New England summer camp when I was thirteen and he was nearly a whole year older. We were two hours from the city and light-years away from parents. We'd talk for hours. We avoided locking braces during my first French kiss. But back home that fall our telephone calls, letters, and visits dwindled. It ended with "time to see other people" after our last rendezvous on the first Earth Day in 1970. I had long clung to memories of that first unparalleled passion. And it had been achingly long since I had experienced kindling someone's desire. I fell into my old relationship habits soon after my marriage ended, before making a major transition that began with deep self-introspection nearly a decade later. In 2007, I traveled unabashedly back to seventies-style casual flings. I let a total stranger pick me up because I had blossomed, as Gail Sheehy assured me in *Sex and the Seasoned Woman*,[2] published the same year I separated. The younger guy and I encountered each other while running in opposite directions along the same path on New York City's West Side. He reversed course to share my stride. "You look great, how about coming up to my place for post-run snacks, then later dinner," he said. I did both and more.

At fifty-two, I opened myself to more than casual interludes. It happened, unplanned, offline. During the prerace marathon expo at one of my favorites races, a running buddy introduced me to a man almost ten years my senior. We all dined together, and the next day this new male acquaintance was waiting for me at the finish line. Marathon Man, as

I will call him, had long beaten me. We launched a multiyear, long-distance romance rooted more in mutual love of running than mutual healthy love for each other. At sixty-two, I diagnosed myself as perennially relationship-challenged. I wanted objective help with understanding me, myself, and I. While surfing the web, I stumbled on Heart and Soul coach Sheryl Spangler in Charlotte, North Carolina. Given that she did online sessions (I lived several hours away), specialized in people over forty, and offered a free intro session, I signed up. Coach Spangler became my relationship whisperer.

She guided me skillfully through a self-discovery process that combined reading, talking, and questionnaires. She helped me uncover the degree to which I had experienced self-doubt and disconnection from my relationship feelings. I learned from her that my childhood exposure to my parents' complex relationship likely affected my choices in boys and men throughout my life. I learned on my own about the impact of ACEs (adverse childhood experiences[3]) on adult lives. I had experienced enough of them in early years to affect my grown-up years. Grappling with these discoveries cleared my way toward the self-love and acceptance that had eluded me in the past. I believed that I would be better off alone the rest of my life than entering into another relationship in which I couldn't thrive as a healthy and independent person without succumbing to old patterns such as being the consummate "fixer." This recognition led to an awesome plan B, now that I had gained the constructive temerity to eternally embrace myself in magnificent love with my being.

After three months of weekly sessions, Coach Sheryl cleared me to enter the online dating marketplace since I had gained clarity about my must-haves, won't-haves, values, and deal breakers. She insisted that I internalize the belief that "my guy is out there, and my job is to go find him." She detailed the launch tactics: (1) don eye-candy attire for a professional photo shoot, (2) develop a concise written profile about my authentic personal passions and desired partner traits, and then (3) blitz the pictures and text across an online site specializing in partnership bliss. I treated this partner quest like shopping online, where you customize searches and peruse product details that meet your specifications. If only there were reviews! Instead, I created a journal to record my impressions of each date, and to keep count of every encounter.

Coach Sheryl noted that, when dating, one never knows what will happen over that first coffee, lunch, or dinner. She urged that I focus on the journey of the moment each time I step out, rather than focus only on the outcome of finding "the one." I came to realize how right she was. I reprogrammed my mindset to embrace the gifts that flowed in and jettison the excess. Even in my pre–Coach Sheryl days I realized I had already received enduring gifts from some dating connections, even when no relationship materialized. I'm confident that I bestowed gifts on others as well.

My long, self-discovery journey included "sensuality restored." Remember that first boyfriend? I found him years later via the web, writing, "Not sure if you remember me." He replied, "Seeing your name brought back a thousand happy memories. Tell me everything." We met for dinner in New York City and a few months later ventured to Atlanta for historical sightseeing and hotel room sharing, where my sensuality was restored. By now neither of us had to worry about locking braces. It was not meant to be a long-term thing, but I'm grateful I got to square that circle from my past.

Our rendezvous thirty-seven years after we first met came into my transition-packed life within a year of my divorce, my father's death, and my qualifying for the Boston Marathon. Remember Marathon Man? When we were seeing each other, he found a house for us in Asheville, North Carolina, to ease the burden of our long-distance romance. I chose to buy it by myself declaring, "I would love the place always, even if we improbably split up." Within two years we did. I kept the house and love it even more. While in Asheville I returned to casual dating. I joined social groups for running and added dancing as a new passion.

During that time, I moved to Washington, DC, for a two-year stay after being recruited for a job there. I decided that the new environment would be a perfect place to reignite the partner pursuit, so I devoted much of my free time to searching exclusively online to find my guy. Geographic criteria: anywhere within a few hours by bus, train, or car. I embraced Coach Sheryl's "you never know what gifts may come your way" wisdom. I replaced my excessive "is he the one?" fervor with a more tempered "be present in the moment" calm. And I did receive more unexpected gifts. I remembered the affirmation that all dates offer benefits; there was five-dollar jazz in Washington, DC. I met this guy for a first face-to-face over a meal and knew midway through dinner I had no long-term interest. But during our conversation about musical interests, he mentioned a long-standing Friday night classic jazz venue at a local church. I became a regular attendee there thanks to that one date.

There was "polygamy is not for me." Knowing what you don't want to acquire may be more important than what you desire. This man was both online and professionally matched to me. On the first date, he bestowed me with gifts and claimed desire for me as an intriguing woman, though over two hours he detailed the woes and hardships of his past three marriages. I later learned that he really wanted two women simultaneously (at a minimum). Since I was still single, I used this opportunity to tiptoe into an emotionally safe-for-me, fun fling because I had no long-term interest in him from day one. He was ten years my junior, so I enjoyed a few no-strings-attached, cougarlike moments.

There was the couch of my dreams in NYC. The lesson from this experience was that fantasies spurred by gazing solely at online photos need reality checks. I spent sporadic time with this man, on whom I had developed an online (ogled over the photos way too long), unrequited crush. We spent a spontaneous weekend in the Big Apple, where I still have my childhood home. I followed him to Soho, where I rarely shop, and stumbled on a couch that he helped me measure for fit. He's long gone. The perfect couch remains.

Finally, there was the gift of the one for all times. By now I was poised to recognize him as my likely partner-to-be. It happened in a New York restaurant on a blustery, late January day. The agreed upon meet time was 5:30 P.M.

I arrived early. He was already seated, sporting a zip-up gray wool sweater and smiling just like his online profile photo. We talked nonstop in teenage crush mode—me at sixty-three, he at sixty-six. The following Saturday we met at a museum. I got home thirteen hours later after we had dined out again, strolled all nine floors of Bloomingdale's, and enjoyed karaoke in Little Italy. We spent the next afternoon at another museum, then the evening with partial Super Bowl viewing at a Greenwich Village bar. We remain on the clock loving each other. After ten months and twenty-four days of online dating, I found the right one—date #31 according to my journal. This new life partner has enhanced my world with joy, passion, and friendship. The fundamentals of teamwork and independence favor us. I love to cook. He loves to clean. I need alone time to run; he needs alone time to read. We love lattes and smoothies in the morning. We love to drink wine in the evenings while watching *Law & Order: SVU*. We agree that calls from our adult children take precedence over anything and everything. We have acquired lessons from past relationships that strengthen our appreciation for what we have found in each other. We respect each other's occasional contrasting views, and we support pursuit of our respective individual creative interests. Our changing bodies have expanded options for sensuality.

My journey took fifty years. The beauty of time has been unearthing the me, myself, and I that became too buried within for me to grasp who and what I wanted. I learned to embrace the inner voice looking out for my well-being, asking myself, "Are you sure he's going to unconditionally love, cherish, respect, and honor your kind, compassionate, quirky self?"

Here are my parting words. Yes, my advice: know and treasure yourself in this season of life before venturing online. Then courageously spread your wings to discover who is out there doing the same in search of you. Document your dreams and desires concisely in your online dating profiles. When you post your photos, use only real and recent ones. Have the courage to be honest. Limit electronic and phone exchanges, then meet in person, in a public place, only when your inner voice approves. Don't settle for not-quite-right. Take a break if needed. Never give up. Repeat!

NOTES

1. Mira Kirshenbaum, *Too Good to Leave, Too Bad to Stay* (New York: Plume, 1997).
2. Gail Sheehy, *Sex and the Seasoned Woman* (New York: Dutton, 2006).
3. Tara Haelle, "Childhood Trauma and Its Lifelong Health Effects More Prevalent Among Minorities," NPR, September 17, 2018, https://www.npr.org/sections/health-shots/2018/09/17/648710859/childhood-trauma-and-its-lifelong-health-effects-more-prevalent-among-minorities.

Late in the Dating Game

WALKED, HOMERED, FOULED OUT

Eugene Roth

In 2004, when I was sixty-seven years old, my partner B of thirty-three years died from complications of myelodysplasia, a cancer of the bone marrow. He was an extraordinary man, deeply sensitive to others, enormously cultivated, a man of fixed moral integrity who was the great love of my life. When he died after five years of increasing debility, I was lost. Now, sixteen years since his death, I am still bereaved, especially in moments of solitude and when I listen to the music he knew so well and loved even more than he loved me. I could not go in or out of the building we lived in without sobbing, and that went on for several years. The loss of one's intimate companion, of one who knew your thoughts almost before you uttered them and whose tastes and interests were wholly aligned with one's own is equivalent to losing oneself. I was accustomed to sharing my life; I loved the life we had together. What was I to do? Online dating was available to me, though the prospect of looking for a new love online was hardly appetizing. Who knew what crazies lurked behind even the most alluring profiles? Who would be interested in a sixty-seven-year-old gay man, especially when youth and beauty are the paramount attractions among gay men?

My unwillingness to live alone, my need for companionship, impelled me to explore the unfamiliar territory of online dating. I reluctantly joined Match. I wanted to meet a man who had experience of life, someone near my age or even older if he were emotionally available and sexually viable. As a longtime professor, I was familiar with ways of the young and for that reason didn't want to meet anyone much younger because they would be unlikely to share my intellectual and cultural interests. Moreover, I didn't want to be anyone's teacher. I had done my time as a pedagogue and retired after forty years of teaching, happily leaving behind the eternal young to their benighted illusions. I wanted someone like B, who could hear "the still, sad music of humanity."[1] I was aware that such an ideal hope was not the wisest hope with which to embark on online dating at my age or perhaps any age.

Hopes high, nonetheless, I began the search of online profiles of gay men within my preferred age range. I had a simple principle of elimination: I rejected anyone whose grammar, spelling, or punctuation was faulty. Life was difficult enough without having to deal with the semiliterate. The first possibility I came across was a man of my age who claimed to be a music critic for a major national magazine. His photograph was pleasing, and I was sure he was not a crazy person because I had read a couple of reviews by him in the magazine, which I admired for their sound judgment and musicological knowledge. I emailed C, and in short order he replied. Certain that he would not turn out to be a serial killer, I invited him to my apartment, expecting that we would have plenty to talk about besides ourselves. When C arrived, I was pleased to find him as attractive in life as in his photo, which is often not the case. He did a brief tour of my apartment, noting the bookcases packed from floor to ceiling and my collection of some four thousand vinyl records. He settled into a chair in the living room; we traded brief biographies and soon were talking about our experiences in the concert halls and opera houses here and abroad.

Conversation was easy; we apparently found each other interesting, but it wasn't at all clear that a spark was lit between us. Before he left, C suggested that we have dinner later that week and go to a piano recital at Carnegie Hall, which we did. A few nights later, C phoned to ask if I would

come to his place on the upper west side for dinner and sex. I was surprised by his bluntness but readily agreed to the invitation. When
I knocked at his apartment door, he complimented me on my shoes,
which indeed were handsome, but I would have been happier had he
responded similarly to my face. Anyway, C prepared a simple steak dinner and as soon as we were done eating, he made his move. It was as blunt
as his original invitation. What followed was hardly romantic and did not
augur well for a continuing relationship, especially because he didn't
want me to spend the night with him since he had a review to finish in
the morning. I felt dismissed, and that was the end of our connection; it
was clear that C was not interested in a long-term connection with me,
and I was ready to move on.

My second attempt on Match was more satisfying. The profile I chose
to respond to was that of a handsome man in his mid-fifties, an actor
whose grammar, spelling, and punctuation were unimpeachable and
who wrote that he was a regular listener to WQXR. The latter meant that
he liked classical music and therefore we would have at least that interest
in common. Not knowing if D, the actor, was crazy, I suggested that we
meet at a neighborhood restaurant for lunch. D was true to his photo.
I was immediately struck by his evident sympathy when I told him
about B's death four months before. He was a good listener. I sensed a
sweet disposition. When lunch was done, I asked him if he would like to
come to my place, which was only a few blocks away from the restaurant.
He said yes, so we spent a few hours talking quietly about our recent
partners. At one point when I was sitting beside D on a couch, I caressed
his face, and he started to cry. I said to him, "Hasn't anyone shown you
tenderness before?" D didn't explain why he was crying, but I was moved
by his vulnerability, whatever it meant. I suggested that we go to the bedroom and become better acquainted. We spent some time in each other's
arms, and I decided that I wanted to see D again as soon as possible. He
lived in a rented town house in Jersey City with his gorgeous Maine Coon
cat, Baron. I had two part–Maine Coon cats myself, Sam and Ramona,

another bonding point between us. D asked me to visit him in Jersey City. I saw him there a week after we first met, and it was then that we had sex for the first time.

It was wonderful to be in the arms of such a splendid man. I wondered about his attraction to me. I'm short, and though my looks won't turn anyone to stone, they won't make one melt either. Our next date took us and our three cats to my country house in Otsego County, New York, where, surprisingly Baron, Sam, and Ramona took a liking to each other—not something cats normally do when they are strangers. Things didn't go as well between D and me. He brought along a CD of a Broadway show—I can't remember which one—which he insisted on playing over and over on my audio system. I hated the music; it was just the sort of popular rock music that I found tedious and meaningless. I admit I'm intolerant and a bit of a snob, but the music was sickening me. I decided that I had to get back to the city and spend some time alone, so I told D that we had to cut the weekend short because I had some serious preparation to do for a doctor's appointment on Monday. Aborted though the weekend was, I still wanted to see D again.

When we saw each other again, D told me that he had to vacate his house because the owner decided that he wanted to renovate the house for his family's use and would not renew D's lease. I knew that D didn't have much of an income and that finding a place to live in the city would be difficult. I liked him well enough; in fact, I was falling in love with him. Since our cats got along well, I thought D and I might do so too. I asked him if he would like to move into my place. He was enormously relieved not to have to search for a new place to live and swept me into his arms in gratitude. Sixteen years later we are still together. D is a wonderful companion. He is kind, thoughtful, intelligent. I feel protected in his company, and he feels loved in mine. We lucked out. I am eighty-three years old now and grateful to have a companion to care for me, especially as I have suffered several serious health crises since we met. In this instance, online dating not only saved me from loneliness but actually saved my life.

However, I had an earlier experience through online dating that proved to be considerably less successful. A few months before B died, when I was shaken by what I knew was coming and the prospect of living alone, I went onto Match for the first time to see if I could bear the awkwardness of seeking a partner. I scrolled through the profiles without finding anyone of interest until I came across the photo and profile of a handsome bearded man of my years who was shown standing in his kitchen looking as if he had just awakened from sleep. He was an art historian and an antiques dealer in a town not far from the country house that I had owned with B for fifteen years. I emailed M, and we had a lively conversation about the Democratic primary contestants that election year. M was very flirtatious on the phone, though I was a bit put off by his flamboyant, campy tone. He thought my voice was very sexy and said we "gave good phone." The latter remark was a sample of the overly sexualized tone of M's talk. I should have taken better note of that; it was not a trait that I admired. My instinct told me that his campy tone betrayed something shallow in his character. But I was intrigued, and we agreed to communicate further by email or phone. Eventually, we would have to meet in person. Titillation by email couldn't go on indefinitely.

I had told M that my lover of thirty-three years had died a few months ago, but I was trying to renew my life and was seriously looking for a longtime partner, that I had no interest in one-night stands or the like. He said he was of the same mind, that he was in the process of ending a long-term relationship with the man who was his business partner and he wanted to renew his life also. I asked him to come to New York to meet me and his reply struck me as bizarre. He said that before he would visit me in New York, I would have to get rid of the bed I shared with B. Further, he said that if we were to have a future together, I would have to erase my history with B. I told him I was my history and if I had anything to offer another man, it was because of my history. In hindsight, the notion of erasing one's history before loving someone new should have put the kibosh on M, but I wasn't hearing him clearly. I was listening only to myself.

I wanted to meet him, so I offered to drive upstate to his house. We exchanged emails before the appointed date; in one of his, he repeated the need to clear out one's history. The night before our scheduled meeting day, I was clearing some of B's possessions out of his bureau and couldn't stop sobbing. I made the mistake of telling M about this in a late-night email. Before I went to bed, I got a telephone message from M telling me not come to him the following day, that I wasn't ready for him. He was probably right, but I reacted with rage. My innards were in turmoil, and I was determined not to be denied. It was about 11:00 P.M. I packed an overnight bag and drove the two and a half hours to M's place. When I parked in his driveway, the house was dark. There was no answer when I knocked at the front door. At the back door, I heard M's startled voice cry out, "Who's there?"

I answered, "Gene."

"I told you not to come," he said.

"Well, I'm not obedient," I replied. M stumbled out of bed and opened the door. He was miffed but said that what I did was "a very ballsy thing to do." I said that I didn't know about ballsy, but I wasn't going to let him deny my pleasure. He reluctantly invited me to share his bed but said that I would have to leave first thing in the morning before his partner/lover arrived. No problem. I would drive the ninety miles west to check on my Otsego County house and return to him in the afternoon. When I arrived back at M's, it was really the first time that each of us got a daylight view of the other. He agreed that I wasn't Medusa and I found him a faithful copy of his photograph. He repeated his comment about my ballsiness in coming to him when I did. He was more than a little giddy, which made me a bit uncomfortable. We talked easily despite the previous drama. He asked me to tell him about my late partner, B. This, of course, was my history, so I wondered about his change in attitude. I began to describe my life with B, going into detail about how much we shared, how central he was to my development as a person in the course of our thirty-three years together. At some point, M stopped me and said that what I was telling him was "all hearts and flowers." When I said that I was simply telling him the truth of my experience, he became angry and told me that I was insulting him and had to leave immediately. I was shocked: Was he feeling diminished by my celebration of B? If so, there was clearly something emotionally and psychologically deficient in the man. Thoroughly convinced now that M was not for me, I drove back to New York.

Now that my stories are done, what do I conclude about online dating when you are old and gray? If you find yourself thinking of seeking love or companionship online when you are past sixty, you are probably doing so because you have lost your spouse or your lover and are surely in turmoil emotionally. What I have to say next is obvious but true: If you are on the rebound from great loss, you are in the worst possible condition for dating online. Steeped in loss and longing, emotionally distraught and desperately needy, your rational judgment will be clouded, if you are even capable of rational judgment then. Online dating is populated by the emotionally hungry and is a haven for fantasists. Self-puffery and outright fraud are common. There are plenty of participants who are potential elder abusers or are online for dangerously selfish reasons. If you are hoping to find someone capable of humane and genuine affection, let alone good sex, you must be on your guard; your instinct for sniffing out deception must be well-developed; your nose for exploitation must be sensitive. There are maniacs abroad. They may not be serial killers but, given one's hopes, the killer you are likely to encounter is disappointment. Know then what you desire and listen for the signs that your desires are not within your counterpart's capacities. And if the signals of incapacity sound, flee. *Sturm und drang* may be exciting, but peace and quiet are blessings and far better for the older person's constitution than the wild fluctuations of adrenaline provoked by dating online.

NOTE

1. William Wordsworth, "Ode: Intimations of Immortality from Recollections of Early Childhood" (1807).

Matchmaker, Matchmaker!

Isabel Hill

"I love being alone," was my mantra. Free after two divorces, I was certainly not putting online dating on my agenda. The tales from my single friends who elected to be out there in the online sea were outrageous. They recounted story after story that qualified as book material—bizarre episodes with men who were married, who asked for money, who wanted to talk online but never meet, who had their "sisters" go online for them because they were "too shy." Men who posed as younger, thinner, smarter, kinder. Why would I stick my toe into this scummy whirlpool? I couldn't. I had seen too many friends sucked under. Besides, I was busy raising my daughter; working on my newfound passion, writing children's books about architecture; fighting a greedy local development project; and seeing a good therapist—all the while holding on tightly to my mantra. But finally, all that good therapy kicked in right about the time an old high school friend came to town.

We had kept in touch, Steven and I, and after his divorce. I had quickly snapped back into a role I had played in high school—confidante/advisor. I knew everything about every girl he dated in high school in our small Alabama town. And now, so many years later, I was helping him date again at sixty-six. He tossed and turned in the maelstrom of online dating, discouraged but never dissuaded. "This is the only way to find someone," he told me, and the process of sorting through clichés was good for him he thought, surfacing things that had gone underground in his years of marriage. The more he launched into these unknown waters, the more I understood why he kept at online dating and applauded him for all that swimming upstream. I didn't hear from him for several months, and then one day, he phoned. He was in New York and wanted me to meet someone. Had he somehow withstood the current and ended up in peaceful waters? I had to hear more.

Lisa was sixty-six, smart, interesting, a petite brunette with soft hazel eyes, and I could tell from their back-and-forth stories that there was a lot of fun, a lot of knowing, and a lot of affection in their relationship. I am prone to snap judgments and right then, I made one. He had met his match and that feeling of possibility was spreading into me. I tried to mask my eagerness for details but cut to the chase. "How *did* you two meet?" Expecting to hear about an eureka moment at a party or dog run, I instead heard the simple, "We met on Match." Then Lisa leaned in and whispered in a kind of stage whisper, "but I hired a matchmaker."

Now, I'm a 1970s feminist, but I do have an old-fashioned streak, so when I heard the word "matchmaker," it struck a tone for me, and Lisa's voice became background for "Find me a find . . . Catch me a catch." I always loved *Fiddler*. A matchmaker—why not? I came out of my cantorial cloud and asked for details.

The backstory was that Lisa had done some online dating and was weary of the task and disappointed with one bad "catch" after another. She had heard about a new-age matchmaker who could help with tweaking her profile and photos, but, most importantly, the matchmaker could critically vet respondees. The search for the perfect match could proceed while Lisa was going on with her daily life, working, doing chores, even sleeping. The matchmaker would take care of the distasteful and overwhelming aspects of online dating, which could be messy, frustrating, and even frightening. Nice to leave the "catching the catch" to someone with experience. But there was one "catch" of a different sort that Lisa warned didn't feel 100 percent okay at first. The way the matchmaker takes away the pain is that she poses as you on the dating site, fending off the bad matches and hunting for the good ones. Delete, delete, delete. Search, search, search. You never even see the bad ones. Well, it didn't sound completely honest at first, but the more Lisa talked about it, the more I bought in. "It was fun," she said. Fun? You found out more about yourself, your values, what makes you laugh, all in the process of putting everything together. Really? Digging deep into self-awareness never seemed to be all that fun. But the idea of outsourcing this job seemed like the only way to go so as soon as I got back home, I googled Julie in Toronto. Yes, it seemed far away, but it's the internet after all; I didn't need to meet Julie, just like I didn't need to meet any of my prospects until she found the right one. Getting rid of scammers, culling through my emails, matching my preferences—I needed a professional. That seemed so clear to me now.

"Helping discerning singles find their life partners," was the way Julie framed her mission. Was that me? Did I really want a life partner? I could figure that out later, I thought, but for now, contacting Julie seemed to be an imperative; I had no time to lose, as a divorced woman in her sixties. "Discrete, confidential, effective" were the words Julie chose to characterize her skills. Perfect for me! Impetuously and determinedly, I emailed her to set up a video chat. A woman in her fifties with short, straight hair, a small scarf fashionably wrapped around her neck, Julie immediately seemed like a good friend. I did, however, wish I had dressed up a bit for the chat, just to perhaps make a good first impression, since there was a chance she could decide not to work with me, but too late, we were off and running. "This is going to be fun," she announced at the onset, and we went on to chitchat about how long we had lived in our respective adoptive hometowns and how each of us got to the place where we were. She, a self-described "connection monster" and "matchmaking addict," seemed driven to put people together in romantic, lifelong relationships and me, a previously self-described independent loner, finally admitting to loneliness and an interest to try one last time at coupling before I settled into solitary life for good. Easygoing, direct, and genuine, Julie seemed honest and authentic. The first step, she explained, would be for me to write up my profile. Then I'd answer two lengthy written questionnaires, one about the match I was seeking, the other about me.

I did as Julie instructed. Then I watched as she shortened and colored my portrayal, using some of the information from the questionnaire. Somehow, she magically added in the job I had had hanging off scaffolding to snap photographs of the Statue of Liberty when Miss Liberty was being renovated. Why hadn't I thought to mention that? I sounded so curious and daring! As to the question of whether to come clean about my attachment to my dog (baggage), my still living-at-home daughter (competition), or my real estate bias (judgment)? Julie said "yes" and "yes" and "yes."

We moved on to choosing photographs. The first two needed to be a close-up and a full length. The third one should convey something special about me. I selected a whimsical, self-referential candid. In the photo, I am taking a photo of a sculpture of dogs taking photos of each other ("Paparazzi Dogs"). Julie loved it. Now for the hard part, the questionnaire about the man I was seeking. It was full of touchy subjects like my preferences of religion, age, education, location, and physical attributes, including a list of deal breakers. Good liberal I am, I whipped through the survey, trying to be open-minded and genuine, unsuperficial. There were no deal breakers; I was open to anyone. Julie immediately returned the survey, and I could hear the wrong answer buzzer as I read her comments.

I had to recalibrate. "This is a time for brutal honesty," Julie insisted. "You're not a bad person if you want someone who went to college and has some money in the bank." It was hard; it collided with the image I had of myself, but I obeyed. I really did want someone six feet tall with hair. And yes, intellect mattered. The athletic section threw me. Sporty, I'm not, yet I could imagine myself with a sports fan. If I became a football widow, wouldn't that be okay? After all, I wanted my alone time. Then again, growing up in Alabama it was . . . football, football, football. I hated it. What if I got a guy who was addicted to football? No football! Julie wanted to know if I played golf. Why was she even asking me this? No golf! Several other questions also gave me pause, "Would you date someone who drives a motorcycle?" Would I? I did in my twenties, but at sixty-six, I had to pass. Julie was aghast at my locational preferences. Though I live in Brooklyn, I selected Boston and Washington, DC, as my geographical choices. A long-distance relationship meant just that—a long distance. Did I really want a perpetual long-distance dating relationship, or was I in it for the real deal? Julie's questions edged me closer to the truth. She knew how to play hardball in a soft way. "You live in a city of almost nine million people, and you are looking to get on a bus?" After a bit more unofficial therapy from my matchmaker, I was in the homestretch. Yes, Brooklyn! Brooklyn was my preference.

At this point, if I never had a date, it was already worth it—the questioning/counseling on dress, religious preferences, and old relationships had lifted the camouflage. It felt so collaborative working with her on my own creative All About Me project, I almost lost sight of the goal; I did want a life partner. And then, the fun, hard part was suddenly at an end, and I had to turn my profile, answers, photos, and my destiny over to Julie.

She was explicit. *She* would be back in contact. I was not to check the online dating site or do anything. I thought the waiting would be hard. But after only four days, Julie had connected with three perspective men. I was taken aback. It was way too soon, even if they were all six feet tall with hair, even if they all seemed appropriate. "No time to wait," she cautioned. Now I had a new problem. Who to choose—Neil, Jonathan, or David? Should I have Julie follow up with all three still pretending to be me? She explained that she would send a follow-up message and continue to build a kind of rapport, using my own words, of course, just to make sure this was a real match for me. Now that I was all in on the "pretend to be me" strategy, I didn't want to give it up. "Yes, yes! You're me! What are you going to say?" Quickly, "my" conversation with Neil moved into territory that Julie felt unequipped to handle—sex and real estate. I decided to first have an initial phone call with him.

Neil had always been close, only a block away for many years. He lived on Third Street, married with children. I lived on Fourth, ditto. He owned a real estate company across the street from my shopping favorites, a health food store and a Lebanese grocery store that he too frequented—twenty-five years, circling, same restaurants, same stores, same schools, same parks, same streets, same doctors. The phone call went pretty well, although I wondered why the hell I hadn't had a drink before I placed it. We covered a few key topics. The bases were covered. He was six feet tall, had hair, wasn't religious, seemed liberal, and now lived several blocks from me. I didn't ask what kind of real estate he did or why he noted in his profile that great sex was his favorite thing to do. Was this scary or funny? He made the next move and suggested that we meet at a local restaurant to hash things out.

In the front of a long, vacant bar, at the Stone Park Café, a handsome, slight, white-haired man fixed his eyes on me as I fumbled with my jacket. "Isabel?" he asked. "Yes, hi, Neil?" I extended my hand as I always do but realized handshaking seemed in that moment off-putting and formal. I was on time; he early, at the ready with a martini at his side. I copied his drink choice as we seamlessly moved into neighborhood talk, a bit of "who do you know," and with our second martinis, on to confessions. "Okay, I want to just get this out there. I know I said I was seventy but I'm actually seventy-two. Seventy just seemed like a round good number," he disclosed.

"Oh, I don't care about that," I responded, and tried to think if there was anything I had fibbed about. Well, maybe that I exercised regularly but what's regularly? Did walking the dog count? I decided to not compete in this creative nonfiction and changed the subject to the real thing I wanted to talk about. Did he support that big development project I had protested against for three years? Thankfully, he did not. He was a successful and thoughtful real estate developer and not at all on board with displacing people or building big high-rises for wealthy people. I didn't have the nerve to ask about sex, but from his humorous quips, I decided that statement in his profile must have been a joke. I was already feeling like I might just have to give up that "I love being alone" mantra for good, because Neil felt like a perfect match. He was my first and only online date, and three years later, we have moved in together and are still happily hashing.

A Cozy, Crowded Bed

Nan Bauer-Maglin

My friend June said, "Get rid of the gray. Everyone lies about their age." I kept the gray but pretended I was seventy-one, my younger sister's age. My other friend Alice said, "Don't waste your time with these dating sites." Online, not much activity. I wrote to some men; some men wrote to me. Then a man, a professor my age, married forty-four years until his wife died, asked me out. I, also a professor, widowed after thirty-six years, said okay to coffee. Turns out he lives two blocks away. Now, the bed is crowded: his wife, my husband, us. It's kind of cozy.

NOTE

The original was published in "Tiny Love Stories," *New York Times*, on March 12, 2019, https://www.nytimes.com/2019/03/12/style/tiny-modern-love-stories.html.

Our Bench and Other Late-Life Wonders

Doris Friedensohn and Paul Lauter

DORIS'S STORY:

1. IN MY LATE HUSBAND'S MUSEUM

I'm naked in the entrance to my house. On the wall in the front hallway, that is. Yes, I tell visitors, that's me: strolling next to my late husband, Eli, as he captured us more than forty years ago on the island of Crete.

In the front room, guests gather around *Ecstatic Over Brooklyn*, a large painting from the 1970s with a pair of flying lovers locked in one another's arms. "The painter's dream?" people ask. "We were lucky in love," I respond. In the living room, a Tunisian couple, both with wrapped heads, glare at one another. In *Elle Veux Trop*, Eli's subjects vibrate with sexual energy— or is it rage? Have they been arguing about money? Or whom to invite to a holiday party? Or the previous night's failure in bed?

Walking through the living room to the sun-drenched dining room, I point to a white epoxy sculpture of Pyramus and Thisbe. We see their naked bodies pressed toward one another on opposite sides of a wall. Are they imagining kisses? Whispering endearments? Suffering in silence? Will love triumph over adversity?

Welcome to my late husband's museum. Enjoy the passions of lovers, the war between the sexes, the yearning and dreamy romance. React, if you wish, to the dead artist's wit, his painterly savvy, his celebrations and existential challenges.

How does a new man fit into such a space? Feel about being there? How does he enjoy a Scotch or a glass of wine when confronted by such autobiographical provocations? How does the artist's widow, after two decades of communing alone with his art, react to sharing her galleries?

2. BACKSTORY

Paul and I have known one another for years. Actually, for decades. We met in the early eighties through women's studies. At feminist meetings around the country, my colleague Barbara Rubin and I exhibited *Generations of Women*, a collection of strong photographs of our students' female forebears. Carrying our black portfolios through hotel and university lobbies in search of the assigned exhibit space, we inevitably ran into Paul. With forty-pound cartons of books from the Feminist Press in each hand, he managed a smile and a greeting. Paul, who cofounded the press with Florence Howe (their Baltimore house was its first home) in 1970, never broadcast that role. He was just doing movement work.

Some years later, when Paul served as president of the American Studies Association (my principle professional organization), he asked me to chair the women's committee.

Loyal to his friends and his causes, Paul always showed up at women's committee events. I appreciated his support.

But it wasn't until 1995, when he invited me to join a team of U.S. scholars for a two-week trip to Japan (marking fifty years after the end of World War II) that we got to know one another. I gave three or four panel presentations with Paul and another half-dozen talks with Ann Fitzgerald, his third wife. The teamwork on both fronts was relaxed and intellectually provocative. Our group of five Americanists worked hard and played well. Thanks to the generosity of our Japanese hosts, we enjoyed banquet-quality sushi, elegant accommodations, inspired department store shopping, and appreciative audiences in a half dozen cities. Colleagues became close friends.

Paul never met Eli. But after his death in 1991, Paul and Annie attended several exhibits of his work, including two or three in the studio attached to my house. After Annie died in 2011, Paul and I began spending time together. I discovered that Paul, almost alone among my friends, loves tripe. My first version of the dish for him was the very best I'd ever made. That stand-out Leonia, New Jersey, meal, on New Year's Eve 2012, launched this tale.

3. The Fish Chef Brings His Own Steamer and Apron

I don't mind fussing with a leg of lamb, baking Asian-spiced chicken, or sautéing leeks and mushrooms to dress up a piece of veal I've bought from Whole Foods. I relish presenting colorful salads, especially when the ingredients have been prewashed and cut by the staff of Julio's in Teaneck, New Jersey. For special occasions and special guests, I'll make tripe or paella. I'll buy oysters or a fancy pâté. I almost never make soup, and I rarely cook fish.

When Paul moved his clothes into Eli's former closet in the bedroom and (a few of) his file boxes onto the floor in Eli's old study, I observed and went on with my business. But when he brought the sixteen-inch fish steamer from the apartment on East Seventy-Seventh Street and his own long, white apron, I took notice. I don't remember clapping or cheering. But that's what my guests (correction: our guests!) have been doing for the past several years, ever since word of the Fish Chef in Residence got around.

Arctic char looks like salmon but is sweeter and moister, especially when poached. And especially when it's purchased at Citarella in Manhattan. Whether at the store on Third Avenue or Broadway, Paul always chats with the fishmongers about how much shrinkage to expect and how

many people such a fish might generously feed. Whatever the size of our
dinner crowd, he reliably buys too much, usually enough for two evenings
of leftovers for the lucky folks in residence. Fish stock is now a regular presence in my freezer. The liquid from one round of poaching is preserved
for the next occasion—and so each fish happening brings with it something like the blessings of history. At least that's a story I like to tell. Our
guests, when recalling the handsomely presented creature, showered with
fresh dill, may mention Paul in his white chef's apron presiding at the
stove. The apron occasionally makes it to the table. If one of our photographer friends happens to be at dinner, I'll find an image of the smiling
fish chef in the next morning's email.

4. THE UNOCCUPIED STUDY

"You'll enjoy Eli's study," I tell Paul. The light pours in every morning
through an east-facing window. The ancient desk chair on wheels is comfortable with a pillow added, and the floor-to-ceiling pine bookcases (full
at the moment with works on art and art history) are the same as the ones
in Paul's own study on Seventy-Seventh Street. While the deep closet has
Eli's file boxes on the top shelf, there's space for Paul to store his files and
extra clothes, too. In a jiffy, Paul set up his laptop and started working on
his lectures. He didn't wait for me to remove Eli's desk files, and I didn't
rush to do so.

About three months later, when it was clear that the arrangement is
working, we removed the Tunisian carpet hanging over the desk (a sou-
venir from our Fulbright year in the late seventies) and replaced it with a
framed hanging purchased by Paul and Annie in Indonesia. Shortly
thereafter, I suggest taking down the collage (by an artist Eli knew only
slightly) on the small wall opposite his desk chair. What would Paul like
in its place? From the storage room on the third floor, overflowing with
small oils, watercolors, and framed drawings, Paul chooses a pale nude of
me from the early 1970s—a seductive, pussy-centered figure at rest. When

he swivels to the left in his chair, there I am, all his—as Eli captured me forty years ago.

5. Lovers on Their Bench

Art imitates life, some like to say. Art tells us what life might be, others retort. Paul and I have it both ways, especially on a fall afternoon in Brooklyn as we survey a collection of Oaxacan folk art. For sale (a benefit for the artists) are more than one hundred small pieces grouped by subject: gardeners, weavers, and doctors; mothers weighed down by their offspring; angels, mermaids, and men enjoying a smoke; also animals more varied than those gathered in Noah's Ark. The figures, rarely more than four inches high, are wryly conceived and brightly painted. Tenderness and humor, explicit in the forms, elicit admiration, especially from those of us who count ourselves as collectors. I linger over the display at the dining room table, moving between the fish, the market women, and a group at a funeral.

Paul, I see, has left the table and joined the checkout line. He stands with his back to the dining room, blocking my view of the object in his hands. When I approach, he's too giddy with pleasure to keep his purchase a secret. A woman in a blue dress and a man in a sailor suit, seated on a sea-green bench, are holding hands. His right arm is behind her back. I recognize the artist, Josefina Aguilar, one of three famous sisters whose market women adorn the bookcase in the front room of my house.

More to the point, I know this situation—this special emotional moment. About two years ago, Paul and I laid claim to "our bench" on a walkway in Edgewater, New Jersey, facing the Hudson. Riverside Church is more or less across the river in Manhattan. The bench, about a ninety-second walk from the entrance to Whole Foods, is ours, we like to say, because it's always empty when we emerge from the market with our coffees and a half hour to kill. Josefina Aguilar's version of our bench now sits on the desk in my study. While the two figures—half a century younger than we octogenarians—are sweetly self-absorbed, I see them grinning at me.

————

PAUL's STORY:

How Could I Fit into Doris's Life?

She had lived alone in a big suburban house in Leonia for twenty years. Her place was filled with her late husband's paintings and sculptures as well as with Oaxacan animals and market women, tiny North African oil lamps, and objects gathered from many years of travel. She had a large circle of friends, with whom she talked frequently and at length on the phone. And she had decided preferences not only about which foods pleased her but about how they might best be presented. My own collection of art and artifacts was probably as large but differed in origins and reflected the tastes of my deceased wife, Annie. I regarded the phone as a kind of threat to stable life. And while I loved to eat, as my girth demonstrated, I never thought about how food looked as it emerged from the kitchen to the dining table. Most of all, I fretted about how I might be regarded by her many friends and relations.

In Leonia, I felt like an intruder. While we stayed in my Manhattan apartment at least once a week—until the COVID-19 pandemic—we did not really live there. The plants needed to be watered, the mail picked up. But we lived in Leonia and had done so definitively since I had been operated on for lung cancer in 2014 and closed my huge office at Trinity College. I had come to Doris's house for recovery. Almost immediately, I transferred most of the contents of my office and a Hartford apartment into a nearby storage unit. A few things found a place in what had been, many years before, Eli's bedroom closet and study. I was moving into Doris's house. We were beginning to live together, to be sure, but in her terrain.

It wasn't that Doris resisted changing things about. We altered the pictures on the walls of Eli's former study, now mine. And a few of my books began to occupy the shelves she cleared. I didn't resist her beautifully curated salads and scrumptious granola, and seldom proposed beefsteak rather than the cherry tomatoes she preferred. But I simply would not have moved an object or a painting or brought takeout to the table in its plastic containers there, as I would without much thought in my New York apartment. Fortunately, I have only a few unconditionally fixed penchants—baked potatoes, sour cream, and crackers with butter among them. And we discovered in our very first sexual encounter that our preferences fit perfectly together. Hallelujah.

Later, we came to see that our upbringings as liberal, secular New York Jews had provided us with amazingly similar cultural experiences—Gilbert and Sullivan songs, rack of lamb, and disinterest in TV. Most of all, neither of us had the inclination to do battle over . . . pretty much anything. I remember a friend answering Annie's query about why she and her husband argued so much: "Why have peace," Marie had said, "when you can have war?" Not Doris and me. "Whatever you prefer" is a phrase common to our discourse, as is filling in the next line in a disremembered song. "Much too much in love to say good night."

I also needed to get to know the physical terrain of northern New Jersey—terra incognita for me. It took me months to find a way of recalling that the next town north is Englewood (Angel Wood, I could remember) and our street is—what is it again?—oh, yes, according to my forwarded mail, Parkside. It helped that most mornings, I ran. Not so far nor fast, but enough to make discoveries. For example, if I went across Grand Avenue and then the railroad track, I could follow a street that dead-ended at the golf course in Teaneck (which I finally learned to differentiate from the other T, Tenafly). There, at the very end, much howling from a dog pound generally greeted my arrival. Some folks fed the dogs and also a fleet of feral cats, who watched me carefully as I approached their hideout and then swung back whence

I had come. Another route carried me past Englewood's sprawling mansions and up the hill toward Jones Road, which seemed to disappear over the freeway. I wasn't learning New Jersey, nor even Bergen County, but I was establishing a substitute for my route up the East River Esplanade from my apartment to around 125th Street. I was fitting in.

The breakthrough may have occurred in November a few years ago. November includes a number of birthdays, including Doris's, and one of our friends usually organized a party at her place to celebrate all the birthdays together. I volunteered—insistently, I think—to make something for the occasion. That something took the form of an arctic char, a delicious salmon-like fish, for which I had bought a long and narrow poacher and had frozen four plastic containers of poaching liquid. A char of three or four pounds is a beautiful fish to behold on a large platter fitted out by Doris with sprigs of vivid green dill. I had the impression that no one among the many assembled friends had seen anything quite like it, and the visual treat was matched, it seemed, by the enthusiasm for the carefully trimmed slices—not to speak of the made-by-Citarella dill sauce. It was clearly a winning contribution to the festivities, and I think there and then, I graduated from visitor to partner.

Over time, we decided to join the local gym, in which Doris had been a nonparticipating member for many years. Its virtue, apart from providing opportunities to read on the exercise bike, was that it offered time we could share, unlike my solitary running. If she liked the gym—and she seemed to since she paid for it—I would like it and even keep up with *The New Yorker*. We could have bought our own exercise bike at less than half the monthly cost, but that would not have provided the common and public gym experience. We were clearly an item there, a rarity among the largely unsocial exercise rats.

We were, likewise, an item at our hairdresser's. Ronnie, the owner and sole operator of his Teaneck shop, provided us with appointments together. "Who's first?" he'd ask as we came through the door. And we were an item at the local fancy food shop, Jerry's, where I got to know the purveyors of cheese and take-home and alcohol. I learned to differentiate Jerry's from Julio's, the Teaneck upmarket greengrocer—home of a fancy salad bar and huge, tasty blueberries. My addition to our circuit was the new cash-only bagel place down the block from Julio's. And while we checked out markets in Hackensack and the H-Mart in Fort Lee, when the pandemic made push come to shove, we narrowed our shopping circuit.

Indeed, the virus threw us back upon one another as nothing else might have. And that has been good. I suspect that an overwhelming event like the pandemic (are there other such events?) makes a relationship or breaks it. We miss seeing friends and relations, yes. We talk with them—especially Doris. But mostly we're with one another—in bed in the morning, watching the PBS News Hour, having drinks after, and then a late dinner. We have a routine, that is, but more to the point, we're in pretty steady contact. Our studies are ten feet apart, but it isn't their proximity that keeps us linked. I send her items from the internet, many during a normal day. Doris supplies me with her latest notes for her new book, *Sheltering in Suburbia*. I look forward to such moments, as her compositions evolve through many emails to her community of correspondents.

But also, sitting in front of my monitor, I frequently look—as is my lifetime habit—to the left. For there, facing me and three or four feet away is one of Eli's nudes: Doris from the neck to the upper thighs. The painting, right at eye level, draws me, draws me in. And that, too, is gray love.

Love after Seventy
and Eighty

Susan O'Malley

When Will, my partner/lover of thirty years, died suddenly in October 2017 of a hemorrhagic stroke, which occurred the same day that the cardiologist told him he could resume normal activities after a stent operation, I was bereft. First, I thought I was going to fall into a hole and die; then I couldn't be in groups of people without feeling claustrophobic; then I was angry that he had died and hadn't seen his cardiologist sooner; and then I missed both physical affection and sex. Will and I had had a very pleasurable love life. What to do?

My friend Margaret, who had been recently widowed after her husband's death from serious dementia, told me to look for widowers; they were the best. Stay away from divorced men. They are too difficult. She had found an excellent way to find a possible partner. Her current writing project involved interviewing leftists who had been involved in the movement. By this method she had found a very suitable, wonderful man with whom she now lives.

I was not ready for any of this. Will's family would question what I was doing, and I was sure my daughter and grandchildren would too. I just wanted to be hugged and comforted. I play cello in the UN Symphony Orchestra, and when the young conductor consoled me about Will's death, I impulsively hugged him, much to his surprise. Masturbation just didn't satisfy the need to be hugged.

I had known Sebastian O'Toole since moving to Brooklyn from New Orleans when I was thirty-two. In 1975 we were part of the group that started a magazine that is still going strong today. After Will's death, Sebastian asked me to have dinner with him or to go to the movies. He was a widower and had been married to Betsy, who did artwork for our magazine. She had died eleven years ago and had been my friend. Both Sebastian and I had had unhappy first marriages and happy second marriages. I had also always found him attractive, although we would often argue about politics.

Although being with Sebastian was fun, it did not solve the hugging problem. At six foot four, he is just too tall for me to hug standing up. I had to stand on my tiptoes, and he had to bend down. I longed to hug lying down. And so, I got up my courage and sent him an email about the need for cuddling and snuggling, particularly in my lonely grieving state. Of course, being a man, he interpreted cuddling and snuggling differently from me. His return email was lovely. He said that after Betsy died, he thought having a love life was over for him, that he was too old (he was eighty-seven), and did not know how to tell me this, but then he thought about my offer and discovered that he felt very good about it. And so, he invited me to his apartment, made a tasty dinner, and asked me if cuddling and snuggling came before or after dinner. I assured him after dinner. And that he wasn't too old.

Sexuality is very different from when my partner and I were younger. With Sebastian, I feel very comfortable, safe, with a sense of completion and joy, erotic but in a different way. When men are not so focused on their orgasm, which may or may not happen, there is more time for eroticism and pleasure together and for the woman to get what she needs. There is more stroking and touching, and lovemaking lasts longer. Sebastian's comment that I have taught him so much about sexuality amuses me—me, a good Catholic virgin when I got married at twenty-two.

When I was younger, I would not have chosen to be with Sebastian. He was too professionally successful. Previously, I had always been with men who were very smart but not that successful, because I wanted space for myself. I still do need space for myself, but Sebastian's success is not an issue.

My daughter Ragan's reaction to my relationship with Sebastian was confusing. I don't think children can imagine their mother having a romantic love relationship, particularly in her seventies (I was seventy-six). Months later she told me that it was her children, my grandchildren, who did not want to meet Sebastian. Will had been their grandfather, and they did not want a substitute grandfather. She had been covering for her children. Ragan said she just wanted me to be happy. She had nothing against seeing Sebastian—she had known Sebastian since she was a little girl attending editorial magazine meetings at the nearby college, where he was a professor, and she remembered him from summer retreats at his farm in the country.

About six months later Ragan did ask Sebastian to dinner. About a week before that, Ragan, my granddaughter, Grace, and I watched the movie *To Kill a Mockingbird* in preparation to see the play. When Atticus (Gregory Peck) appeared, Ragan said to Grace, "That is what Sebastian looks like." I giggled and said, "Well he is a bit older, Grace, but he does look like an academic." The morning after we all had dinner together, Ragan texted me: "Sebastian O'Toole is a lovely man, and he always has been."

Another concern in older people's relationships is aging, sickness, and accidents. The December before COVID-19 struck, Sebastian fell down the nineteen steps in my Brooklyn brownstone. It had been a wonderful evening: he had attended a UN symphony concert that I had played cello in at the New School. Afterward, we had taken a cab to Brooklyn in a stormy rain, drank wine, talked, and laughed. I don't know when I had been so happy. In the middle of the night, when he got up to go to the bathroom, Sebastian fell down the nineteen steps. I let out a bloodcurdling scream that caused my tenant and her boyfriend to come running up from their apartment to discover Sebastian lying bloodied at the bottom of the stairs and both of us stark naked! Amazingly, Sebastian got up, blood dripping from his head, and walked back up those steps. I think his height and slightly inebriated state may have saved his life. I agonized about calling an ambulance—it was 3:00 A.M. and raining—which made thoughts of the ER less than reassuring. Not to mention that Sebastian refused to go and said he wanted to stay in bed with his arms around me. So, I kept him awake and talking to make sure he didn't have a concussion and watched as the blood from his head wound finally stopped. Then I waited until morning to call a doctor friend who had admitting privileges at Methodist Hospital. Dr. Fein said I should call an ambulance immediately. He would call the hospital to alert them. Watching the paramedics carry Sebastian back down those nineteen steps, strapped securely to a chair, was certainly a relief. Sebastian had two tiny neck fractures and a small brain bleed as a result of his fall and spent a week in the hospital. In addition to Sebastian's fall, he's had a heart valve operation and pneumonia during our two years together, and I developed breast cancer, so gray love comes with many bumps and detours. I must say, though, I liked it when Sebastian introduced me to his nurse practitioner as "his sweetie."

And then there was COVID-19. I probably quarantined more days before I saw Sebastian than I spent with him. If I had never left his apartment in Manhattan, I would not have had to quarantine, but I live in Brooklyn and have family, friends, and a pianist with whom I play my cello. Also, Sebastian could not stay at my house because of the stairs.

The rule for quarantining his daughter rightly insisted upon was ten days of quarantine followed by a gold-standard COVID test, including quarantining until I got the test results—or fourteen days of quarantine with no test. This was because of Sebastian's precarious health. The first summer of COVID we spent a month together at his farm in western Massachusetts. I quarantined alone for fourteen days there. We met only for meals outside. Then we spent the final two weeks physically together. In the fall, we got together in Riverside Park, masked, and bundled up against the cold wind because I hadn't done my quarantine. After Thanksgiving I quarantined again for only ten days, but unexpectedly tested positive for

COVID with the most reliable test. Although I had no symptoms, I quarantined for another ten days. I developed no symptoms and was deemed COVID-free by a doctor. Then I spent five days with Sebastian. Thank goodness his daughter insisted on my being tested. My asymptomatic COVID-19 could have infected him. That might have been the end of our relationship.

For months our relationship consisted of emails and phone calls. Every evening we would say we loved each other. Sebastian wished me sweet dreams, and we would send one another music and photos. Sebastian writes funny and very literate emails; they sustained me. Last week we spent five days together after a four-month separation because I had been diagnosed with breast cancer resulting in a lumpectomy and three weeks of radiation. We were both two weeks beyond our second vaccine. Recently, we invited similarly vaccinated friends for dinner and feasted, talked, and all hugged each other. I had been apprehensive, but it felt good. It is reassuring to love and be loved again—unexpected at our ages—but so pleasing.

Where Is This Going?

Barbara Abercrombie

Many years ago, at a party in LA, attended by all three of the men I would end up loving in my adult life—my first husband, the man who would become my second husband, and Joe—it was noted by the man who would become my second husband that Joe and I were flirting and seemed attracted to one another. My first and then current husband did not notice, or most likely didn't care, but my second husband mentioned it for years after.

When Joe called me for a date thirty years later, I was long divorced from my first husband, and my second husband had died two years and two months earlier. My grief for him was no longer raw, but I still couldn't listen to opera, I still felt as if my life had been ripped from under me, and I still missed him in a way that only those who had lost a spouse or partner could understand. Later I told Joe that if he had called even six months earlier it would have been too soon.

We had stayed in touch over the years. He'd dated some of my girlfriends and had been to parties at the house in Santa Monica that I shared with my second husband (where I was careful not to flirt with him), and he'd written an essay for an anthology I'd edited. So we had some history beyond the night we'd flirted thirty years ago. We were friends. We were both writers. We both had dogs.

Even so, I was caught off guard when he called and suggested getting together for dinner. I hadn't dated anyone for a very long time. I had married my first husband three weeks after I met him, and my second husband had been one of my closest friends, so it never felt like dating before we married.

Out of my nervousness over having a real date, albeit with an old friend, I suggested a playdate with our dogs. I'd recently seen Joe's dog Skeezix on Facebook celebrating his fourteenth birthday. Skeezix could meet my dog Nelson, who was also getting on in years. Dealing with dogs would be a diversion. Who could be nervous with their dogs? But Joe was set on dinner with just the two of us, and then maybe another time for a dog playdate.

My nervousness resulted in asking Joe a lot of questions on the way to dinner. Questions that sounded like advice for dating straight out of *Seventeen* magazine circa 1964. *What are the five things I should know about you?* I actually asked him that as we drove east on Sunset Boulevard just before we reached the 405 Freeway. I know the exact spot because to this day, four years later, my question still makes me cringe. But dinner was wonderful; we never stopped talking and we laughed a lot. It was both easy and deeply strange. Easy because we had so many mutual interests and friends, and strange because I had not dated anyone since 1964.

We had that dog playdate the following Saturday morning, then kept on seeing each other. We both worked—he's a movie critic and I teach creative writing—so we were busy with our own lives, but I'd go to movie screenings with him, and we'd find restaurants that had outdoor dining and take the dogs. Sometimes he'd bring DVDs over to watch at my apartment and I'd cook dinner. No wonder I had flirted with him thirty years ago—he was tall and attractive, funny, sweet, and very smart, and after a month or so of dating I could listen to opera again. I was seventy-eight years old, and he was eighty-four.

Then we went away to the mountains for a weekend with the dogs. In the middle of the first night Joe woke me and asked, "What is that?"

"What's what?" He nudged my leg under the quilt, and I moved my foot around and felt Nelson's warm little body. He had gotten into bed and crawled down under the covers between us. "It's Nelson—he always sleeps with me," I said.

There was silence as Joe absorbed this information. Then we heard the *click click* of Skeezix's nails as he paced the room. Joe had put his doggy bed at the other end of the room, and Skeezix kept coming over to our bed to make sure Joe was still there.

"Maybe you should put his bed closer to ours," I said as Skeezix kept *click*ing back and forth across the room. So, Joe moved Skeezix's bed next to ours, and Nelson remained under the covers with us.

Sleeping together was more complicated than dating, and we quickly learned things a lot about one another. For instance, I sleep under white clouds of down quilts with piles of fluffy pillows; Joe sleeps under a blue electric blanket with one firm pillow under his head. He needs total darkness for sleep; I get claustrophobic if curtains, let alone blackout shades, are drawn. I can exist on very little sleep; he becomes extremely anxious and cranky when his sleep is interrupted. I also learned that he had a problem with Nelson sleeping with us. I was surprised. Who didn't like sleeping with their dog? Joe, it turned out. He didn't even like sleeping with his own dog, let alone Nelson. So, I bought a little doggy bed and blanket for Nelson and from then on, with astonishingly quick adjustment, Nelson slept in his own bed every night, with or without Joe in my bed.

"Are you in love?" asked my cousin Sally. She had googled Joe and approved.

"I'm in like," I said. "Deeply in like."

He had been divorced in the eighties, and since then had many girlfriends but hadn't lived with anyone for three decades. As someone who had been married for most of her adult life, I was curious about what was it like to date, to be a serial dater for all these years. I'd quiz him on why it didn't work with such and such girlfriend. "It just wasn't going anywhere," he'd say over and over.

That first year we both moved, but not in together. It was like musical houses. Joe sold his condo in Santa Monica, a town I'd lived in with my husband for twenty years and moved into a rental in west LA because it was closer to screenings for his work, and I moved out of my small temporary apartment in west LA and bought a house in Pasadena near my daughters and grandchildren. One daughter lived right down the street from my new house. Joe was startled to discover I could decide to buy a house and move with such alacrity. I was amazed he could move without being homesick for his old neighborhood in Santa Monica. Where was this going, this relationship of never-ending talk and laughter and loving movies and books and our dogs?

Early on we had discovered we had a mutual friend, a playwright in New York, and both of us had recently read an article about his living arrangements—he lived in an apartment next door to his wife's apartment. We laughed when we found out we'd read that article and had thought the same thing—what a perfect way to live.

Now that we were living twenty miles apart, we began to fall into a just weekends, all weekend, every weekend together sort of relationship either at his new apartment or my new house. The dogs traveled back and forth with us, happily adapting. We were adapting too. Joe put up with my down quilts and pillows with sun blasting through the windows at dawn in my house, and I managed the blackout shades and electric blanket at his place.

"You mean he leaves every Sunday night?" asked my friend Victoria with deep envy in her voice.

"Or I leave," I said. "But we're not sure where this is going."

We planned trips and began to travel. If things weren't feeling right between us, I'd think, *We can just go on this one last trip and then we'll evaluate the situation, decide if we want to stay together.* But I loved traveling with him. He was considerate and easy to be with and we never stopped talking. Then we'd come back to LA with our weekends-only together and hectic weekdays working, his crankiness over sleep and mine over the need for sun at the crack of dawn, and plan another trip, and I'd think, *Well, after the next trip we can decide where this is going.* I kept bouncing from the need to figure it all out, nail it down, move in together or not, and give us a label other than girlfriend/boyfriend (partners?), to realizing how delicious independence felt.

By now I knew I was beyond like and into love. Our history together was becoming precious, our trips, sharing friends and family on both coasts, visiting his daughter in Oregon, and spending time and holidays with my daughters and their families in Pasadena. Once, deep into one of our *where is this going* moments, I thought of the celebration we could have if we gathered all our friends and family, this much-loved community of ours, and I said, "Maybe we should get married! What better celebration than a wedding?" Then I quickly added, "But let's not live together." And Joe laughed.

We loved each other; it was that simple. The details at our age were not that simple though. What if the big earthquake hit when we were twenty miles apart? What if one of us got sick?

Then came the pandemic. It was just us. We were each other's pod, we only saw my family from six feet away, outdoors and masked, or we had Zoom calls with his daughter in Oregon or my brother and his family in New York. Joe was the only human being I could touch or have inside my house or drive with in a car. There were no trips, of course, and there was no end in sight to the pandemic. He streamed movies at his house for his reviews and I taught my classes on Zoom from my house, and we continued to spend our weekends together. The second week into lockdown I adopted another dog, Nina, a sister for Nelson. Joe and I both grew many pots of cherry tomatoes on our separate patios and got our groceries from Instacart. Feeling guilty while most of the world suffered, our relationship flourished like our cherry tomatoes and new dog.

We are stunned sometimes when we realize how old we are. Eighty-one and eighty-eight! How I wish we had decades left, but we're both aware that one of us could drop like a leaf at any moment no matter how healthy we are right now. And we're also aware that this relationship could not have worked if we were younger. I learned a lot in my second marriage; it was a happy marriage, full of trust and deep love, and made me a far better partner than I ever was with my first husband. And Joe certainly is a better partner through his succession of girlfriends.

It's been four years now, and we still flirt; we still are attracted to one another. We have never run out of things to talk about. And one of us still leaves every Sunday night. Sometimes we wonder where this is going.

Maybe we're already there.

Pleasures and Complications

LIVING APART TOGETHER

Susan Bickley

Once upon a time, long ago and far away from Boston where I grew up, long before online chatter consumed us, I found myself in Madison, Wisconsin, divorcing my high school sweetheart after a fourteen-year marriage, with a small child and shared custody. It was 1974, and the little fishbowl of Madison seemed quite different from the big city of Boston, so much so that just about any unmarried man I knew or met seemed to be the former spouse of someone I knew well. So, with hope of romance all but obliterated from my horizon, I discovered Single Book Lovers. It was described as the answer to the thinking person's quest for companionship and romance, compliments of Bob and Ruth from Swarthmore, Pennsylvania. Their list of single men or women promised access to a wide array of singles, all of whom would be "Single Book Lovers." I pitched this to my friend Sharon, who was in a similar boat, and we agreed, we were in.

Single Book Lovers was indeed a candy store of seemingly alluring potential mates, and Sharon and I took it on with gusto. Its real promise for me, a librarian and passionate reader, was access to people who liked to read. The application required naming one's five favorite books, which turned out to be a great screening device. Nine out of ten men included self-help books such as *I'm Okay, You're Okay*, which immediately landed them in my "Not to be considered" pile. But one guy's list totally won my heart. When I met him, though, he was nothing like the interesting list he had put together. My confidence in the sorting tool was shaken. It turned out, his best friend was a college librarian, and she had done the list. That ended that relationship, though I did consider asking him for the librarian's number.

Between us, Sharon and I had two years of adventures with many different men. But neither of us found a candidate for a long-term relationship. So, we made the decision to drop out. Having agreed to that, Sharon added, "But, there is one more profile here. I have had it in my desk for two years. I think this guy is too intellectual for me, but you just might be a perfect match. So, as the last act of this fruitless campaign, please consider writing to him." This guy did have an appealing profile. He was the real deal—a reader to his very heart, a book collector, a romantic guy who, after three divorces, still believed in marriage. His answers on the application turned out to be absolutely true to who Alan was—a reader, a romantic, a cowboy at heart, never out of his jeans if he could help it. After studying the artful profile for some time, I wrote to the guy whose list of books would make any book lover swoon. And sure enough, I married the guy a year later. This piece is neither about him nor the thirty-seven years of marriage we enjoyed. He was stricken with a disease in the ALS continuum that robbed him of many pleasures during his eighties. He succumbed peacefully to the cruel illness at eighty-three in 2017.

After contemplating the long years of his illness and given the complications of any long-term marriage, I was surprised by the enormity of the loss I experienced. Even an expected death leaves one bereft, alone, and uncertain of the future. Many months later, after settling the estate and an unexpected tax audit, I packed my grief along with my computer and clothes and took advantage of what had been our little escape—a condo nestled into Sarasota Bay, with a view of a bird sanctuary filled with blue herons, roseate spoonbills, and many other Florida birds. I allowed myself four months of leisure, walking, reading by the Gulf, and having breakfast with the birds as they harvested the bay floor for abundant fish and shrimp. This was a luxury, and, by the end of my stay, I decided I would take a step toward my new life. I signed up for a Match account on my last night in Florida.

Waiting for my flight at the Sarasota Airport the next day, I brought up my new Match account on my phone. Suddenly the screen was filled with tan, healthy-looking, rather appealing men, all of a certain age. Not feeling at all sure what I wanted to do about it, I looked forward to getting home and thinking about what I wanted the future to be.

Reentry took some time. I let friends know I was home and went to rehearsals with my group the Raging Grannies—a women's chorus of social justice activists. These women are my soul mates and sustenance. We support climate actions, immigrant rights, Black Lives Matter, and more. We don't lack for places to go and people to support. It was good to be home.

It took a while before I screwed up the courage to look up Match on my own turf. What a shock! While the Florida photos had been very appealing, the corresponding Wisconsin views were something else. Most men in Wisconsin, it seems, feel it is not important to have a profession-ally taken photograph. Imagine the array of men aged seventy-five to eighty-five taking selfies of their bearded faces, sitting in ancient reclin-ers looking as if they had just emerged from the North Woods. What a contrast to the Sarasota experience! When I limited my search to Madi-son, the array was somewhat improved. I allowed myself some time to con-sider my options and then began making contact.

My seventy-eight-year-old self was determined to find the good in people, not to have overly high expectations, and to consider this an exper-iment with no predetermined ending. That was a good thing. Many men my age and older are stinging from a divorce, in search of someone who will cook for them, or hoping for a companion. The men on the app seemed to lack vitality, humor, and wit. We were in the Age of Trump. Suddenly one had to spell out one's political views. I added to my profile the words, "Please do not contact me if you voted for Trump or even thought about it." I eliminated from my list men who wrote on their profile that they were "middle of the road." No time for wishy-washy political thinking!

I knew that after three years of hard caretaking, I needed to be cautious and unhurried about jumping into anything. At this age, it's scary how small a step it can be from independence to flat on one's back. Finally, I was enjoying my health and independence. These seemed essentials to relish and slowed me down in my search for companionship. I stopped reading the daily Match feed and joined a boot camp for women over fifty. There were lots of women like me in the group, out of shape from years of caretaking. I was the oldest in the class. The combination of lifting weights and building strength was the best thing I could have done for myself.

After a few months away from the Match site, I decided to peruse the new listings to see if I was missing anything. "What have we here?" I whispered to myself as I spied a new face among the usual suspects. Here was a guy with a head full of gray hair with a great photo. He wore a handsome black shirt and stood against a fence filled in with a beautiful array of colorful wildflowers. He identified himself as a liberal, a former teacher, a reader, and a widower. We set a date to meet at Michaelangelo's, a favorite State Street gathering place. I was often fearful before meeting a match I did not know. Would this one be the River Falls guy who murdered the women he met on a dating app? In this case, it seemed unlikely.

He was the guy in the photo. Adorable. We got coffee and sat down. He asked what I had been doing on the square, and I told him about the peace vigil I attended with the Grannies. So far, in my Match history, no one I met had heard of the Grannies. But Mike said, "What? You are a Raging Granny? I love the Grannies." By the time we were asking each other about politics, I opened my bag and put my Granny apron on the table. What leapt out is the large button that says, "Now Governor Walker, you have pissed off Grandma." Turns out Mike was the head of the Recall the Governor group at Madison College, which moved us to the amazing feeling that we were on the same page!

We made a date for the following week.

Mike confirmed our date by email the following day and also confirmed the feeling we both had, that we just might be on the way to creating our own little space of sanity and happiness. Those were his exact words. That was a promising beginning.

Mike's profile was like mine in that we were both widowed, though he, at age seventy-one, was seven years younger than I. We both were looking for the rare combination of friend and lover, and we both had plenty to do, but we acknowledged that it was difficult to find that one person to share what life had to offer. We were fortunate to each have children who were happy, if not somewhat bemused by our finding each other. His grandchildren seemed to like spending time with us, especially as I was a former children's librarian, often showing up with books for them. My daughter and Mike got along from the first meeting. All of this went so easily; it was clear we had become an item.

Mike lived in a big, old house from the 1920s filled with photos of his kids and his wife and members of their families going back generations. It had stairs everywhere, and I knew from the first moment that my knees and hip would not be happy living there. My condo, purchased to escape from a house with lots of stairs, was perfect for me. It had two bedrooms, two baths, a generous amount of space, and no stairs. It was becoming clear to me that I was really enjoying having my own bedroom for the first time in many years. If I woke in the night and wanted to read, no one would be bothered by the light. The first time I watched a movie in my bed when I could not sleep felt like a new and joyous discovery.

Mike never doubted we were going to work things out. We began speculating about what kinds of arrangements would suit us. Over the summer, we played with ideas that usually started, "What if—" Eventually, it came down to, "What if we found a condo in my building and you lived down the hall?" When a unit became available on my floor I called immediately. The realtor explained to her client who was asking to see the condo and why. She exclaimed, "But her husband just died too!" Maybe it seemed that it was too soon to be in a relationship, but it hadn't occurred to us that we were rushing or that we were on some unseemly timeline. We were just happy. We were also conscious of time working against us.

His offer on the condo was so straightforward, it was accepted within the hour. Mike now had three months to downsize most of a life. The man was undaunted. Somehow, by his closing, his house was sold at a great price, the remaining goods were moved in, and at this point, we could decide how we wanted our lives to evolve as we began our "living together down the hall."

One of the many things that makes us so compatible is each of us having had full lives before we met. He had different groups of friends, a best friend, two daughters, and four grandchildren. I had the Grannies, other close friends I would see for lunch or for coffee, two daughters, a son-in-law, and a grandson. This was Madison. There were lectures at the university, the wonderful book festival with readings and lectures. The movie scene was vibrant. The Overture Center had symphonies and plays and visiting artists. Suddenly, we had time and interests, and we just had to decide which we might do together, which we might do on our own, and which, if any, we would let go. It was a joyous abundance.

Soon, however, the coronavirus was upon us. As healthy as we were, I was already eighty years old. Our love affair now on *terra firma* was still fraught with the existential questions we face at this age. My mother died at my age and had suffered from dementia. Who of us knows how this will turn out? March fifteenth, we were staying home. Now there would be so many things we would not be doing as planned. As the political scene was heating up, the Grannies were sidelined. A bunch of older women, with a million and two preexisting conditions among us, could not protest at a time when the country erupted in protest. The Grannies were reduced to supporting each other on weekly Zoom meetings. We vowed to live to vote in November no matter what. We all made it to that day and beyond. We voted by mail, ceremoniously hand-carried our ballots to a safe box, and hoped to live long enough to see the results. By November, Wisconsin was the new virus hot spot in the country. We were all on borrowed time.

So, what now? Many of our friends had moved from the big family house into condos or retirement living. If they were married and home

24/7, there was a lot of stress. If they were single and without family nearby, they were often lonely and isolated. Creating a safe bubble with others with whom you can share meals and visit during the COVID-19 pandemic is essential. Mike and I wonder how we were prescient enough to decide not to share my condo. Surviving marriage with both parties at home and no outside social life, or the alternative of living totally alone, both offer challenges we are fortunate not to have. We used to have a whole village to dilute the intensity of living together, but the coronavirus has brought something new: we are asking a partner to be our everything.

Living apart allows us to keep our weekdays for our own projects. It turns out that while I have always called Mike a monk, I am actually pretty monkish myself. His days are spent working on his math projects, which he publishes on his webpage and which have a following. He reads voraciously, and he walks a few miles outside in almost any weather. He Skypes with his best friend, texts with his daughters, and prepares his own breakfast and lunch. My days are spent maintaining the larder and maybe preparing something special for dinner, but otherwise reading, writing, doing other projects, checking by phone on friends who are alone, and walking at least a mile if the weather cooperates or acclimating to my new rowing machine if it is too cold or wet to walk. I do a lot of reading. We both do the *New York Times* Spelling Bee puzzle daily.

Most nights, we cook dinner together, an evolution since the first time I cooked dinner for Mike. As I fixed dinner that first time and Mike was sitting on the couch in the living room, I realized this would be a problem. I suggested that if I was in the kitchen working, perhaps he could be in the kitchen helping. That changed everything. Mike is now a happy and talented sous chef. As I am increasingly hampered by arthritis in my hands, he opens cans, peels potatoes, and chops carrots. He clears the table, cleans up in the kitchen, and empties the dishwasher. It is a real partnership.

Financially, we have our separate bank accounts. But we have a shared fund to which we both contribute and replenish as needed. We split our grocery bill, the takeout bills, the presents for the children. When my daughter was almost laid off from her job at the university, Mike said, "Tell her not to worry. We can help her." This is a man with a gentle manner and a kind heart. He is generous in every way.

My dear friend said one day, "Suzy, you are the only woman I know who at your age is in a loving relationship and having sex on a regular basis." For so many reasons, many people our age are not able to keep this physical dimension in their relationship. We are most fortunate. There is a powerful attraction here. After years of being alone, we both celebrate the warmth, the depth, and the satisfaction that develops over time together.

With an underpinning of joy at finding unexpected love, having no illusions of permanence or guarantees of survival, surrounded as we are by huge spikes of the virus, we do find ourselves on an unexpected island of happiness and gratitude.

If I had to make a prediction, I would say that we shall continue to save each other. In the midst of all the political stuff, the fears for our children, the planet, our health, there is something keeping us going. We have created a happy place. We make life easier for each other. Vaccines are increasingly available. We are finding joy in small things: the occasional Wisconsin cherry pie, a fire in the fireplace with a Saturday movie, reading together on a rainy day, knowing that we are here for each other, even when we are apart—and down the hall.

Parallel Matches

Anonymous

Two matches responded simultaneously.

One: Let's meet. Two: Can't now, maybe later.

Dated One for three months. Nice, but no etchings.

Then One left town for three weeks.

And Two wrote back: Let's meet.

Dated Two twice. She had a knee replaced.

He tended to her. They got very close.

One returned; took him to see her etchings.

Now he stays at One's on Fridays, Two's on Saturdays.

Both know. Each prefers monogamy.

How to choose? Must he?

Temporary shrink didn't help.

A friend gave good advice. He didn't take it.

What's this lucky man to do?

NOTE

The author is a late-seventies widower who, after three years, is still seeing both women, also seventy-plus. These events occurred six years after his wife died and followed several Match.com dates and two prior relationships of several months each—though not simultaneous.

Reflections on "Old Love"

Sarah Dunn

"Today I am eighty-four!" I announce repeatedly. I say this with a with a mixture of pride and trepidation. "Remember, eighty-four is just a number," Marilyn retorts. She is seventy! "Happy birthday," my son Dan, who is fifty-eight, sings on the telephone. Then my daughter and her family exclaim, "eighty-four is cool!" and proceed to sing "Happy Birthday." Paul, the man I have been seeing for the past seven years, sends a singing card by email. I am ecstatic! I feel powerful. Yet a creepy feeling about aging rests on my neck and then works its way up to my brain as I sit reading in my red leather chair. How much of what I just read would I remember for my book group discussion on Saturday? Disconcerted, I answer the real and imaginary voices. Yes, eighty-four is just a number, but a number with multiple meanings. Yesterday when I saw an Argentine movie, I only remembered a few important scenes for the Zoom discussion. Last month, I even forgot my son's birthday for the first time in fifty-seven years. So, when my younger friends repeatedly say, "Eighty-four is just a number," I smile and shrug my shoulders knowingly.

Eighty-four says time is short, the end is near, the future is ephemeral, plans are for next week or maybe next year. Eighty-four asks me to reflect on the good and reckon with my choices. Though one may do this at any point, the urgency around choice and action is now specific and limited. I repeat the number eighty-four. I reminisce about my divorce at thirty-two and my old boyfriends. Mostly, however, I think about raising my two children as a single mother while obtaining a doctorate and finally meeting Paul at a professional meeting when I was seventy-seven. I guess my musings are mostly about "old love," about being in a confusing, difficult, nontraditional relationship for more than seven years. When I call it "old love," I don't mean the feelings are different, but rather the consideration of what it means to be in a relationship at eighty-four is different. No longer are there many plans for the future or discussions around raising a family. No longer do I feel the need to live with someone or be in an exclusive relationship. Yet because I no longer feel invincible, I need someone who is there when I am sick or helps me when I walk funny or lose my balance. At the same time, the need for companionship, intellectual connection, warmth, holding, and sex are all still present and central to what I call "old love."

I was seventy-seven when we first went out. We had spoken several times at conferences, and each time I was drawn to Paul's warm smile, the mischievous twinkle in his eyes and the ease with which we talked. Yet it wasn't until the weekend before Thanksgiving that Paul sent an email asking if I would like to meet on the following Saturday to discuss retirement! Retirement? "Hmmm?" I mumbled questioningly to myself. After all, it was now 2012 and he had retired in 2003 and I in 2006. Was there really something he wanted to discuss? I smiled knowingly as I accepted the invitation. When Saturday morning rolled around and I was in the kitchen preparing breakfast, I could feel my legs stiffen and my hands become sweaty as the ordinary became onerous. Even making my usual breakfast of English muffin and eggs required thought and focus, all of which seemed elusive as I contemplated my first date in seven years.

How to present myself? What to wear was my first consideration. It needed to be casual. Yet I do not wear pants as I am conscious of being overweight. Black is my choice, the usual East Coast color, or non-color as my son who lives in the Midwest often teases. Yes, my black circle skirt and a black wool sweater are perfect. Not only would they show off my intricate silver jewelry, but it would also help me look significantly slimmer. All good!

As I began getting ready and applying makeup, anxiety moved my eyes to the kitchen clock. As it went from 6:15 to 6:30 and on to 6:55, my application of mascara became shaky. Promptly at 7:00 P.M., just as I finished applying my eye makeup, the bell rang. With apprehension, I opened the door. There, standing in the doorway, was the graying, mustachioed man with the inviting raspy voice. Immediately it felt comfortable and homey to have this man in my house.

We talked for over five hours—no food, no drink, but much warmth. We moved through politics, film, and our personal histories, realizing how much we shared. In addition to shared interests, we were also both leftists, children of immigrants, divorced with two children, and academics. As the evening was ending and we hugged goodbye, he said, "I have something to tell you." My heart raced as he awkwardly blurted out, "I have had a girlfriend for over thirteen years who I see on weekends, yet I am unhappy in this relationship and need to leave but can't." Wow, what a bomb he just lobbed between us! Clearly this was trouble! Bewildered and angry, I just stood there and looked at him. After several minutes of silence I replied, "I need time to think this over." He smiled and answered, "I will call you next week and really hope you will not run away from our warm connection!"

An invisible tear ran down my cheek as I said goodbye. So much tied us together. At seventy-seven I had found so much in this one person who was only partially available and could not really be a part of my life. How to think about a limited relationship that in some ways met so many of my needs and in other ways did not meet many more? Besides, I was deeply attracted to the poetic look of this American scholar. And what of this other woman? What did it mean to be in a secret relationship, and what kind of betrayal was I thinking of entering? Thus, I mused, while also thinking about how wonderful it felt to be so connected to this man despite his partial availability. These musings continued over the next few days.

Lonely, in need of warmth, physical contact, and emotional caring, I finally let go of my trepidations and questioning and agreed to see him again when he called the following week. At the time, the limits were less important than the pleasures. And so it went.

We started a weekly Wednesday liaison. He would come to my house, and we would talk, maybe watch a film, eat lunch, and make love. It was warm, sexually exciting, loving, and significant. Sometimes we went out to a midday film and ate out. I had one rule, he had to stay at least five hours. I wanted a relationship, and this number was my way of ensuring a connectedness that moved outside of a simple sexual affair. Yet after three years, a sadness developed around being an outsider in his life; never being able to meet his family or friends, and never being able to accompany him to the important events in his life. I hated secrets and could never keep them, except for those my friends needed me to keep. My own secrets always slipped out. I did tell several close friends and I even got him to accompany me to lunch at one friend's house as well as come to brunch with my kids and grandkids. Though my kids knew about Paul, they always remained silent when I spoke about him. My older granddaughter called him a "player" and the others never asked questions or really engaged when I mentioned Paul's name. Only my daughter-in-law, an ardent feminist academic, encouraged me, when she said, "At eighty you need to enjoy yourself! Have fun! Time is short!"

So, Paul remained in my life discretely and minimally, while I never entered his. He did try to bring me into his life by sending the correspondence he had with his grandkids. In this surreptitious way, I watched them grow and develop into thoughtful, loving, and intelligent young adults. I rooted for them in their struggles through school, friendships, and life choices. I forged a relationship with them even though none of them knew I existed.

By 2016 things shifted. Paul moved emotionally farther away. We now saw each other only every two or three weeks. Excuses intervened! I became anxious as I wondered what was happening. Perhaps he decided to give all this energy to his primary relationship in order to make it work. Yet we continued. We celebrated my eightieth birthday with my friends from Chicago. But in the spring, when I went to North Africa, communication between us fell off. By June, when he went to Cuba, I did not hear from him for over a month.

I had mulled the relationship over for more than three months, and though I loved him, I loved myself more. I was hurting and needed it to be over. Finally, after a month, an email arrived. "I'm sorry it did not work out! "It"? What is "it"? And what does "not work out" mean? Enveloped in anger, I spent the summer brooding that all he could write about a four-and-a-half-year relationship was a three-line emotionally detached note.

In September, I received a second note, "I've started a new relationship with a woman I have known for over forty years, and I finally left Ann." Unprepared for this third person, who was sixty-eight, I cried for the first time and continued crying until no more tears came. The hurt was deep, deeper than expected. It was about this third woman; it was about his claims of being unable to leave his partner for me that pierced me and opened a deep wound.

Dumbfounded, agitated, and distressed, I burned two pots and melted down an electric water kettle. Its foul smell seeped into the lobby. Several residents knocked on my door in overwrought concern that I was burning down the building or at the very least causing poisonous air to penetrate the lungs of the other co-op owners. Embarrassed and in extreme distress, I embellished a half truth about distress over my granddaughter being sick. A few weeks later, I went in for knee surgery, and though Paul kept writing friendly notes, I did not answer until the loneliness of my recovery prompted a response in December. Brief emails passed between us but after four months of me being home alone working on my knee recovery, several longer emails arrived, and we started to communicate more regularly. Finally, in a phone call, I found the courage to ask, "When did this new relationship with Denise begin?" "In June 2016," he replied. He had known her professionally and personally for more than forty years.

All my confusion from the year before became clearer. The big question, the most troubling question, I now asked, "How were you able to finally leave Ann?" "The therapist you suggested really helped," he answered. My mouth hung open as tears dropped and my hand slapped down the phone. Mummified, I sat with my hand on the phone and my mouth refusing to close. I must have looked much like the painting *Howl* by Edward Munch. It was certainly a howl that emerged. It was a howl from deep inside, a howl that hurt and triggered a kind of layered scream, layered with pain, anger, and betrayal. I felt stupid about the ways I had been duped. Many months before, when he told me he brought Denise to his grandchildren's graduation, I had asked if he was interested in Denise. "Oh, no," he exclaimed. "I was just bringing her because she has known these children since they were very little."

But leaving is not always simple, and pain is not always the deterrent it should be, and age that brings wisdom also brings loneliness. It is not that easy to give up warmth, comfort, and affection, and so the pain remained. However, the man whose betrayal was enormous kept writing in friendship. I answered tersely and with much caution, but I answered. Finally, in the spring of 2017, we met up as friends. The spark was there, but I pushed it down hard. We walked and talked. He confessed he missed me a great deal. *Good*, I thought; nice to hear! We went to the movies and talked over dinner. It was pleasant and comforting. It was just what I needed and wanted—nothing more. However, within six months the relationship shifted to a caring friendship with sex.

So, what is this about I asked? At thirty this would never happen—the world is your oyster! At sixty, this would be unlikely to happen. After all, you are a feminist and politically engaged. Yet now, in my eighties, this "old love" feels different. Now it is about comfort, reassurance, and pleasure, and not the promise of building a future or living together. It is about confronting the end of life and knowing there is someone special who helps you through these difficult days of old age—with "old love."

Over the years much has gone on between Paul and me, including a nine-month break up. Yet at eighty-four, the limits are less important than the pleasures. As I move toward the end of my life with feelings of deep caring for someone, with physical pleasure, and a warmth that brings forth a youthful energy, I find it all too hard to give up. Can someone love two people at the same time? Is my relationship with Paul a betrayal of feminist politics or a betrayal of another woman? I ask myself these abstract questions frequently but continue to live in the concrete pleasure of Paul being in my life.

A Vine of Roses

Mimi Schwartz

Soon after my mastectomy, my friend Penny gave me a gift that I shoved in the closet. It was a framed poster of a woman with one breast, her arms raised in victory to the sky. Across her scar is a vine tattoo. This was 1988, when the media had started writing about breast cancer, using titles with "tragedy" and "terror," signaling hysteria and doom. So that's what I knew when the doctor found my lump. A woman with breast cancer was either "victim" or "survivor," and I remember seeing no images. Visuals, evidently, were too shameful to print.

Yet here was this woman, not tragic but brazen—and I kept thinking about her when I took off my bandages and confronted the jagged red scar. And again, when my husband and I made love. And again, when I started back to work. Within a month, the one-breasted woman was out of the closet and over my desk to look at every morning. I began saying, "I had breast cancer" instead of "I have breast cancer" even though, at age forty-eight, I had no guarantees for anything.

I considered breast reconstruction, but then I heard of a neighbor ending up with uneven breasts and a cousin of someone having three surgeries because of a leaky saline implant. A tattoo fantasy—mine with a vine of tiny roses—seemed easier. I didn't seriously consider it because, back then, tattoos were for Hells Angels and drunken sailors in sleazy parlors on a street of bars. But I did whisper to my husband one night, "Maybe I'll get a tattoo on the scar!"

"Do it if you want," he said, kissing what was no longer there. "But you don't need one."

It was the perfect answer, along with the one he came up with when I wept after misplacing my prosthesis, and he went off calling, "Here, Titty, Titty!" Self-pity had no chance. Tears went to laughter and to trust. I didn't get a tattoo.

My scar has faded to white, along with another over my belly button after a GI bleed (too much Advil), and at seventy-three, I'm again thinking of tattoos to cover my scars. Since Stu died—it's been two years now—I'm trying to figure out my body without him. I've started to go to the movies and dinner with other men, but intimacy seems like a leap, even if I still had two breasts. I miss curling around someone at night, but can't see myself making love, especially with the lights on. And worse, walking around casually naked and lopsided in the morning!

I'm reconsidering breast reconstruction, but then I wonder if I should add a facelift, liposuction, tummy tucks, neck lift, the works. And I still won't look as new as the kitchen chairs I reupholstered. So no, I'll just stick to my rule about medical procedures, which is the same as for the comma: If in doubt, leave it out.

Yesterday I found half a dozen websites displaying tattoos over mastectomies. Most are enormous, like the barn owl in pink and gray, its wings flying over half-hidden red leaves. And the blue arctic fox with its paw on a saved nipple, its tail draped over a bare shoulder. And a toga of giant pink flowers set on emerald leaves that wind their way from shoulder to scar to hip to butt. I would disappear in such designs, and I'd miss myself. Only one tattoo, "Bad Ass Chest Piece," done by Tina Bafaro, made me imagine possibility. It's an Art Deco brassiere in swirling reds, blues, and browns that you'd never find in Victoria's Secret. The tattoo initially went viral, and Facebook shut it down, saying mastectomy tattoos are taboo. But it is back up again—and I saw it. We've at least come that far.

This morning I passed a young woman in a scooped-neck shirt with "Brooklyn" tattooed like a banner across her chest. It's ironic how the generation that avoids commitment is fearless about such permanency. I, who lived with one man for fifty years, would worry: What if I move to Queens or Tokyo? Would I want my Brooklyn past so prominent for my life? I let the tattoo idea go again, thinking, I'm too old and impatient. I can barely sit still for an occasional manicure; plus, it would hurt, even a small tattoo like my vine.

Enter my four-year-old granddaughter, Karen, with a tiny rose on her arm. It's temporary, her mother assures me, taken from a book of designs she found at the toy store. An hour later, I'm in that store buying one— no, two books of tiny flowers, stars, hearts, and other joys of color no more than an inch big (including the princesses and white horses, which I will give to Karen).

Back at home, I choose a rainbow for my mastectomy scar and a blue rose for above my belly button, and standing before the mirror, I peel, press with a damp towel for thirty seconds, and I am tattooed. I love them, these shifting shapes of self-definition. And if I land in someone's bed, like this guy I'm seeing who likes surprises, he might delight in the rainbow. When it fades, I could switch to a peace sign over my belly button and two roses where my left breast was. I'll leave space in between to show a pale scar of connection like a thin laundry line. History unhidden.

NOTE

A shorter version of this essay first appeared in *Post Road* and then in Schwartz's memoir in essays, *When History Is Personal* (University of Nebraska Press, 2018).

From Texas to Ohio

Bonnie Fails

I am currently living with a man I fell in love with through the EliteSingles dating service. At the time of our meeting three years ago, I was seventy-three and he was eighty-two. He lives twelve hundred miles from my home (I in Texas and he in Ohio), does not drive, and uses a walker. Additionally, he is a published children's poet, an advocate for the underdog, a great conversationalist, a beautiful man, and very romantic—our personalities meshed. The only thing of importance came down to all that is ever important: we truly understood each other. The deep attraction and need to give and receive love were very present.

Online dating was something I never considered, even looked down upon, thinking the world remained as before in the dating realm. This snobbery disappeared after my husband of forty years died. As I got used to being alone, I also started feeling a horrible lonesome feeling not relieved by dogs or friends.

I began by asking my friends if they had single male friends as I was very open to dating. The phone would ring occasionally, and each new encounter, although coming with great references, only ended in laughter or tears. *The Frogs!* I even found out that some of my dates were my friends' online dating rejects, but my friends felt we might work instead.

After a year of many women's lunches, rejecting dates with men, and joining and leaving all the social clubs in town, I became interested

enough to listen to the pros and cons of online dating. I became marg-
nally open to it.

Christmas arrived that year, and I felt like I was suffering through a
month of Sundays without someone to share it all with. On one of these
days, as I was standing in front of the Christmas tree, my daughter-in-law
announced that my pain was seeping out of me for all to see and she was
going to help me do something about it. And she did. Her gift to me
was a membership to a dating service, which she set up, writing my profile
and putting my "oh yeah" photograph on the site. I was compliant and
even a little excited to see what would happen.

A new life was heralded in for me the moment I opened up the site.
I went to my profile and saw a heart had been left for me. I read this man's
profile, and seeing he was a published poet, I googled him. After reading
his profile and the pieces I found online, I decided I would like to get to
know this man. The problem was he lived twelve hundred miles away, so
the probability was slim. Still, I left a message and a phone number. He
called the same evening, and we started daily three-hour conversations.
Thus started a new chapter in my life.

After a few days of long FaceTime conversations, we both canceled our
memberships to the dating service. Arnold was the only man I ever had
contact with through the site, and I was quite sure of my decision. Additionally, we changed our Facebook statuses to "in a relationship," which
caused quite a stir among our friends and family.

After two months of FaceTiming (up to five hours day and night), we
decided to meet in person, both feeling a strong commitment to the other.
I flew from Texas to Ohio with only feelings of anticipation for this new
chapter in my life. The moment we first saw each other and started hugging, the feelings of lust and love intensified. Because of the hours we'd
spent over the phone and on FaceTime sharing our separate lives, we did
not feel like strangers. The love story started, and after being together for
a month, we did not want to live apart. We made life plans to share each

other's homes during different months, so I flew home to get the belong-
ings I wanted to have in Ohio.

After I returned to Ohio during a beautiful spring, a respite from a hot
Texas summer, we started talking about taking a couple of trips to Texas.
He had a few health problems, and it became obvious that it would be a
difficult trip for him to visit me in Texas. We made the decision that I
would stay with him and go home for a visit every once in a while, and
this is how we managed my homesickness—I would go to see my family
when the mood struck. It worked well.

We have been together for three years with a lot of laughter and fun.
Being with a man who uses a walker has never been an issue, as I just saw
it as a part of aging. We went places and made the necessary adjustments
in our life. COVID-19 came and brought changes; it did to all of us. For
me, the hardest part has been not being able to return often to my home in Texas,
where my family lives. I have a house there and miss my own world.

Life goes forward with changes and in our case that included health
problems for both of us. I have rheumatoid arthritis in my hands, making
care of another person impossible. Arnold has psoriatic arthritis; after
months in and out of the hospital, he has lost much of his ability to walk.
This has been a great love, but decisions to stay or return to my home in
Texas are pressing on us.

Till Illness Do Us Part?

Angela Page

Dating is hard enough when you're healthy, but after sixty, it can be tricky. There's a 75 percent chance that either you or a prospective partner or date will have at least one or more chronic ailment. Some may even have life-threatening illnesses.

The top issues that affect the over-sixty crowd are diabetes, heart disease, eye conditions, cancer, depression, joint pain, arthritis, dementia, and Alzheimer's. Other common issues are asthma, COPD, ED, and Crohn's. Don't forget the rising STDs among seniors. But with increased longevity, new drugs, and advanced treatments, it's very possible today to be in a relationship even in your sixties with someone a decade or two older.

Who would ever think you might be in a May–December romance as a senior?

I was sixty when my aunt Rose introduced me via email to her attorney's friend, Joe, who was seventy-eight. He wanted to spend the winter in south Florida, where I lived, and build a social circle. Joe was divorced with an adult son living in California. Joe was about six feet tall, bald, wore hip glasses, and looked dignified. He seemed energetic, was an affable salesman, and ran his own window company. We were both graduates of New York University, exactly twenty years apart. We discussed a house swap for the winter, as I needed a temporary place in New Jersey for my new job. Oddly my company headquarters was a half-hour drive from Joe's condo.

Joe and I had lengthy daily phone calls. Our conversations intensified as our chemistry grew. After a few weeks of talking, he disclosed his prostate cancer diagnosis. He claimed it was under control with medication.

We met in person after two months of phone calls. I traveled to New Jersey to start my new job, and we hit it off at first sight. We clicked in and out of the bedroom, and he declared he was in love with me. We quickly moved into each other's homes.

Joe was robust, energetic, and fun. He was concerned about the age difference, but I had experience as a young woman with a man thirty years my senior. I knew the territory of raised eyebrows and being mistaken for a daughter. Joe and I looked young for our ages, but you could still see a generational age difference.

I am a New Jersey native, and Joe had spent the last fifty years living and working not far from my childhood home. He was a secular Jew and had sworn off dating Jewish women. He seemed pleased I had no religious affiliation, and neither did my family. As a Latina atheist, it was always assumed I was Catholic or at least Christian. I was resentful when called a shiksa.

Joe and I had common tastes in theater, film, and music. He took me to his favorite restaurants, and we went dancing. He showed me to his childhood Brooklyn beach neighborhood and showed me where his ashes should be scattered at sea.

Our visit to his choice of final resting place led me to raise the issue of incapacitation and end of life. He said he hoped I would be there for him. That thought prompted him to propose in a very cavalier tone, "Should we get married?" "It's like you're inviting me for a deli sandwich," I responded. At that point I knew more about his finances and noted that I had more to lose than he did if we were to marry. He agreed and shortly after, unbeknownst to me, he did draw up a will, including medical and financial powers of attorney.

Ten months into our relationship, I noticed Joe was losing weight and stamina. I still wasn't allowed to attend his doctors' appointments or see his reports. Even his son was kept out of the loop. I was very afraid of caring for a sick man. I considered breaking up with Joe, but I procrastinated since I still loved him, and the thought of leaving was too much to think about.

By the time I was allowed to be involved in Joe's medical appointments, his cancer had metastasized. He was a difficult patient, skeptical of doctors, and one oncologist didn't want to see him anymore. The oncologist had encouraged him to have advanced drug treatment and radiation, but Joe had refused, and his prognosis was not good.

I contacted his son, who was too busy with work and could not fly to New Jersey. He was also annoyed with Joe's condition. "I have no time for this," the son said. Even after the son understood the gravity of his father's condition, he still did not plan to visit. They argued daily by phone. It was heartbreaking to listen to them. I was devastated for Joe and could not imagine a child ignoring and dismissing a parent who was seriously ill. I knew they had conflicts, but as far as I could tell, he had been a good provider and father. It appeared there were unresolved issues from Joe's divorce twenty years before when the son was a teenager.

When the son found out I held the power of attorney, both financial and medical, he went ballistic. His son argued that I was only a girlfriend and had no business being in charge. Joe countered back, "Consider her my wife," and said he wanted to die in love and "don't ruin it." Joe also boasted about my credentials in dealing with a dying partner. Twenty years earlier I had been caregiver to my husband who died of cancer at age forty-five.

The son didn't let up his attacks on Joe and me. I wanted to leave the situation, but it felt inhumane to leave Joe. Somehow, I felt this was the universe's plan all along. As painful and stressful as it was, maybe I was destined to be by this man's side to the end.

His condition went downhill quickly. I was now managing his medical care and finances, hiring caregivers, and dealing with his son long distance. His son complained I was spending too much on home care and should not deplete Joe's dwindling funds. He asked Joe's doctors and the hospice nurse to find a free facility.

I was determined to honor Joe's wishes to die at home and with dignity. If Joe ran out of funds, I planned on moving us into a cheaper condo and to liquidate his business. But he died only a few weeks later at home by a picture window and still "in love."

The son held a memorial service and scattered Joe's ashes off the Brooklyn beach. None of Joe's close friends, longtime business partners, nor I were invited. We had only been together twenty months when he passed.

Dealing with an ailing partner is not uncommon. My neighbor, Janet, who is ninety, had a boyfriend in his mideighties. They became quite close, and Janet spent a lot of time with him. Janet's children were concerned, as this boyfriend was not in good health. They kept close tabs on Janet to ensure she didn't move in with the boyfriend, co-mingle finances, or even secretly marry him. Unfortunately, Janet, at ninety-two, became his caregiver and held his hand to the end. She had no regrets.

My cousin Anna, in her midsixties, dated Sam, who was eighty-three. He invited her on an island cruise. They slept in same cabin, but Anna was not ready for intimacy. "You'll tell me when you're ready," Sam announced. He had trouble walking, and Anna ended up on shore excursions alone. She knew there wouldn't be any rolling in the waves with Sam like in *From Here to Eternity* but was hoping for at least some romance. She realized she couldn't cope with Sam's needs and broke up with him after the cruise.

There are other stories of women and men over sixty trolling for elderly partners with view toward financial gain. In many cases the children intervene, but sometimes these people get away with caregiving for a short time and become an heir.

Chronic illness can be deal breakers for many people. Experts recommend that you reveal a big health issue early in the dating process, but not too early. They say you should expect rejection but hope for acceptance. If you are the one disclosing, the reaction of the other person can be telling.

It's also possible that either of you could develop a chronic or serious illness once you're in a relationship. It's best to be prepared and have arrangements made. Be aware of each other's plans; be in sync as well as in contact with their next of kin.

If you end up as a caregiver, you could face dealing with a partner's family, finances, and medical decisions. If you are not married, the family may keep you out of the loop. If you do marry, get advice on shielding yourself from financial responsibility for their care.

In some cases, a serious illness or chronic condition becomes too much for a relationship to survive. Everyone has different thresholds. Sometimes the connection, intensity, and attraction you have to the other person will outweigh even the worst health situations. That was my case even though we were only a couple for a short time.

Dating in our senior years can bring love, joy, and companionship. We just must hope that gift is not short-lived.

What Remains Has Just Begun

Tierl Thompson and Idris Walters

TIERL THOMPSON

It all started with a picture, when I ordered a print from Idris, an old acquaintance. Or did it? Now I wonder. Did I unconsciously want to reach out, over a fifty-three-year time span, toward someone I once knew? I would once have dismissed that idea as fanciful. But now I'm beginning to believe that life and love do indeed move in mysterious ways and that not all decisions are fully conscious. Something within me led me toward Idris. A chance thought, a chance conversation. Eventually, a persistent want.

Some time ago, my lifelong friend Joy and I were recalling our school days, as we were often wont to do. "I wonder what happened to those guys we hung out with who lived above the deli?" we asked. The deli was where Joy and I had part-time jobs serving food. Pouring boiling water over pre-cooked spaghetti, as I recall. We must have been drawn to it by the word *LOVE* painted in large letters on the outside of the building and equally drawn to the architecture students who had written it and lived in the flat above the shop. It was 1967, the "summer of love" in Oxford.

"Let's google them," we said, and chose the first name that came to mind, Idris Walters. And there was a website with his original artwork on it. "Isn't it beautiful?" said Joy.

Years later I was looking for a print to grace a large wall in a bungalow I was renovating by the sea in Norfolk. And I remembered Idris and those lovely, nature inspired, abstract prints I had seen on his website. They had stayed with me. I wanted the feel of one of them on my wall. When I went back to the website, it wasn't hard to choose which print. There was one in particular that spoke to me of the coast in Norfolk. It was called *Sunlit Field Edge*. I emailed the address on the website, "Hey, I don't know if you remember me? I knew you in Oxford back in 1967?" It seemed that a warm, welcoming voice came back, as far as you can tell with emails. "Certainly do remember you," he said, "and that's actually one of my favorite pictures."

A beautiful print was bought. A correspondence started, stopped, came and went, and unexpectedly some two years later, intensified. We wrote for months before we finally met, telling each other anything and everything about our lives, about the turns they had taken since 1967. In our emails we made jokes, played on words, shared memories, music, inspirational ideas, and showed care for each other. I sensed kindness, warmth, a kindred spirit, someone I could trust with my innermost self. Eventually I found myself experiencing the delicious, unfamiliar, and disconcerting sensation of falling in love—with a man I hadn't seen for fifty-three years, falling in love by email, no less. And having a completely unexpected emotional and sexual awakening.

You see, finding my way to Idris's picture wasn't even the most remarkable thing. More remarkable was that I had been single for twenty-two years and had been a gay woman for most of my adult life. I had come to feel that relationships, romance, and most definitely sex, had somehow passed out of my life. I famously told my friends, or anyone interested in me, that I was done with intimate relationships. The thought of being with someone could become quite frightening. And yet this wasn't scary. Much of the time when I was single, I felt contented and peaceful. I was happy to bring up my daughter single-handedly without further conflicts in relationships. Occasionally, privately, I grieved over the loss of the lusciousness of sexual desire, because I genuinely thought it had gone, never to return. Sometimes I would look enviously at the companionship of other couples, particularly elderly ones, wondering how they did it, how anyone did it. "The grass is greener," I would tell myself with a shake. "I'm fine, my life is fine." "Never say never," my friend Judy said, but I didn't believe her.

At age seventy, when I least expected it, when I wasn't looking for someone, I found that my hormones were crashing through my body and I was falling romantically, passionately, head over heels in love with a solitary artist. A man I once knew. What was to be done? It took me some time to summon the courage to tell Idris how I was feeling, which was "lovesick" according to my diary at the time. Lovesick at seventy? Really? For someone usually so cautious in affairs of the heart, this was all so unexpected, but strangely it never felt unwelcome. This all happened during the first COVID-19 lockdown in 2020 and I was racked with questions. Was any of it real? Was it lockdown madness? When the restrictions eased, Idris and I met up. Everything I had felt remained true. I was not to be disappointed. Idris offered me a sure, steady, loyal, unashamedly romantic love, the likes of which I had never experienced. We laughed. We loved. We talked. We had, and still have, rather blissful sex. I found it surprisingly easy to be a sexual being again and we faced the challenges of our aging bodies together. We found a supportive companionship that grows by the day, by the week, by the month. We have been blessed and wished well by my gay friends and our families. To my amazement, rather late on, I find myself in the unimagined joy of a happy and fulfilling relationship.

This is gray love, love in our early seventies. Is this usual? Do other people have these resurgences of sexual desire, love, and romance? Perhaps I will find out from this book. Is there much that's different about gray love? I do know that I don't want to abandon too readily the self that I carefully established during my single years. Despite our longings and the difficulties of living two hundred miles apart, Idris and I resist the idea of complete immersion, of losing ourselves in each other 24/7. We have often said we don't want to lose the people we fell in love with—our independent selves. All those single years certainly helped me not to fear being alone. Hopefully we can bring stronger selves into our relationship and respect our differences rather than gnaw away at the other person because of our insecurities and want them to be like ourselves.

And yet the bittersweet side of gray love is the awareness of our advancing years and the inevitable, eventual decline of our health. How long do we have together? I think more often these days about mortality. I'm fearful sometimes that something will happen to one of us. But if I've learned anything to date it's to try to live more in the moment. And if anything is guaranteed to make you feel young at heart, it's sex, love, and romance. So, let's celebrate gray love. It's a gift from the mysterious powers that be, for the end of our days.

Idris Walters

In 1967, Oxford was the perfect place for a young man to imagine who he might, one day perhaps, become. A place of historic awakenings, the sun shone madly, it seemed, all magical year-round: a city of aspiring dreams alive with nuance, imagination, and promise. Literature, music, and art were compelling forces for radical change and exciting alternatives to just about everything on earth, appearing like thieves in the night, colorful pranksters by day. It was under the glare of a light representing an apparently inevitable new age that I first saw her, fell somewhat smitten, and made her acquaintance. She had an unusual name, moved among us like fresh air itself and was a friend of a close friend. But my courage abandoned me. I kept a safe distance by way of an adolescent fear of rejection and maintained a merely agreeable social connection. Although we soon moved swiftly on, we enjoyed a memorable share of the blessed 1960s, a time when a whole day could seem to pass in a minute or two, so enchanting was it, and a year so full of new ideas could easily last forever.

Then, quite suddenly, fifty years flew by. Peer groups scattered nationwide. In separate worlds now as they picked over the leavings from the inaugural feast of a glorious new age, that very same new age was almost imperceptibly subdued into subservience by the prevailing politico-cultural establishment and its blind obsession with greed-and-growth economics. Though the curtains had been terminally drawn on the remarkable sixties, they battled on against convention in their different ways: she had become a committed lesbian, editor, teacher, and political activist while he remained largely heterosexual given to furious bouts of creative self-immolation. Unawares, they overlapped and crossed paths time and time again, at one point living within a couple streets of each other in London without even knowing it. Sustained relationships of all kinds were, in any event, continually under threat from unrealistic expectation, obligatory promiscuity, and taboo-breaking indulgence. Kind, creative, healthy children were born as courageous single parenthood became more commonplace: a daughter for her and a son for him. But by the time one century stumbled uncomfortably into yet another they had each, eventually, and perhaps even finally, settled into living contentedly alone. Hard work, diligence, and effort had secured reasonable conditions for the single life in retirement. A certain mindful solitude in approaching advanced age seemed an attractive and viable option with, inevitably, many a broken dream left returning sadly to silence out in the rain.

I remembered her so well when her unusual name appeared out of the blue in my inbox. I blessed the impudent forces of circumstance and enthusiastically recalled my attraction to her from a full half century earlier. She had remembered me too and, having logged on to my gallery website, expressed some interest in purchasing a particular artwork. Things moved quickly from there into a lengthy email exchange. A surprisingly organic connection, uncertain at first, then bold and fearless, then intimate and revealing, demanding, in turn, perhaps, a meeting on neutral territory, by way of a catch-up, or even a brief home visit. As intensity developed, we discovered that our hitherto very different lives had concluded for us both in long periods of heroic celibacy. With a combined one hundred and forty or so complex and challenging years to review and compare, we began— sight of each other unseen for more than fifty years—to enjoy a truly unexpected and thrilling desire, insistent and almost entirely absent of fear. I eventually, nervously, drove to the coast to meet her at last and, thankfully, all went very well. We began to feel that love, from whence it had lain trampled for years in the mud, had come back to us for serious consideration. I live in an old stone house in the middle of nowhere in the far north of the country and she occupies a bungalow close by a raging sea to the south and east. But we are a tiresome two hundred miles of hard road apart.

We get together in a pandemically correct "support bubble" about twice a month, and we have convinced each other that while "enough" is always a good thing by definition, you can always use a little more "enough." I have, finally, come to understand what forever really means, the true gravity of a kiss and how rich in quality the future, however short in years, can yet become. We speak every two days on the telephone and communicate constantly across the internet. There are emails first thing in the morning and emails last thing at night. Our times apart are marbled with numberless, often flirtatious social media communications. To me she is the calmest, kindest, most chic, and most beautiful of creatures, elegant both inside and out, that I have ever known and my only regret is that the energy of our new kind of love is confined in these days by COVID-19 restrictions and cannot radiate beneficially amongst others as it might otherwise do.

So, at the supposed twilight of their days, they have discovered a companionship more honest, caring, playful and thrilling than had ever seemed possible—an astonishing physical intensity, well-mannered and lustful, not performance-related, characterized by love, laughter, respect, and a rare lack of self-consciousness. Sometimes he goes to her. Sometimes she goes to him. They take long walks and talk endlessly. They relax into almost disreputable passages of slow-time spent in desirous passion, their hard-won identities unchallenged and complete, their differences—a welcome diversity—accepted and thence binding without prejudice. Their children are supportive without condition and a true freedom seems to have, at last, been achieved.

For myself, I love her totally and cannot conceive of living without her. Our relationship is as erotic a gender-defiant fairground of sensuality as it is emotional, intellectual, and empathetic. She represents for me all that is going on around me, what it has all been for and about along with what it may yet become. I feel that we have each been singularly blessed with the other at the eleventh hour to coincidence. To have loved and lost so often and so painfully, to have been loved and been lost as many times again and then to love and be loved to a new perfection in one final blaze of glory is, unashamedly and surely, an affirmation redolent of eternity itself.

At Once

Dustin Beall Smith

It's mid-July 2014, and I'm attending a seventieth birthday party for my girlfriend Betsy's younger sister. It's a sunny afternoon and fifty-odd guests are packed into an airy Massachusetts summer house a few minutes' drive from the ocean. I suspect that Betsy, whom I've been seeing for less than a month, has abandoned me in order to assess from afar how I hold up amid this heady academic crowd. So far, I've happily engaged in conversation about the most recent status of SETI's search for exoplanets; the pedagogical merits of math circles; and the precession of the equinox as posited by the Greek astronomer Ptolemy. But not once has anyone asked my name or how I happen to be in the room, which makes me think they must already know. I feel like the groom whom no one has met until the wedding reception.

I place my sweaty glass of water on a cork coaster and plunk my butt down at the end of a long, comfy sofa. I scan the large room and spot tall, elegant Betsy, more properly introduced as Elizabeth Dane, holding forth in a group that includes five or six distinctly interested older men. Suddenly, an attractive woman about half my age sits down eagerly on the other end of the sofa and slides toward me with an expression of great anticipation. I don't want to be inquired into at this moment, but she slides closer still. "What I want to know," she says, excitedly, "is how did you get so lucky?" And with that, she points to Betsy, who, at that very moment, is glancing smilingly over her shoulder in our direction.

———

Elizabeth and I were born three weeks apart in Boston's Mass General, in the Year of the Metal Dragon, 1940. Our paths converged more closely fifteen years later at the Putney School in Vermont, a coeducational private school with a mere two hundred students. Despite the intimate class sizes, neither of us can recall exchanging a single word during our three concurrent years there. Not even at our graduation in 1958, where, after enduring a long speech by Eleanor Roosevelt, we received the high school diplomas that now hang next to each other in our upstairs hall. These personalized documents, illustrated in watercolor by a fellow student, depict long-limbed Betsy hanging upside down from a bending birch branch, her hair swinging freely and me sitting with my back against a very different, less yielding tree, reading a book with the name CAMUS inked on its cover. She seems the very picture of a carefree studious girl, and I a bad boy, already anticipating a future filled with existential rebellion.

All of which is to say that we didn't really meet until our class's forty-fifth reunion, a weekend event in June 2003. I was nearing the end of a monthlong swing through New England, visiting friends I hadn't seen in years. I'd also recently ended an intense five-year relationship with a woman twenty-three years my junior. So, it was in a blissfully free *why-not* mood that I joined the registration line in the new arts building. I pinned a name tag to my green linen shirt, pocketed the weekend schedule, and began perusing class memorabilia spread out on Kraft-papered tables and pinned to portable partition walls. I funneled through the display like a leaf caught in a stream, until suddenly I found myself stopped in front of a tall, graceful woman with walnut hair and green eyes. Her dress was a mustardy color, as I recall. She wore an expression of slight puzzlement and had an expectant youthful air that conveyed an interior sense of humor about this whole reunion thing.

"Hello, Betsy," I thought, surprised that her name had come to mind so easily. She held out her hand as though to keep me at a distance. I hadn't been about to hug her, but her instinct to prevent me from doing so seemed immensely sage, since the antennae in my fingertips had already detected (if not yet decoded) the potential for intimacy. Not that it mattered. Such promising moments aren't exactly uncommon in life. And she wore a silver wedding ring. I won't pretend to remember or try to characterize exactly what we said in that moment or during the next day's alumni events that led up to the dance on Saturday night. But it was the dance that did it.

As a high-school student, the prospect of choosing a partner and committing to a slow dance would have sent me outside for an illegal smoke with my buddies. But time can sharpen the libido's appetite in surprising ways, even as it winnows the options. I remember folding Betsy's right hand into my left and drawing our elbows close between us. For a while, we didn't even bother to move our feet to the music; we just swayed in place. The compelling quality of her touch—our mutual touch—the smell of her hair, the tenor of her voice in my ear, the ease with which we'd come together, completely surprised me. I began to wonder if maybe, at age sixty-three, I'd finally found. . . . But the notion was absurd: she was married.

Nevertheless, we left the dance together (having danced with no one else) and stepped into the soft night air. We walked along a moon-dappled dirt road that led downhill to the Alumni House. When I spied a huge bullfrog sitting boldly in the middle of the road, caught dramatically in a patch of bright moonlight, I stooped to pick it up. It obliged me by sitting patiently on my palm as I introduced it mock-formally to Betsy, whom it seemed to like. I took that as a good sign and said so. The frog's apparent trust in us relieved me of whatever caution I might have otherwise brought to this moment, and I put my arm round Betsy's waist, drawing her close to my hip. We stared into the creature's unblinking gaze for several minutes, before I bent down again and offered it release, which it took another few minutes to accept.

We continued walking along the dirt road, talking about our marriages (two each, Betsy's second entering its fourth decade). I learned about her career as a professor at Hunter College in New York City, and about how she and her husband and their two adopted children had moved to Helena, Montana; and how subsequently, when the kids were grown, moved again to Tucson, Arizona. I described how my career as a key grip in the film business had come to its natural conclusion and how I'd just that month completed my two-year pursuit of an MFA at Columbia University's School of the Arts. "I have no idea what I'll do now," I told her.

We parted at the entrance to the Alumni House and slept in separate preassigned rooms. After breakfast on Sunday morning, Betsy traveled back to New York City with a fellow alumna. She was scheduled to fly out of LaGuardia the next day. I drove back to the city alone, then called her from my apartment, convincing her to meet me the next day, before her flight. We met at my apartment and walked the winding paths of Central Park for several hours, ending up at a small French bistro just off Madison Avenue, where we lingered over tea and fizzy water and lemon tortes for four hours. The late-spring weather seemed to fuel an undeniable mutual attraction, and perhaps inspired our amazement that our paths had never crossed in the city. We'd been undergraduates on campuses a mere block apart in the early sixties; she at Barnard, me at Columbia. We discovered that we'd once lived in back-to-back buildings on the Upper West Side; we'd even both raised children on that side of town; perhaps even unknowingly stood on the same street corner waiting for the light to change or in the bread line at Zabar's.

Betsy flew back to Tucson that evening. The following day, she emailed me saying how much fun she'd had and expressing her desire to visit again soon. She often flew to the city, she said. I replied recklessly that I'd enjoyed her company so much I'd follow her to Timbuktu, if necessary. Inevitably, my name came up one too many times in Betsy's conversations with her husband, which led to some drama between them, which resulted in her decision to break off any future contact with me. And that was the end of that.

Then a decade later in 2013, I read in the fall issue of the Putney Post an entry under Alumni Notes, written by one Elizabeth Dane, in which she mentioned the death six months earlier of her husband from brain cancer. She described her newfound readiness to move on from the life they'd shared—to look for new paths. She concluded the entry with this sentence: "It is amazing to me how the human spirit can be consumed by immense sadness and at the same time can countenance the boundless thrill of being alive." I emailed a reply with my condolences and expressed my interest in hearing her thoughts about "new paths," should she ever want to share them. Several seasons passed. No response. I had bellowed the embers of what I'd remembered as a mutual desire only to discover that those embers must have grown cold. Hardly a surprise, I told myself. So much had changed in our lives.

I'd been teaching in the English department at Gettysburg College for ten years. At the urging of a few matchmaking colleagues, I'd hooked up with a bright and savvy woman twenty years my junior, a writer and editor, and a newcomer to the college. During our time living together, we'd carved out a little niche in the world of literary nonfiction and I'd published a prize-winning (though hardly money-making) memoir-in-essays. When our live-in relationship lost its luster, we agreed to part ways. I became the monk I now figured I was destined to be. I could walk to the college, devote all my time to students, and still hit New York City to see my daughter whenever I chose. At age seventy-three, I was done with love relationships.

After the May graduation of the class of 2014, I drove to New York to mull things over: see friends, take down the storm windows, watch sunsets from a bench down by the Hudson River. One afternoon I clicked on an email message addressed to the Putney Class of '58. It was Betsy, asking if anyone was thinking of going to our fifty-sixth reunion, and if so, would they be able to provide her with a bed in the city and a ride to Vermont? I had zero interest in going to a fifty-sixth reunion, but I was definitely interested in sharing my bed. Which is how, precisely eleven years to the minute after our first cautious encounter in the new arts building at Putney, I opened my apartment door to encounter Betsy already leaning across the threshold like a runner toward the tape, as if even the time it would take to open the door fully would prove unbearable.

That night, all night, we lay on my king-size loft bed, with its view of the river, our seventy-four-year-old bodies smoothed magically young again by the forgiving light of yet another full strawberry moon.

———

It's now spring 2021, the season in which we will both turn eighty-one. We live in the spacious house Betsy purchased when she moved to Gettysburg to be with me. It sits a few miles from the college campus where I still teach. We revel in our lives together. We enjoy our gardens and neighbors— many of whom are teaching colleagues—and like most of them, we call ourselves husband and wife, though we've never had a formal ceremony, never sworn to have and to hold forever forward, "for better, for worse, for richer, for poorer."

When we came together, the quantifiable struggles hinted at by the words "better" and "worse," "richer" and "poorer"—all the predictable angers, resentments, jealousies, infidelities, competitiveness, and professional demands typical of marital relationships—had already been played out. Grievances of any kind now seemed petty and inconsequential when compared with the luck and joy we felt at having found each other in such a circuitous yet oddly intentional way.

Before the pandemic hit, we traveled in Europe, spent partial summers out west, and entertained current and former students. During it, now, we Zoom with friends, read books, share podcasts, and talk endlessly. We support our respective passions and private pursuits (writing for me and music for Betsy), and until recently we have enjoyed good health. We seem to have obviated the need to engage most of the rocky shoals warned about in the marriage vow, having negotiated them in earlier years. We honor our very different and divergent histories—our essential solitudes—which is where real steadiness in marriage can be found.

Now, having received a particular medical prognosis, we are forced to consider the inevitable approach of a new kind of solitude: for one of us it will consist of going on alone; for the other it will consist of going alone. Death *will* us part. It's part of the "I do." But death cannot erase, for either of us, the living certainty that we grabbed the moment to come together when that moment presented itself. Knowing that we had little time, we wasted none. To think of oneself as courageous, to know for certain that one has been demonstrably courageous in love, is the real "I do." We can now say to each other, *We did it.* We did not shrink in the face of all the obvious and often comic absurdities of late love: the ghosts of former loves; the incremental loss of hearing and even memory; the incessant entropy of human flesh and bone—any one of the realities that might have served as a persuasive excuse not to act, a convincing argument that it was too late for love.

It is always too late for love. But the risk left untaken, the love not dared, the ring not snatched at once would have made of all our ongoing joy a hollow "what if."

Acknowledgments

Gray Love is dedicated to two terrific people who are no longer with us: Linda Mason Hood and Jon-Christian Suggs.

We thank all the contributors for sharing their intimate personal stories. Without these there is no book.

Many people—too many to name—helped by introducing us to potential contributors.

We want particularly to thank Doris Friedensohn, June Jacobson, Rich Klin, Avis Lang, Jacqueline Lapidus, Paul Lauter, Stacey Parkins Millett, Kurt Lane Ross, and Florence Tager, for their editorial assistance and general support. A special thanks goes to Yael Ravin for her excellent editorial work on the introduction.

The folks at Rutgers University Press have been extremely responsive and cooperative with this project. Thank you, Kimberly Guinta, editorial director; Courtney Brach, publicity manager; Vincent Nordhaus, production editor; assistant editors Jasper Chang and Carah Naseem; and Unaisah Quazi, editorial intern. Also, many thanks to Cassie Gutman, copyeditor, and Sherry Gerstein, production editor at Westchester Publishing Services.

We appreciate all these contributions, but none of these folks are responsible for any errors that may make the final cut. We, Nan and Dan, take full responsibility for those.

Notes on Contributors

The pseudonyms Elizabeth Locke and Sarah Dunn and Anonymous are not included here.

BARBARA ABERCROMBIE teaches creative writing in the UCLA Extension Writers' Program and has published sixteen books—novels, picture books for kids, writing books, poetry, and anthologies—plus many essays in national publications. Her latest book is *The Language of Loss*.

NAN BAUER-MAGLIN has put together eight collections (six with coeditors) on topics such as stepfamilies, retirement, feminism, death, dying and choice, and older parents. Her latest book is *Widows' Words: Women Write on the Experience of Grief, the First Year, the Long Haul, and Everything in Between*.

SUSAN BICKLEY, a retired teacher, librarian, and editor, lives happily in Madison, Wisconsin, an isthmus surrounded by reality.

JUDITH UGELOW BLAK, a U.S. citizen living in Denmark, is a retired high school economics teacher. At age sixty-four, her first piece of nonacademic writing was published in *Tick Tock: Essays on Becoming a Parent after Forty*. She is currently writing a novel about an older mother finally coming of age in her sixties.

PHYLLIS BOGEN is a retired clinical social worker (nursing home and private practice). She raised three children in Washington, DC. In 1995, she moved to New Jersey to be near her children and grands. For fifteen years she volunteered as a mentor to a single mom with three children.

LAURA BROADWELL is a writer, editor, and content creator living in Brooklyn, New York. Her essay "Life in Balance" appears in the collection *Tick Tock: Essays on Becoming a Parent after Forty*. She is a current contributor to the *Park Slope Reader* and other local and national publications.

JIM BRONSON is a scientist who was the founder of Performance Dynamics, an organizational development company in Mountain View, California. He is a long-term mindfulness meditation practitioner and leads retreats from time to time.

A former journalist and marketer, STEPHANIE MUMFORD BROWN now runs Wiseacre Press, where she's trying to compile the missing owner's manual for the second half of life. Her first book is *No Bad Dates: A Guide to Online Dating and Beyond for Women Old Enough to Know Better*.

PHYLLIS CARITO is a retired college administrator and creative writing teacher. The highlights of her published work include two poetry books, *barely a whisper* and *The Stability of Trees in the Winds of Grief*, and a novel, *Worn Masks*.

BONNIE FAILS is a retired psychotherapist from College Station, Texas. She now lives in the countryside with family and a huge yellow Labrador.

ALICE F. FREED is professor emeritus of linguistics at Montclair State University. She is the author of *The Semantics of English Aspectual Complementation* and coeditor of *Rethinking Language and Gender Research: Theory and Practice* and *"Why Do You Ask?": The Function of Questions in Institutional Discourse*.

DORIS FRIEDENSOHN, liberated from college teaching twenty-five years ago, writes about travel, eating, and everyday life. Her food memoir, *Eating as I Go: Tales from America and Abroad*, tracks her adventures and opinions through 2005. Current essays examine adaptations, pleasures, and disappointments during the pandemic season.

SANDI GOLDIE was an elementary school teacher until she rewired as a life coach when she stopped teaching. She is a cofounder of the British Columbia climate solutions education organization, DrawdownBC.

ISABEL HILL is an urban planner, architectural historian, and award-winning documentary filmmaker who recently turned to writing to nurture her creative spirit. She is the author and photographer of four children's books about architecture, published by Star Bright Books.

DANIEL E. HOOD is a retired academic who has published in his specialty area of sociology. He was on faculty of a handful of colleges and universities in the New York metro area, both public and private, for four decades. His latest book is *Redemption and Recovery: Parallels of Religion and Science in Addiction Treatment*. His memoir essay, "Better Late Than Never," was recently published in *Tick Tock: Essays on Becoming a Parent after Forty*.

JAN JACOBSON is a writer and psychologist living in Asheville, North Carolina. In college she rode a boxcar for several days from California to Missouri in the heart of winter. Her adventurous spirit thrives to this day.

NATASHA JOSEFOWITZ is a business consultant, keynote speaker, poet, syndicated columnist, and author of twenty-one books. She taught the first American course for women in management at the University of New Hampshire and San Diego State University. Natasha earned her master's degree in clinical social work at age forty and her PhD in social psychology at age fifty.

MARGIE KAPLAN is a mother of two, a grandmother of three, a therapist in private practice for more than forty years, a psych professor for the last quarter century, and an avid journaler of fifty-plus years. She is a lifelong New Yorker who loves the outdoors, walking, reading, and playing Scrabble.

JONATHAN NED KATZ is an independent scholar and the author of innovative books on the history of sexuality and gender, including *The Invention of Heterosexuality* and *The Daring Life and Dangerous Times of Eve Adams*.

CANDIDA B. KORMAN is a professional writer, amateur tango dancer, and an incorrigible story vampire. She lives, writes, and dances in New York City.

PAUL LAUTER is Allan K. and Gwendolyn Miles Smith professor of literature emeritus at Trinity College. His most recent book is *Our Sixties: An Activist's History*. He remains general editor of the groundbreaking *Heath Anthology of American Literature*.

Brooklyn-based JEAN Y. LEUNG, a graduate of New York University, has written about Asians in America and abroad in publications such as *A Magazine* and the *Wall Street Journal*. People, plants, and food are some of her passions.

DAVID LEVY has worked as a potter, taught ceramics at an alternative high school, and was a music teacher at a residential school for children dealing with developmental disabilities. Before the pandemic, he played flutes in local hospitals. His current work in photography and music can be seen on YouTube under "Water Prayer Songs by David Levy."

Living in Glen Cove, New York, close to her two grandsons, HEDVA LEWITTES is professor emerita of education and psychology at SUNY Old Westbury. She has published articles on women's development, teaching critical thinking, and in the field of contemplative studies. She is currently working on an article about her sixty-year friendship.

ERICA MANFRED is in her late seventies; she moved to Florida alone seven years ago, driving her trusty Ford Focus from upstate New York and hasn't regretted it. She writes about aging and technology and other subjects regularly for SeniorPlanet.org, LifeExperienced.com, and her own newsletter, SnarkySenior.com, and is published in the *New York Times* and *Washington Post*, among others.

CYNTHIA MCVAY splits her time between the Hudson Valley and St. Croix, where she writes, paints, rows, and forages. Her work can be found in *Orion*, *University of Pennsylvania Gazette*, *Mondays at Ten*, and other literary journals and anthologies.

STACEY PARKINS MILLETT retired from a full-time career in philanthropy, health equity, and community development. Now she writes creative fiction and nonfiction in multiple genres and lives part time in her native New York City home on the Lower East Side and part time in Asheville, North Carolina.

LINDA WRIGHT MOORE is a retired journalist and communications professional living in suburban Philadelphia. She loves gardening, photography, and poetry and is at work on a memoir. She is eager to travel and get back to dance classes as soon as COVID-19 departs for another universe.

SUSAN O'MALLEY, professor emerita, City University of New York, is author of *"Custome Is an Idiot": Jacobean Pamphlet Literature on Women*. She has been on the editorial board of *Radical Teacher* for forty-five years. For the last ten years she has been on the executive committee of the NGO Committee on the Status of Women/NY (UN) working to further the international women's movement. She plays cello in the UN Symphony Orchestra.

ANGELA PAGE is a freelance writer, author, and film producer based in South Florida and Los Angeles. Author of the recent comedy suspense novel, *There's a Dead Girl in My Yard*, as well as the novella, *Suddenly Single Sylvia*, which includes a boomer dating guide.

IRVIN PECKHAM has been a writing teacher at the secondary and college levels for forty-three years. He retired four years after the death of his wife of forty-one years.

AMY ROGERS is a longtime contributing writer who explores food and culture for the NPR station WFAE and other outlets. She was awarded an Arts and Science Council (NC) Creative Renewal Fellowship for her work covering social justice through culinary connections. As an editor and workshop presenter, she has helped hundreds of people hone their skills and find satisfaction in their writing.

EUGENE ROTH was a professor of English literature at Adelphi University for thirty-three years, specializing in the Renaissance. For seven years until his retirement in 2000 he was also associate dean of Adelphi's Honors College in liberal studies.

MIMI SCHWARTZ's memoirs include two about marriage: *Thoughts from a Queen-Sized Bed* and *When History Is Personal*. Other books include *Writing True* (with Sondra Perl) and *Good Neighbors, Bad Times Revisited*, about what her father's German village in the 1930s taught her about negotiating decency then and now.

DUSTIN BEALL SMITH is the author of *Key Grip: A Memoir of Endless Consequences*. A former professor at Gettysburg College, he retired from teaching in 2021.

STEPHANIE SPEER received her master's degree in humanistic education from Goddard College. As an educator, she founded a private school for young children and provided training programs for adults working in health-care corporations and not-for-profit organizations. Her Buddhist studies and mindfulness practices have permeated all aspects of her life.

NEIL STEIN is retired from being a longtime owner of a real estate office in Brooklyn, NY. When he is not working on his backhand, he writes a blog, essays once described as "slices of life." Nowadays, since *Seinfeld*, they may be best described as being "about nothing."

TIERL THOMPSON is a retired sexual health education teacher/consultant. She has an ongoing interest in writing, dreams by the sea, and hopes to stay engaged with progressive politics in these turbulent times.

VINCENT VALENTI is a retired screenwriter, an amateur songwriter, and a professional spectator living in Brooklyn.

IDRIS WALTERS is an architectural illustrator, graphic designer, and now-retired journalist. Incurable romantic and furious Celt, he remains in pursuit of quality in all things.

SUSAN OSTROV WEISSER is professor emeritus of English at Adelphi University. She has published four books and numerous articles on the subject of women and romantic love.

WILLIAM WIESNER is a retired university administrator and divorce mediator. He has written a book of poetry titled *Seasons of the Wolf* and a whole lot of memos. He currently volunteers as an explainer in the Butterfly Room at the American Museum of Natural History and as a greeter in Central Park.

RETT ZABRISKIE has served the Reformed Church in America as pastor, denominational executive, and interim minister in twenty-nine congregations. As the word "retired" does not appear in scripture, he hasn't.